Five Ps Leading Teams to Top Results

OL IVER'S SPOT

A LEADERSHIP STORY

Dr. Patrick Leddin, PMP

Author photo by Susan Speece

ISBN: 147011898X
ISBN-13: 9781470118983

Contents

Introduction

Every year, businesses invest millions, if not billions of dollars to generate sales, launch new products, improve customer service, increase employee effectiveness, and reduce inefficiencies, all in an effort to ultimately deliver maximum return to their stakeholders. Process improvement initiatives, computer systems sporting acronym-laden names, and continual reorganization efforts often lead the pack. At times, desired results are achieved and the investment is validated. However, all too often, initiatives die on the vine due to leadership changes and lack of continued funding, or the muffled conversation that the effort should have never started in the first place eventually wins the day.

This book contends that the answer to achieving amazing results often lies not in new strategies or sweeping programs, but in the ability to develop leaders and teams that drive accountability, commitment, and engagement. Unlike significant changes to policies, processes, or procedures that can be expensive, time consuming, and gum the works, causing employees to dig deeper into their anti-change fighting positions, organizations that focus on developing leaders and teams benefit from an immediate and positive impact on business performance.

To achieve new results, companies must rethink business as usual and embrace pragmatic and arguably more effective approaches. Successful accomplishment of strategy doesn't happen at the corporate headquarters. It occurs at the front lines, where individual employees and their leaders interact and make decisions on how to employ resources every day. Unless that part is done correctly, no strategy, no matter how grand it is, matters.

This story discusses how one group of leaders in one company worked to get it right. The story is a work of fiction, and the characters exist only in the author's mind. However, the five Ps outlined in this book are grounded in reality and represent how leaders and their teams can work together to accomplish remarkable results.

The reality is that many team leaders and employees don't operate under this simple five-step process. It isn't because they are bad people who don't want to perform well. It's simply that most of them aren't given the opportunity to engage their passion and potential in their everyday roles. Companies will be far more effective when frontline employees and their leaders embrace a simple planning and execution approach.

A Leadership Story

Chapter 1: A New Reality

There's that feeling again, Susan Walker thought as she trudged down the narrow hallway. In all honesty, the word hallway was inaccurate. A hallway suggests some sort of walled-in structure. She was actually navigating a pathway that cut through the manufacturing floor. Outlined in yellow safety tape, the path shifted occasionally, as packaging lines were reconfigured, people repositioned, new products launched, and innovative manufacturing techniques tested. Moving the tape appeared to be a never-ending process that slowly weaved its way through the entire plant, only to begin again the next year.

Trudging and the associated mixture of feelings—doubt, anxiety, and a dash of fear—did not come naturally to Susan. Typically, the most upbeat person in a room, she was known for her contagious smile and her ability to share kind words. Infusing energy and positivity into daily interactions was her calling card, but even she had her limits, and they were now being tested. As she walked up the flight of stairs to the conference room, her mind continued to question the situation. How is it possible that I feel so anxious and out of place in an organization where I've worked for years?

With the question barely formed in her mind, she turned the corner, entered the conference room, and observed that the Monday morning staff meeting was about to start. Susan scanned her colleagues' faces, recognizing the all too common mixture of frustration and apprehension. Her gaze settled on Michael Thomas, the tall and fit Vice President of Sales, and the two briefly made eye contact as he slid into his usual seat. Michael's hesitant nod of solidarity confirmed Susan's belief that she was not alone in her concern. Susan offered an uncomfortable smile in response.

The weekly gathering had been a Monday morning seven a.m. staple for years. Operating on autopilot, she settled into her normal spot at the table. Her trusty coffee mug, filled to the brim with the required dose of morning caffeine, transitioned from her hand to the worn conference table as if it knew the routine. Familiar banter filled the room, as her colleagues discussed the arrival of spring and the warm weather and flurry of weekend activities it brought with it. The conversations were comforting, but all recognized that beneath common dialogues lurked the beginning of another uncomfortable session that had become all too regular over the past few months.

It's only been ninety days, Susan thought. How is it possible that so much has changed? Just three short months earlier, she had passed the four-year mark as the company's Human Resources (HR) manager and fifteen years as an Outdoor Essentials' employee. Gifted in a number of areas, she was most talented as a relationship builder. Her cheery disposition, combined with genuine concern for others and great listening skills, made her a sounding board for her colleagues as they struggled to make professional and at times personal decisions. In her first forty-eight months as HR manager, Susan grew very comfortable in her position, enjoying both her role and the relationships developed with her team, the organization's 350-plus employees, and her fellow leaders.

Contentment wasn't just reserved for Susan. Sure, the company had experienced tremendous growth over the years, and with that growth came its share of challenges, but for the most part, employees and leaders new what to expect from their jobs and were able to put in their week's work without an inordinate amount of stress or frustration.

Susan reflected on the company's founder, Barbara Cray. Barbara's departure was the unintended catalyst for many of the changes. When JWL Adventures approached Barbara and made her an offer she "couldn't refuse," the company was quickly sold and the plant manager, Sam Finch, was named Outdoor Essential's interim president. A plain talker from rural Wisconsin, he grew up on a dairy farm where he learned the practices of hard work, straight talk, and team building. In his previous role as Plant Manager, Sam helped lead the organization through a fairly stable period and managed to get things done in his consistent, no-frills way. Sales were consistent, suppliers reliable, and Outdoor Essential cutting-edge products kept the competition at bay. With only Barbara to answer to, Sam was given tremendous latitude to deal with company's day-to-day business. However, all that had changed in a dramatic, arguably shocking way. Shortly after Barbara's departure, JWL Adventure's senior leadership became increasingly involved in company's business.

Alex Morgan, JWL's President & CEO, decided to leave Outdoor Essentials intact as a separate business and began the search for Barbara's replacement. Alex chose to let Sam fill Barbara's vacancy in the short-term until the completion of a formal hiring process. Although Sam was a strong candidate for the position, the process had to be conducted to ensure all interested candidates had the opportunity to apply. From the beginning, Sam struggled in his interactions with Alex and his management approach. A stoic figure, and a man who said little and appeared to judge all, Alex seemed the antithesis of Sam. An impressive résumé complete with the best educational experiences and powerful positions in both start-up and global organizations, Alex Morgan had mastered the art of lofty rhetoric, confusing metrics, and intimidation.

Enough about the past, Susan thought to herself. I need to focus on the present and the task at hand.

In typical fashion, Sam started the meeting with a few pleasant-ries in an attempt to calm everyone's nerves and put the group at ease. Although appreciated, all in attendance knew that Sam's efforts were simply postponing the inevitable. They were right; in a matter of moments, the conversation turned to the organization's performance on Mr. Morgan's key metrics. Jane Hudson, JWL Adventure's performance improvement manager, retrieved a large stack of documents from her bright red briefcase and distributed them to everyone in the room. She appeared emotionless as she started her presentation.

Despite her small frame, Jane packed a verbal punch. Susan and her colleagues often referred to Jane as a condensed version of Mr. Morgan, as she was a smaller, more concentrated edition of the man. Per usual, Jane was dressed, or at least accessorized, in red; while everyone else in the room wore Outdoor Essentials traditional attire of hiking boots, blue jeans, and signature shirts, Jane sported a full business ensemble. Jane demanded attention and results.

Many interpreted Jane's dispassionate demeanor as a reflection of her calculated, no-nonsense approach to her work. They believed that she was simply acting as a surrogate for Mr. Morgan and would use the recently installed metrics program to replace every leader in the room. In reality, the leadership team's assessment was only half-true. Jane did report directly to Mr. Morgan and was "on loan" to the Outdoor Essentials to drive improved performance and align the newly acquired business with JWL's corporate culture. They were also right in thinking that, if the organization continued to miss established goals, Jane would likely recommend to Mr. Morgan that he replace Sam and everyone else in the room.

What they did not know was how Jane truly felt about the situation. In earlier years, she would brazenly walk into a company intending to either fix leadership or replace them. She had the brains and willingness to do whatever she believed the situation dictated as well as the backing of her boss to make it happen. This approach had served her well; she made a name for herself, and the promotions quickly followed.

Sam first met Jane when he was summoned to JWL's Corporate Headquarters, along with leaders from other business interests, to update the new boss on a number of issues. Sitting in the back of the room, waiting for his turn, Sam watched in dismay as the other briefers were subjected to a barrage of questions from both their boss and Jane, who sat to Mr. Morgan's right. Eventually, Sam found himself standing on the receiving end of the duo's attacks. After taking his share of verbal abuse, Sam licked his wounds and headed to the airport in a daze. He replayed the episode a number of times in his mind, acknowledging that he couldn't avoid Mr. Morgan, but he'd do his best to steer clear of Jane Hudson in the future.

Despite Sam's desire to avoid Jane, she had somehow steered herself right into the weekly Monday morning staff meeting. What he didn't realize was that Jane was not thrilled about it either.

Had someone observed Jane walking to the meeting, they would have noticed a person exhibiting similar discouragement as those around the table. Head down, she plodded toward through the facility carrying her bulging bright red briefcase and an even heavier burden on her shoulders. However, unlike the others in attendance, who brought their dejection into the room and parked it around the conference table, Jane chose to leave her doubts and worries at the door and put on the mask of the focused, aggressive professional. She was very much the person her reputation indicated. Mr. Morgan sent her to get a job done and she was going to do it, no matter the collateral damage. However, unlike past companies Mr. Morgan had dispatched her to fix, she truly liked this group and wanted to see them be successful. She saw potential in Sam, admiring his passion and the manner in which he interacted with his team. It was this admiration that drove her to be even more focused and direct. After all, that was how she had gotten things done in the past, and she was going to bring her best to help this leadership team. If nothing else, she was going to instill the importance of improving their performance. She may have hoped for them to succeed, and was willing to give them the information they needed to run their business more effectively, but ultimately success lay in the hands of the seven people in the room and the 350 or so staff who reported to them.

Always the perfectionist, without an item out of place, Jane adjusted her jacket to ensure that just the right amount of shirt cuff was exposed. Most in the room believed that she was dressed more for an investment banker meeting than a weekly leadership team session. One could only wonder what those on the production floor thought of her "corporate attire." She began. "Last quarter Outdoor Essentials missed twenty-one of the twenty-four established metrics." She paused to allow her comments to take an effect on all in attendance and surveyed the dejected faces in the room. As she continued, Mel Taylor, the once jovial, now painfully unhealthy and increasingly agitated operations manager, let out a sigh that seemed to express the group's collective sentiment.

The leaders watched as Jane presented one confusing performance chart after another. "Frankly, the next quarter is not looking any better. The lead indicators we have in place suggest that the low performance will continue. Your six sigma projects are way behind schedule, and most metrics, including number seven, 'Incremental Return on Invested Capital,' and number fourteen, the 'Employee Productivity Index,' are moving in the wrong direction. Moreover, it's my understanding that several key supervisors and employees will be out in the coming months for required technical and product training. Combine these absences with projected personnel losses, and the situation will only get worse. I assure you that

Mr. Morgan is very concerned with the company's performance. Sure, Outdoor Essentials has done well over the years, but things are changing, and Alex Morgan is not one to accept mediocrity."

Ouch! Susan thought. *Mediocrity? That stings.*

As Jane continued to talk, Susan's mind began to wander. Her mental escape was not from lack of concern. She cared greatly about the future of the organization and its employees. She had simply heard the "bad news" so often that the escape served as a coping mechanism to deal with the stress brought on by these meetings. Jane's monologue continued for the better part of thirty minutes. As the meeting drew to a close, Jane reminded them of the need to "meet the numbers" and "improve performance." She ended with a finishing blow, "Mr. Morgan has told me several times that Outdoor Essentials needs to embrace excellence and begin providing the return on investment that he and the board expect."

When Jane finished her presentation, Sam regained control of the meeting and worked to end on a positive note. "Look folks," Sam began, "I know that we're going through some tough times. Jane has painted an ugly picture for us. We can't hide from it. We need to show some improvements quickly. Each of you knows what needs to be done, so just get out there and do it..." Sam's words trailed off, and the leaders began to slowly rise and work their way out of the room.

Walking to the door, Bill Engleman, the organization's financial manager kept playing Sam's last words over in his mind. *Each of you knows what needs to be done, so just get out there and do it.* He wondered if he really knew what needed to be done. So much had changed. He felt as if the new performance metrics were paralyzing him, his team, and the entire organization. Past leaders had used metrics, such as revenue growth, net income, and production throughput to measure company performance. These were easy to understand and people knew how to relate their daily work to them, but Mr. Morgan's metrics seemed overly complicated and disconnected from everyone's daily work.

Bill walked out the door and right into the "meeting after the meeting." He joined the conversation, and the group huddled in the hallway grew as the leaders came out of the room. Terse statements suggested that most were frustrated with the situation. Sensing their concerns and recognizing that the hallway was not appropriate for a heated discussion, Susan suggested that they meet for lunch the next day to chat about the situation. Everyone agreed, and the impromptu meeting quickly disbanded.

Chapter 2: Reflection

Sam Finch made a quick departure from the staff meeting. He paid little attention to his leadership team gathered in the hallway as he rapidly covered the distance between the conference room and his office. After a brief stop at his assistant's desk to check messages, his schedule confirmed that, in an hour, he was participating in a conference call with Mr. Morgan for the weekly senior leadership session, or as Sam called it, "the grilling."

Sam hustled into his office, collapsed in his chair, and reached for his keyboard. A quick touch brought his computer back to life. He entered his obligatory password and watched his e-mail inbox fill with twenty-seven new messages since he had left his desk ninety minutes earlier. Eight of them were marked 'high priority.' "And they told us that technology was going to make our lives easier," Sam muttered to himself.

He pushed back from his computer, rose to his feet, and walked across the room. The photo on the wall caught his eye, and he paused for a moment to enjoy the image from his family's farm and reflect on his not-so-distant retirement when he would return to his homestead. Hanging adjacent to it was a photo of Sam dressed as Elvis Presley, Sam's favorite performer. The photo was taken at an Outdoor Essentials' annual Halloween party where Sam won the award for best costume and the hearts of his employees for his willingness to fully participate in the event. He moved to his office doorway and looked out at the production floor. From his vantage point, he could see most the two main production lines that produced the majority of outdoor coats with the bright orange "OE" that was the company's trademark. Several people walked through the space, and an occasional forklift rolled through the facility and into Sam's line of sight. The machinery made an indiscernible noise that inhabited the workspace the entire day. Sam was used to these sounds. He had heard them day in and day out over his many years as an Outdoor Essentials' employee.

Sam was one of the first five people to join the company. He started on the "manufacturing line," which consisted of a few cardboard tables, several sewing machines, and a lot of heart, energy, and desire. As the company grew, so did Sam's responsibilities. Over the years, he had played a role in manufacturing, sales, product development, quality, and customer service. Sam ate, drank, and slept Outdoor Essentials. He loved the products, the people, and believed in the company's mission. Yes, Sam had spent most of his days—and far too many late nights—working his way from the manufacturing floor to the front office.

As he watched his colleagues go about their daily work, Sam couldn't help but think that they deserved a better leader. Times were changing. Mr. Morgan was demanding more of the company, and Sam was unable to insulate his team from the new level of scrutiny they faced. Many times he had thought about retiring, and he had been poised to do so at the end of the year when an unexpected sale of the company changed everything. Suddenly, he was in consideration for Barbara's position. He was excited about the chance to lead the organization he cared so much about and let it be known that he was very interested. Although several other candidates had been identified, Sam clearly had the upper hand. He felt confident that he would be selected. After all, no one knew Outdoor Essentials as well as he did. His confidence was his demise.

With little preparation, Sam traveled to JWL's headquarters and strolled into the interview session where he met Mr. Morgan's line of fire. The two had yet to meet, and when Mr. Morgan had unleashed a series of questions about the company's performance over the last several years, trends in industry, the growing global marketplace, and the need for transformation, Sam's lack of preparation was revealed. It was clear that Sam had a good handle on the people in the company, but his comments on specific performance aspects and anecdotal examples failed to provide the strategic vision, statistical rigor, and overall sophistication Mr. Morgan had expected. Sam left the interview session demoralized. It had felt less like an interview and more like an inquisition, and he knew that his performance had been poor. Sam was not surprised when Mr. Morgan informed him that he was not prepared to appoint him as Outdoor Essentials' President, but would name him as the interim leader until a "suitable replacement could be found."

Those were Mr. Morgan's exact words.

Sam was constantly reminded of them. They often woke him in the middle of the night, and they consumed his thoughts throughout the day. Deep down, Sam knew that he was the right person for the job. In the beginning, he felt that he could convince Mr. Morgan to place him permanently in the position if given enough time. However, Mr. Morgan's appointment of Jane Hudson as the new performance improvement manager and the organization's performance to date on Mr. Morgan's twenty-four key metrics was wearing on Sam. He estimated that his time in the position was limited to another ninety days if the company didn't show marked improvement.

★ ★ ★

Three doors down, Susan Walker was also reflecting on the situation. Her mind returned to the questions she had been asking herself prior to the start of the weekly staff meeting and the subsequent conversation with her colleagues. She was considering her career and the situation she found herself and the organization facing.

A flurry of questions swirled in her head. Did I move up the ranks too quickly? Am I in over my head? Should I work on my résumé and find a new job before things get worse and my choices become limited? How can I leave the company and the people I care about without a fight?

Before she could form an answer to any of these questions, there was a knock at her door. She looked up to see Sam. He was on his way to the conference room to take Mr. Morgan's call and had stuck his head in to ask about some HR issues that might come up during "the grilling." Susan gave him the information he requested and took a moment to ask how he was doing. Over the years, the two had formed a trusting relationship, and both felt comfortable confiding in the other. She could tell by the look on his face that he was stressed, and his comments confirmed her assessment. Susan shared that she and her colleagues were equally frustrated, and that they had agreed to meet the next day for lunch to talk over the situation.

At first, Sam was defensive. He questioned what they were up to and why they would meet without him and away from the office. To ease his concerns, Susan invited him to come along. He responded, "Susan, I'm sorry if I questioned everyone's intentions. This whole change in ownership and our poor performance is eating at me. Frankly, I'm at a loss. I don't know what to do next. I used to be so confident in my role and the direction of the company." He paused to collect his thoughts.

Susan jumped in, "Sam, we're all in the same place. That's exactly why we decided to get together away from the facility. If you're going to be upset at anyone, be upset with me. I'm the one who suggested we meet offsite for lunch." She paused and looked at him earnestly. "To be honest, the 'meeting after the meeting' in the hallway was becoming heated. I didn't want anyone to let their emotions get the best of them, especially in the open, where anyone could hear the conversation. We all want to see you succeed." Sam's expression softened. "In fact, it would be wonderful if you could join us tomorrow. I think getting away from the office would be good for all of us."

"I might just take you up on the offer," Sam responded. Looking at his watch, he added, "I've got to go. I don't want to be late for the grilling…I mean meeting." With a quick smile, Sam turned and walked away.

Chapter 3: Short-Notice Gathering

The restaurant was overrun with customers, but most of the patrons were eating outside. Spring had arrived, and after a long winter, people seemed pleased to enjoy the first warm afternoon of the year. In her typical fashion, Susan arrived at the sandwich shop fifteen minutes early. She had a natural desire to take care of people and ensure everyone felt comfortable, so she secured a corner table and began arranging chairs. She had been to the sandwich shop two weeks earlier with her husband and felt that it was the perfect location for the short-notice gathering. The food was good, but more importantly, the restaurant was located a few miles from the Outdoor Essentials' facility and the table arrangement allowed for private conversation. Susan had hoped to avoid running into other company employees or have other diners overhear their conversation. Although they weren't going to discuss anything too sensitive, Susan felt more comfortable knowing that they were far less exposed than the hallway where the conversation had started.

Susan was relieved to learn that Jane Hudson would not be available for the discussion. Not that Susan would have invited Jane, but the fact that the performance improvement manager was out, harassing a part of Mr. Morgan's kingdom, made things easier. After all, what would Susan have said to her? "Why yes, Jane. We're all going to lunch, but we'd prefer you not tag along. To be honest, most of the discussion will be about you, Mr. Morgan, and the twenty-four metrics the two of you have been beating us up about. In fact, I hope we can get our heads around how to get the company moving in the right direction and getting you assigned someplace else." Susan was glad she was able to avoid that conversation.

Not surprisingly, Michael Thomas was next to arrive. Towering above most of the patrons crowding the entrance, Michael was easy to spot. The "Sales Guy," as Susan called him, was every bit of six foot six. Rumor had it that he was a decent basketball player in college and had made a bit of a name for himself among the avid fans at his alma mater. Watching him effortlessly weave his way through the lunch crowd, Susan had no doubt that he was a former athlete.

Susan waved him over and invited him to take a seat at the table. Michael secured the chair that would allow him the best view of the restaurant and took a seat.

An outgoing type, Susan wasn't surprised when Michael started the conversation. "Thank you for organizing this meeting. I'm concerned about the direction of the company, and I'm glad we'll have the chance to talk about the issues as a leadership team without the prying eyes and ears of Ms. Hudson."

"My pleasure. I thought it better that we all got together sooner, as opposed to waiting any longer," she responded.

Before either could continue their conversation, Bill Engleman walked up to the table. He explained that Mel Taylor was at the counter placing their orders and that he would hold the table if Susan and Michael wanted to order too.

Fifteen minutes later Outdoor Essentials' leadership team, including the interim president, was seated around the table, exchanging small talk and eating their meals. Sam waited until all were settled and started the discussion.

"Firstly, I wish to extend my thanks to Susan for setting up this get-together."

Everyone nodded in agreement.

He continued, "Listen folks, I know that things have been trying the last few months. Mr. Morgan and Ms. Hudson have been pretty hard on the company. I wish that I had the answers for how to best address the situation, but I'm at a bit of a loss. I've known each of you for years, and I trust your judgment. I'd like to hear your thoughts on the situation."

No one at the table was shocked by Sam's approach. Although guarded the last few months, he had always been the type of leader who welcomed—actually encouraged—input from the team. All were glad to see this side of him reappear.

Without hesitation, Mel responded, "I'll go first. To say that I'm frustrated with the situation would be an understatement. I've been running operations for several years. I know how things work, and I'm getting pretty tired of having someone from outside our company constantly telling us that we're underperforming." Mel's face got redder and his voice louder as he continued, "I don't know what's going on above us, but if I hear the word 'transformation' one more time, my head's going to explode."

Thinking it might happen at that very moment, Bill Engleman jumped in. "I think I know what Mel is saying. I've been working in the financial management world for years. I'm concerned about some of the metrics they're using to measure our performance and the way they approach interacting with us."

Susan agreed. "You guys are right, and I'll take it a step further. Not only am I frustrated by the situation, but our people are too. They seem to be feeding off of our aggravation, and I'm seeing them focus less and less on their work."

The discussion continued with each leader sharing concerns. They spent the better part of the next half an hour venting. After each shared their ideas and thoughts, Sam took charge. "I appreciate each of you opening up and sharing your feelings. I'd sum it up by saying that we're all in the same place. As painful as it is to admit, I own much of the blame for our problems. I wish I could go back and change some things, but I can't. I think that our best move at this point is to focus on improving Mr. Morgan's twenty-four metrics. I'm open to any thoughts about how to make some positive strides. Remember, my door is always open." Sam paused momentarily as he looked at his watch. "My goodness, time has gotten away from me. I've got to get back to the office for a meeting with a vendor. Let's plan to do this again soon. Thanks for your time. I value each and every one of you and believe that we will work through this together."

Everyone at the table returned the sentiment, conveyed their willingness to keep the dialogue moving, and committed to looking for solutions to the challenges they faced. One by one, they excused themselves from the table. Susan was the last one to leave. As she headed to the door, she reflected on the conversation over the past hour. Well, she thought, we didn't manage to come up with a solution like I'd hoped, but I think it was a good use of time to get the issues on the table and to express our support to Sam.

She stepped out onto the sidewalk and paused for a moment to enjoy the sun. She started toward her car. Along the way, she passed a bookstore. The sign read "Oliver's Spot." A sticker in the window indicated that the establishment had been a member of the Reader's Guild since 1968. She glanced at her watch and decided that she could spare a moment to look around.

As Susan swung the old door open, an old-fashioned bell announced her arrival. The door's inability to shut squarely revealed the building's advanced age. The creaky floor echoed the sentiment. One glance confirmed that the store was much different from the large bookstore chains. It didn't have a coffee bar, there were no comfy chairs to sit in, and stacks of books signified that organization was not high on the priority list. Deciding that sifting through the piles was more than she had time or energy to tackle, she reached for the door-knob. She stopped when she heard a man's voice asking, "May I help you?"

Chapter 4: Chance Meeting

Susan turned to see an older gentleman peering out from behind the cluttered counter. "How can I be of assistance?" he asked again.

"Well, I'm not certain what I'm looking for, and I don't have much time. Perhaps I can come back another day," she responded.

"That would be fine," he said, "but I know my way around here pretty well. Why don't you tell me what you are interested in, and I'll see if I can dig something up for you." As he came out from behind the counter, Susan got her first look at Oliver Stanton. He wore a crisp pair of khaki pants and a dark blue shirt. It appeared to be a button-down, but Susan wasn't quite sure as a smock covered most of it. He had a full head of disheveled white hair, and he was squinting at her over a pair of reading glasses. His unkempt hair and strained eyes revealed that he had been deep in thought. People were always telling him that if you put a book in front of him, a bomb could go off and he wouldn't notice it. The assessment proved true, as he had barely noticed Susan's entrance.

Susan paused to gather her thoughts. Out of desperation from her work predicament or curiosity about this interesting character, she decided to take him up on the offer. "Yes, perhaps you can help me." He took a few steps closer as she continued, "I'm looking for some information. Do you have a section on organizational performance?"

"Absolutely. We have a number of books that address organizational performance. Some are in our management section, and others are kept with our leadership materials. If I may ask, I've noticed that people use the phrase to mean different things. When you say 'organizational performance,' what do you mean?"

Sensing the gentleman's genuine desire to be of assistance, Susan began to clarify her thoughts. "Well, I'm looking for something that will tell me how an organization can work together to accomplish a number of performance metrics." Although she started slowly, the words soon came quickly. "Where I work, we're trying to do a number of things as part of our everyday duties. Then we have a laundry list of metrics in place that we are being held accountable to—"

Before she could go any further, Oliver interrupted, "Please excuse my jumping in, but I believe that I'm starting to get an idea of what you are looking for. May I ask a couple of other questions?"

Although not one to be easily offended by the interruption, Susan appreciated his politeness. "Of course," she responded.

Removing his glasses with his left hand and steadying a stack of books with his right, Oliver asked, "When you say 'a number of metrics,' how many are you referring to?"

Without hesitation she blurted out, "Twenty-four!"

"Well, you certainly knew that number." A full smile and brief nod of the head encouraged Susan to continue.

"Of course I do, we hear about them every week," she added.

Oliver raised his left hand, glasses held firmly in his grasp, and motioned for Susan to pause. "And of these twenty-four, are they all equally important, or are some more important than others?"

"That's a great question. I really hadn't thought about it that way."

Susan cast her eyes downward as she reflected on his question.

He followed with another. "And when you said that you have the everyday work and then the metrics, does that mean they're in conflict with one another?"

Susan answered, "They sure seem to be. The week usually starts with a meeting that focuses on the twenty-four metrics and whether we are or are not performing." She paused to consider if she was telling too much to a perfect stranger. Deciding that it was safe to continue, she added, "But soon after the weekly meeting is over, we go back to our normal work. Although we have the desire to improve on the metrics, we never seem to get there."

"Very interesting," Oliver said, almost to himself. "So, if I understand you correctly, you have a number of performance measures your company is supposed to perform against. You also have daily work that seems unrelated to those measures. Even though you want to do well on the measures, you can never seem to get to them because of all the other work that needs to be done. Is that about right?"

"Yes, that sounds about right," Susan answered, half embarrassed.

Recognizing both her sense of embarrassment and the reality that her situation was not unique, he calmly continued, "Who created the performance measures?"

"I'm not exactly certain who specifically created them, but I know they were handed down from people above our organization."

"Hmm...that's interesting," he said, not in a judgmental way but in a manner that suggested he was absorbing what she had told him. "So what happens if your company manages to win on all the metrics?"

"We get to keep our jobs," she said with a smile.

"Okay, I get that." Oliver smiled in return. "But what's the big win? In other words, if you win on all of the smaller metrics, what's the big thing that happens or doesn't happen?"

"Honestly, I don't really know," she replied.

"You know what," he said with a wink, "until you figure that out and can explain it to your people, everything else doesn't really matter that much." He paused to let his words soak in, and then he continued, "Here, we have many books on organizational performance.

I know that I've ordered them, stocked them, sold them, and I read the majority of them. And you know what? They all say pretty much the same thing." Susan listened intently "I'm more than happy to sell you a book or two. I'm just not sure what they will do for you. Books are helpful, no doubt, but I think you would benefit most from a conversation. If you're interested, I'd be happy to chat with you a bit more."

"Wait a second, aren't you in the bookselling business?" she quipped.

"I'll be honest. Selling books has been a great career for me and I've enjoyed it immensely, but I'm much more interested in helping to solve problems. Some folks even think that I'm pretty good at it. Give it some thought, and if you're interested, pay me another visit sometime. It would be great to share with you the five steps teams follow to get things moving in the right direction."

"Five steps?" Susan asked.

"Yes, five steps. I've learned from decades of reading books," he said, motioning to the stacks of books surrounding him, "that there are five things organizations do well to drive exceptional performance."

"I have to admit, you have certainly piqued my curiosity."

"I'll tell you what," he said as he searched for a piece of paper on the cluttered countertop. "I'll give you the number here at the store. If you want to come by and discuss this further, give me a call and we can set up a time to chat. You can even bring some other folks along if you want." He tore off the bottom half of a sheet of paper and scribbled down his name and number.

Susan was taken aback by the offer. "Thanks," she said as she glanced at the paper. "So you're Oliver, as in Oliver's Spot?"

"Guilty as charged," he replied.

"Nice to meet you, Oliver. I'm Susan." The words were barely out of her mouth when the bookstore's phone rang. Oliver excused himself to get it. Susan turned and headed for the door.

Step 1: Gain Perspective

Chapter 5: First Impressions

Had someone told her a week earlier that she would have been sitting in the old bookstore the following Thursday afternoon, Susan would have thought that person crazy. However, there she sat, and the only person she considered crazy was herself. Sitting adjacent to her was Bill Engleman, the company's CFO, who was contemplating his own sanity after already deciding that Susan had lost hers. When she talked him into meeting Oliver Stanton, he was skeptical. After arriving at the store, surveying the cluttered shelves, and catching a glimpse of Oliver, he was certain that the pressures of Mr. Morgan's metrics had pushed her over the edge.

When Susan left Oliver's Spot two days earlier, the discussion had intrigued her. On her way back to the office, she had decided that Bill was the one colleague she could confide in about the conversation at the small bookstore. Over the years, Susan and Bill had often bounced ideas off one another. Each found the other to be the type of sounding board every good leader needs. Her attempt to track Bill down proved futile. He was buried in a mid-year budget review with no chance of surfacing anytime soon. Even if he had come up for air, she knew better than to try to talk to him on the heels of an afternoon budget session.

The next morning, Susan was standing in front of Bill's desk. She asked for a few minutes of his time, and without giving him an opportunity to object, she launched into the story about the bookstore, its owner, and their brief but interesting conversation. Bill learned that

Susan had tried to talk with him the previous day because she was slightly interested in paying the bookstore another visit. If they had met then, he probably would have talked Susan out of it. There was no changing her mind now. Her desire to visit the bookstore again had grown over the course of the night. By morning, she was resolved to have at least one more conversation with Oliver.

Susan wasn't a bit surprised at Bill's response. If she lacked in skepticism, Bill certainly made up for it. He leaned back in his seat and chuckled as she described her initial interaction with Oliver. "Come on, Susan," he said, his eyes narrowing, "this guy's goal is probably to sell you a dozen books—or better yet, get you to buy two or three for every employee in the company."

Defending the bookstore owner, Susan retorted that he had had the opportunity to sell her a book the day before and had elected not to. She added that he seemed like a kind older gentleman who was genuinely interested in helping them solve their problem. Bill countered that perhaps he was just a lonely old man desperate to drag some people into the store for an afternoon of conversation over a cup of coffee. Although she disagreed with Bill's assessment, she wasn't in a fighting mood. She conceded that it was possible that additional time spent at Oliver's Spot might be a waste, but she was willing to run the risk if it meant the possibility of learning something that would make next Monday's staff meeting even a bit more bearable.

Her final comment stopped Bill in his tracks. "You can laugh at me if you want and choose not to come, but a few hours invested with Oliver might be a small price to pay if it brings a hint of relief."

Even Bill couldn't disagree with that argument.

When Susan and Bill arrived at the store, Oliver was on the phone and a co-worker was helping a customer at the cash register. Oliver gave them a smile and pointed to the back room, indicating that he would be there in a few minutes. The pair followed his direction and made their way to the "meeting room." As they moved from the public portion of the establishment to the employees-only section, they were not surprised at what they saw. The clutter of the store extended and perhaps intensified in the back room. Both wondered how Oliver got anything done in such a cramped, untidy storage area.

Although the room was messy, it was evident that their host had prepared for the visit by arranging a table and chairs and organizing several stacks of books on an array of topics both on and adjacent to the table. Susan's quick count indicated that there were a dozen stacks with no less than fifteen books. On top of each stack was a five-by-eight index card with a topic hand-printed in all capitals. She walked around the folding table and grabbed a seat next to a large stack of books. Perched at the top was a card that read "Performance Management." Bill sat next to her. He too noted the stacks and read the card on the pile labeled "Strategic Planning" to his left.

The two said little to each other. Both were absorbed in their own thoughts and paid no attention to the phone conversation in the other room. They only became aware of the phone call as it reached its conclusion. As he finished the call, Oliver's voice grew louder. "Absolutely, it's my pleasure. I'm glad I could be of assistance. I'll talk to you soon. Goodbye." His final words were still making their way to the back room when he entered the storage area.

Susan introduced the store's owner to her colleague. She kept the introduction brief, mainly because she didn't know much about Oliver. As she turned to Bill to finish the second part of the ritual, she looked her colleague straight in the eye. He nearly stared a hole through her, indicating that he was ready to leave. Meeting his stare with a calm smile, Susan spared the details on Bill's bio and suggested that they get started.

Always a gracious host, Oliver offered his guests something to drink. Both declined. He picked up a white carafe from a table in the corner, poured water in a ceramic mug, and began to peruse the teabags stored in a wooden box. After several seconds of deliberation, he selected one. "Yes, this will work just fine," he said to himself. He removed the teabag from its packaging and placed it in the hot water. As he walked to the table, he discarded the wrapper into a small trash can.

The portable table wobbled slightly as Oliver placed his mug in front of the third seat. He sat down and looked first at Susan, where he benefited from her ever-present smile, and then at Bill, who failed to provide a similar benefit.

Oliver wasn't shaken by Bill's demeanor.

"Okay," he said, "let's begin."

Chapter 6: Ground Rules

"I have to admit that I didn't think you'd come today," Oliver said to Susan. Turning to Bill, he added, "And I certainly didn't expect you to bring someone with you. This is a pleasant surprise."

"Well, since we're coming clean on things, I must admit that I'm surprised that I came as well. Don't get me wrong," she said with slight hesitation, "I'm not intending to be disrespectful. It's just we met only briefly. I'm not sure how you can really help, and I'm guarded about sharing much about our company."

"That's fair enough," Oliver said. "Why don't we lay down some ground rules for our conversation? You're right, we know very little about each other. Perhaps we could agree to what should or shouldn't be shared." He paused to gather his thoughts. "I don't know about the two of you, but I often find that setting some professional ground rules can be helpful."

Susan and Bill shared a look of relief. "That sounds like a good idea," Bill responded. "What do you have in mind?"

"First, I can see that you work for Outdoor Essentials," he said motioning to the logo on their shirts, "yours is a great company that enjoys a wonderful reputation in our community. Beyond the general scuttlebutt in town, I know little about your business and I see no need for that to change. For the purpose of our discussion, your business is none of my business." As Oliver spoke, the tension seemed to leave the room. "I don't need to know the details about what your employees do or how your business is currently performing. In fact, I suggest that you convey only what you feel comfortable sharing. I imagine that we'll mostly discuss general ideas about organizations, how they perform, and what I've learned about improving performance. How does that sound?"

Susan's eyes brightened. "That sounds good," she responded. Bill nodded in agreement.

"Second, as Susan and I discussed on the phone, let's meet for one hour today. There are no commitments or expectations beyond that. If the two of you find the conversation helpful, that's great, and we can get together again to continue. However, if you decide that this meeting was a waste of your time, no harm done. In fact, I recommend we make no commitments today about getting together again. You two can talk about it after you leave. Susan has my number."

Bill and Susan both agreed that this was a good approach. Susan added in her usual upbeat tone that they did value his time and expected that the session would be beneficial.

"Third, you might be concerned that you're committing your company to some sort of consulting agreement and that I will hand you an invoice when you leave. Let me assure you, this is not the case. I'm not a consultant—I'm an avid reader. Consider this more of a book club." As Oliver explained ground rule three, he watched Bill's face light up. Again, his tablemates nodded in agreement. "I have one last ground rule." He looked at Susan first and then at Bill. His face conveyed complete sincerity. "I'm an open book," he said. "Ask me anything you like. My only goal for our time together is to help the two of you help your organization—nothing more."

Oliver's ability to put people at ease was evident. They both believed him.

Bill and Susan indicated that the ground rules seemed sufficient. Their new teacher asked a few general questions about Outdoor Essentials. He inquired about their industry, the size of their teams, and about how long each of them had worked there. Staying true to the ground rules, he didn't ask any details about work or performance specifics.

Susan took the lead. She explained that Outdoor Essentials employed about 350 people and offered a full-range of outdoor clothing and apparel through a network of distributors and via the company's growing on-line presence. She described in general terms how the company was organized and the recent purchase by JWL Adventures.

When she finished her brief overview, Oliver walked to the chalkboard, cleared his throat, and rolled up his sleeves. He turned to Bill and Susan and began his lecture. "The other day when Susan visited the store, she asked me about books on organizational performance. As I explained to her, we stock many books on organizational performance. Every year many texts that deal with various aspects of improvement hit the market. Just take a look at the stacks I assembled this morning." He pointed to several and paused for dramatic effect. "These stacks represent what various authors have written about the subject from a number of different viewpoints. Whether writing from the perspective of general management, leadership, statistics, marketing, or a wide range of other functions, they collectively make the argument for a number of steps that leaders and their teams should follow to be most successful."

"Five of them, right?" Susan added.

"Yes, I believe the ideas distill down to five essential steps. Over the years, I have shared these five steps with many people. Some were leaders in large organizations; others worked in the smallest of teams. Not only do these leaders agree with me when I explain the steps to them, but I have heard some amazing stories of the results they achieved by applying these steps."

He turned and picked up a piece of chalk sitting in the small trough at the base of the chalkboard. The board appeared to be decades old and was framed by a border of dark wood that rested on two sturdy legs. The legs sat on caster wheels, and although it had the ability to move, it appeared to have been positioned in the same place for years. On the left and right sides of the frame were two brass knobs that could be loosened so that the entire board could rotate, revealing the other side and, no doubt, more writing space. The chalkboard reminded Susan of her childhood. Her fourth grade teacher had had an identical board. Susan thought that if Ms. Ryan were still teaching today, she and Oliver would be the two people still using these chalkboard relics.

Oliver interrupted her daydream. "Ever since I was a kid, I've consistently done two things. First, I asked lots of questions, so much so that I drove my parents, teachers, and friends crazy. Second, I read everything and anything I could get my hands on. These two obsessions served me well in school and later in business."

Susan and Bill glanced around the place.

Oliver watched as the two looked about. "Now, I know what you're thinking." He looked pointedly at the mess surrounding them. "How did all this questioning and reading serve him well in business?" Without hesitation, he answered his own question. "Prior to purchasing this store some ten years ago, I owned a regional chain of bookstores called AC's."

Bill jumped in. "I'm familiar with that name. There were a couple of them here in town. I also think there were some upstate."

"Actually, just prior to selling them, there were three throughout this city and fifty-four stores in total," Oliver explained. "Things were going great and the business was thriving. Then one day, I received a phone call on behalf of a national competitor. They asked if I was interested in selling. At first, I said no, but they eventually put an offer on the table that I couldn't refuse." His smile revealed that the offer must have been quite sizeable. Susan and Bill both considered how Oliver's situation was similar to what had recently transpired at their company. "After the deal went through, I hung around for about six months to help with the transition. Then I decided to try my hand at retirement. It didn't take. I started hanging around this place a lot and eventually made an offer to buy this store. In many ways, I'm back where I started. It's a different store in a different part of town, but I'm the same guy surrounded by books again."

Before Bill or Susan could add anything, Oliver turned to the chalkboard, drew a circle in the middle of it, and wrote the words "YOUR TEAM."

Oliver turned to face Bill and Susan and continued. "Let's begin with a brief discussion about the implementation of strategic plans. Of course, the execution of a strategy can break down for a number of reasons. Perhaps the strategy is not well thought out; thus, no matter how well implemented, the desired results will not be achieved. Other times, as the organization begins to implement a strategy, a major shift occurs that causes senior leadership to move in a different direction and discard or significantly revise the plan."

Bill and Susan both nodded their heads, suggesting that they had seen each of these situations play out in the past.

"However," Oliver continued, "from my experience, most strategies succeed or fail based on the decisions that teams and their leaders make every day. This happens because teams choose on a day-to-day basis how to apply the organization's resources. In doing so, they may elect to behave in ways that align with the strategy or run in opposition to it. Let's face it, at some point, the grand strategy eventually lands on a team's shoulders, and it's their job to implement it. The best organizations are separated from the merely good ones not by their ability to plan, but by their ability to implement the plan. Successful implementation of a plan happens—or doesn't—at the team level.

"Is it fair to say that both of you lead teams and that your organization is made of teams, whether they be groups of three, ten, or fifty?"

Susan confirmed Oliver's suspicions. "Yes, our company is made of teams. Some, like mine, are small with only a few employees, while others are much larger."

"Wonderful, that's what I suspected," Oliver responded as he turned again to face the board. He drew a second, much larger circle, around the original one. This circle was made of dashed lines with the words "Step 1: Gain Perspective" neatly printed at the top.

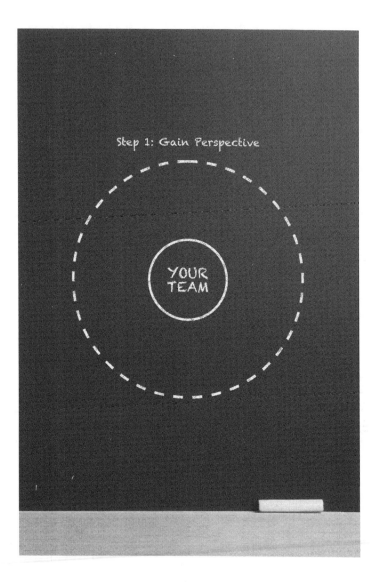

Oliver glanced over his shoulder and observed both Susan and Bill copying his illustration in their notes. Poised to explain step one, Oliver waited for them to finish their sketches. When both had completed the task, they looked first at one another and then at their teacher. With that, the most important lesson of their professional lifetime began.

Chapter 7: Begin at the Beginning

After neatly drawing the dashed circle and labeling it "Step 1: Gain Perspective" on the chalkboard, Oliver explained the importance of perspective. He informed them that many books on organizational performance begin with some notion of understanding what is going on inside or outside the organization that will directly or indirectly affect a team's ability to implement the strategy. He emphasized terms that both of them recognized, such as Strengths, Weaknesses, Opportunities, and Threats Analysis, or SWOT, and 360-degree organizational assessments. He further explained that very few books provided detailed specifics that leaders could actually employ to meet the demands of their current situation.

As Oliver talked, both Bill and Susan were amazed by his ability to adapt to the situation. It had only been a few minutes since he had learned that they worked for Outdoor Essentials. Nonetheless, he had modified his language and approach to relate to the specific challenges they faced in their roles in a mid-size, newly acquired company.

"Perspective is all about determining what matters to those who matter to you. It helps you understand how the company is currently performing, what is possible, and what is simply not going to happen. When you work in any organization, some things are within your control; however, many things are not. Thus, gaining perspective affords you and your people the opportunity to put your best efforts and resources in action against those that really matter."

"Hold on," Bill interjected. "I have to stop you there. What about all of the things I've read and heard about setting grandiose goals and objectives? Aren't we, as leaders, supposed to be visionary?"

"Don't get me wrong," Oliver responded. "I'm not saying to squash creativity and initiative by not dreaming big. I'm saying that before you go charging down a new path, put things into perspective. There may very well be times in your career where you can set lofty goals to take your team in a new direction. There are also times where the goals are essentially dictated down to you, and your wisest move is to act on those goals first, deliver the results, and earn the right to take on the next challenge. Setting a grandiose goal or objective for your team might be exactly the right thing to do. I'm simply saying to pause first and assess the situation. In any business, grand plans without funding and senior leadership support are hallucinations. Perspective helps you determine what's possible and important today based upon current realities."

"Okay, I understand," Bill replied. "You aren't saying dream small, you're saying dream smart."

"Exactly!"

"Well, how do we do that?" retorted Bill.

"That's precisely what we're going to discuss next. We'll use a tool I call the Perspective Matrix." Oliver turned to the board and wrote four words: Who, What, How, and Which. Underneath each, he wrote a question.

Perspective Matrix

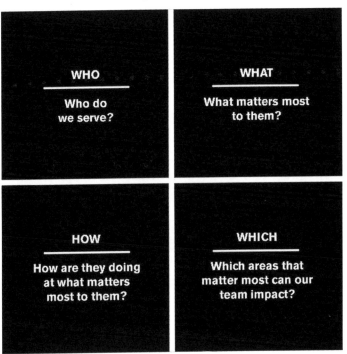

"I know these are simple questions, but the answers are critical. The first focuses on who we serve. All too often, teams think they exist simply because the company's structure dictates their existence. They have a box on the organizational chart. Therefore, they have a rightful seat at the table. Although this is true to an extent, all companies, business units, teams, and individual employees exist to serve others."

Susan stopped taking notes and looked up from her paper. Her eyes gazed toward the ceiling and her head tilted slightly to the right. Oliver sensed her concern and paused.

"If we were the corner coffee shop that might be easy to answer, but in our world, things are more complicated. I have all sorts of people that I serve. I have my direct boss, and I have the other leaders in the company. I also have individual team members who rely on our team for a number of issues, and I'm quickly learning that I answer to other HR people in the corporation who dictate what we can and can't do. In addition, we are increasingly assigned to ad hoc teams at JWL Adventures that place demands on our time."

Bill added a short, "Ditto," and the ball was back in Oliver's court.

"Fair enough. I suggest that you invest some time developing a complete customer list. You can prioritize them later, but for now, just capture all of them." Susan and Bill nodded, and Oliver returned to the chalkboard. "Once you have listed your whos, now consider what matters most to them. In some instances, answering this question can be achieved by reading through some documentation. If your boss just generated a plan for the future, read it to see what matters to him or her. In most cases, though, answering this question requires an actual face-to-face conversation."

Susan and Bill both saw the humor in the statement. Other than a formal staff meeting or a quick conversation in the hallway or the production floor, neither could think of a real conversation in the last several days with anyone who might appear on their list.

"You can phrase things any way you'd like. What you are trying to find out from each person is what matters most to him or her." Oliver smiled wryly, "You will have to trust me on this one, but I think you'll be surprised to find that many people haven't thought through their answer to this question."

"I'm sure our boss's boss has," Susan added. "Remember, we have twenty-four different metrics that he measures and we talk about every week at our staff meetings."

"Yes, I remember." Oliver reflected back on his first conversation with Susan. "But I would suggest that we're confusing a couple of different issues here. In most companies, we tend to measure what can be measured without truly thinking through what's most important. Consider my bookstore. I can measure all sorts of things: how many customers come in every day; how many books I have in stock; how many items each customer purchases; how many times I'm asked for something that is out of stock; how many times I'm asked for something that is in stock; how many people call every day with questions; how quickly I answer the phone when they call. The list could go on and on. The key isn't measuring everything. The key is sorting through all the possible measures and identifying the ones that if focused on and improved really make all the difference in the world.

"Here's my challenge to both of you. Go back to your company, talk to your teams, talk to those who matter the most to your teams, and try to answer the questions for the top three customers you support. Second, seize the opportunity the next time the twenty-four measures are discussed to ask the question, 'Of all these measures, which ones really matter the most?' You can fully expect at first that you will be told that each one is essential. I encourage you not to accept that as the final answer. Push back a little bit by saying something like, 'Okay, I imagine they are all important—otherwise we wouldn't be talking about them. But if you had to identify the few critical ones, which would they be?'"

Surprisingly, Bill responded first with a hearty, "You know what, Oliver? We've got nothing to lose. I'll commit to both tasks and to coming back here next week if you're willing to discuss how things are progressing."

Susan added that she would do the same. They wrapped up their discussion as they walked out of the back room and through the store. Trailing behind them, Oliver called out, "I look forward to hearing how things go. Let's plan on getting together the same time next week.

After we discuss how things are progressing, I'll share the second step with you."

As they walked out the door, both turned and smiled at Oliver. Susan mouthed a quick "Thank you" to him as they stepped into the afternoon sun.

Chapter 8: Gaining Perspective

As they drove back to the plant, Susan and Bill talked about the session with Oliver. They both agreed that, over the next day, they would spend some time on their own working to answer the questions he had outlined for them. Both felt that they could take a fairly good stab at answering the questions for those individuals or teams that they felt represented the top three most important customers. They also agreed that they would get together prior to the next Monday morning staff meeting, share their progress with each other, and decide how they would tackle asking questions about Mr. Morgan's twenty-four metrics.

Friday morning arrived early for Susan. She was up well before dawn and was in her office long before the overnight production team finished its shift. Despite her initial reservations about answering Oliver's questions, she found the process invigorating. She started by creating an exhaustive list of all the people who mattered to her team. Admittedly, had she answered the question, "Who matters to your team?" off the cuff, she probably would have replied that there were only a handful of people or teams that mattered. However, after ten minutes of pondering the question, she had a fairly exhaustive list of over thirty individuals or teams that mattered. *Now the hard part,* she thought. Somehow, she had to narrow the list down to the few that mattered the most. Her first pass through the list quickly cut it to less than fifteen names. A second time through and she was down to eight. *Eight isn't bad,* she thought, *but it's a far cry from three, and Bill and I agreed to three*. Then she remembered something that Oliver said. He mentioned that when prioritizing, you have to separate the merely important from those that matter the most.

She looked down at the list of eight names and said to herself, "Okay, Susan, if my team failed to deliver on our responsibilities to three teams or individuals on this list, which ones would have the biggest impact on our future?" The answer jumped out at her. She crossed out five names, leaving herself with the name of Sam Finch (her boss), Mel Taylor (the operations manager), and the name of a JWL Adventure's team she was recently assigned to. Leaving Sam's name on the list made sense. She figured that, if the boss wasn't happy, nothing else mattered too much. She added Mel's team because he was understaffed and faced several HR-related challenges. Lastly, she included the JWL team because the team members were working to help restructure several HR policies that would influence both her company and the entirety of the JWL corporation. The powers that be called the team IMPROVE. It stood for Internal Management, Policy Review, and OVersight Enhancement. When she first saw the name, Susan had chuckled to herself, thinking, *Welcome to the world of large companies where it isn't a real project team if it doesn't have a catchy acronym.*

She set out to identify what mattered most to each of them. She started with Sam and listed a number of things that she felt were important to him. Some were items that she had heard him talk about numerous times. Others were assumptions that she had made based on what had mattered in the past to Barbara. The list was becoming rather lengthy and, as she tried to assess current performance, she began to realize that there were a number of blanks on the page. She decided to transition to Mel's team and quickly found herself in a similar predicament. Susan then turned her attention to the IMPROVE team. She found this one to be a bit easier to address. The team was fairly new, but they had developed some initial project outcomes they were looking to achieve. Thus, listing what mattered most was easy. Identifying current performance was quickly accomplished too, since other than establishing their initial charter, they had really failed to accomplish anything of value to date.

Staring down at a piece of paper peppered with names, some sketchy assumptions, and plenty of blank spaces, Susan decided her next step was to talk to Mel. She figured that she could wait to talk to Sam until she better understood the process. As for the IMPROVE team, that might need to wait a bit longer until she had a chance to sit down and talk to the team's leader, who, frankly, was out of her office on business travel more often than not.

★ ★ ★

That afternoon, she managed to catch up with Mel. Susan and Mel spent the better part of an hour together. At first, he was distracted, and his permanently red face suggested the stress he was under. After five minutes or so, though, the conversation became very productive.

Susan started the discussion simply by saying, "Mel, I'm trying to help my team focus its energy on what truly matters the most. To do so, I have listed a number of customers that we serve, both within Outdoor Essentials and JWL Adventures, and then narrowed it down to the few that seem to be the highest priority at the moment. Your team landed on the short-list, and I was hoping to spend some time together making sure I understand your priorities." She added a warm smile, conveying her sincerity.

Mel responded enthusiastically to her inquiry. He looked at the list of issues she had identified for his team. He confirmed most, deleted a few, and added a couple. He then assessed how his team was performing in each area and helped her think through where the HR team might be able to provide some support. In the end, they came up with four or five areas where the HR team might be able to provide both short-and long-term assistance.

As she walked out of Mel's office, he stopped her and said, "You know, Susan, the last thing I like to do on a Friday afternoon is add another meeting to the calendar, but I'm surely glad you stopped by to talk. I've been up nights trying to figure out some of the performance issues we're facing and never seem to get to the staffing and training challenges. I'm glad that we took the time to discuss them. I know we didn't solve anything specifically, but I feel as if we might be on our way."

Susan replied, "Mel, I should thank you. I appreciate you helping me to better understand the challenges you guys are facing. It really helps me to put things into perspective." The word "perspective" had barely left her mouth before she found herself smiling a bit. At the same time, she swore to herself that Mel's ever-red face had lightened a few shades over the course of their conversation.

★ ★ ★

First thing Monday morning, Susan was sitting at her desk reflecting on her conversation with Mel the previous Friday. Bill Engleman arrived at her door. "Boy, you're in early this morning. Are you scrambling to get your perspective homework completed?"

Bill's question brought her back to the present. She spun around in her chair and responded to his inquiry. "To be honest, I didn't get all of my homework done, but I did make some really good progress. I'm excited to compare notes about what I've learned so far."

In his typical fashion, Bill responded with a somewhat cynical, "Well, I would say that I'm excited to share what I learned. But frankly, until my second or third cup of coffee, I barely get above 'disinterested' on a Monday morning. However, I *did* learn some interesting things over the last couple of days, and I want to hear how things went for you." He glanced at his watch to check the time and, realizing he only had a few minutes, he excused himself, saying, "Susan, let me run to my office, drop off a few things, grab my perspective notes and a cup of coffee, and meet you back here in ten minutes."

Before she could respond, he was gone.

As promised, Bill was back in ten minutes, and the two sat down at a small table in the corner of her office to share their work. Susan went first and described her approach to identifying her team's customers and then narrowing the list to the top three. She discussed her challenges with filling in the form and her decision to meet with Mel in person. Susan emphasized the value of the conversation, and Bill even seemed to smile when she mentioned that Mel's face had appeared to lighten by the end of the discussion.

When it was Bill's turn, his explanation was less descriptive than Susan's, but it was clear that he had made some great progress. He too had narrowed his customer list to three. Like Susan's list, Bill's included Sam, the interim president. He too had decided to wait until a later time to approach Sam. They immediately agreed that they would approach Sam together later that day, after his conference call with Mr. Morgan. Bill continued with his customer list. He had identified two groups within the company that required attention because of the specific ramifications their current actions had on the budgeting process. Like Susan, Bill had seized the initiative to talk to the group's leaders and had used the discussion to complete his *Perspective Matrix*.

Both were pleased with their progress and agreed that the process of putting things in perspective was valuable.

The discussion turned to how best to approach the Monday morning staff meeting. Although Bill was rather hesitant to come right out and ask Oliver's question to Jane Hudson, Susan was willing to address the issue straight on with Mr. Morgan's surrogate and let the chips fall where they may. She added, "Bill, we go in there every week and get beat up by Jane. What's the worst that can happen if I ask a question or two?"

The comment had barely emerged from Susan's mouth when a reminder popped up on her computer screen along with a chime to catch her attention. "Well, we're about to find out," Susan said. "The meeting starts in five minutes. We need to get going." The two of them sprang to their feet and headed to the conference room.

Chapter 9: Staff Meeting with a Twist

As per usual routine, the leadership team filed into the meeting room and took their seats. Susan's mug rested in its customary position, and once again, the casual conversation about the weekend ensued. This time, however, Bill and Susan were clearly absent from the discussion. Instead, they were focused on the task at hand. Their job was to use Oliver's suggestions to challenge Jane Hudson, Alex Morgan's surrogate, about the twenty-four metrics and identify which ones mattered the most. The meeting continued as usual until it was Jane's turn to present. The chart with Mr. Morgan's metrics appeared on the screen. As she worked her way to the front of the room, everyone sat in silence, waiting for the weekly thrashing. Jane had barely begun her presentation when Susan interrupted. "Excuse me, Jane," she said. "May I ask a quick question before you get too far into your report?"

Jane turned toward the voice. The room was silent for a moment, not because of any particular tension, but simply because all were surprised that someone actually had a question. Frankly, the team had an unspoken agreement about the metrics discussion, whereby, as Jane produced the latest results and shared Alex's disappointment in their lack of progress, the leaders remained quiet, took their dose of weekly feedback, and got out of the room as quickly as possible. What was Susan thinking, breaking protocol? Any question asked was only going to slow down the process and make the pain last longer.

Jane was as shocked as the rest of them. "Please go ahead," she replied.

Susan cleared her throat, sat up a bit straighter in her chair, and began. "I've been thinking about the metrics we review each week. If you had to identify those that were *most* important to Mr. Morgan, which ones would they be?"

Just as Oliver predicted, Jane responded, "Well, they're all important. If they weren't important, Alex wouldn't have asked us to track them."

Following Oliver's suggestion, Jane replied, "Oh, I didn't mean to suggest that they some weren't important. I just wonder if you could name the top few. You know, the three or so that matter most at this moment, what would they be?"

Surprisingly, Jane had an answer. Without hesitation, she said, "Okay, I see what you're asking, and frankly had you asked that question last week, I probably wouldn't have had a good answer for you. However, late last week, I met with Alex to discuss the beginning of a business planning effort he's about to start. In the discussion, he identified his top four objectives, or pillars, as he calls them. Please keep in mind that these aren't solidified and will likely change somewhat as they are refined; however, since you asked, I'm willing to share. I don't think Mr. Morgan will take issue with my sharing his preliminary ideas with you in an effort to answer your question."

In an instant, the mood in the room changed. First, in the group's eyes, Jane moved from Mr. Morgan's minion to someone who appeared to be, even if only slightly, on their side. Second, instead of wanting to run for the door, the entire leadership team was anxious to hear what Jane had to say.

"Let me pull up a presentation I'm working on, as it captures the essence of my discussion with Alex." Jane purposefully walked over to her laptop, which was connected to the projector in the back of the room, to search for the file. As she looked for it, Jane thought that Alex might very much care that she was sharing the information with the Outdoor Essentials' team. In fact, he hadn't even seen, much less approved, the materials she was about to share. But in that instant, Jane was concerned less about possibly upsetting her boss than she was about helping the new acquired company's leadership. It was her hope from the start that she would be able to help them win on the metrics. This was her first and perhaps only chance, and she wasn't going to let it pass.

"Yes, here it is." Jane motioned toward the screen. On it appeared a slide that read, "Preliminary Business Planning Direction." "Again, I should include the caveat that this is a draft and hasn't been fully vetted by Alex, so please keep the information to yourselves. In the coming weeks, he will refine these thoughts as he prepares for a business planning session that will take place soon."

Glancing at his calendar, Sam added, "Yes, I believe the session is scheduled for three days in mid-April. I've been asked to be there; however, other than putting the dates on my calendar, I have little insight into the agenda."

"My understanding," Jane responded, "is that you and Mr. Morgan's other direct reports will be going through a planning session focused on the development of a two-year business plan. The discussion will include reviewing the results of an internal and external assessment that is underway and the creation of strategic goals and objectives that build on Mr. Morgan's preliminary strategic direction." Jane moved onto the second slide, which displayed the words "Pillar One: Operational Excellence."

What transpired from the time Jane put up the "Pillar One" slide until Sam made his adjournment announcement amazed Susan and Bill. They watched Jane explain Mr. Morgan's four pillars of success. In addition to the 'operational excellence' pillar, pillars two through four focused on sales, innovation, and people development. The dialogue was robust. The team members were energized and began to see how the twenty-four metrics tied or, in some cases, *didn't* tie to the newly stated priorities. Suddenly, the complex metrics began to make sense to the leaders.

At one point, Michael Thomas, the former basketball player and current Sales VP, grabbed a flipchart and started capturing items on the paper. He looked like a basketball coach sketching out the final play for the win at the buzzer, as he drew lines connecting the twenty-four metrics to the four pillars. From the time Susan asked her question, the meeting continued for another hour, ending only when Sam stood up and said that he had to run in order to get ready for his session with Mr. Morgan. Had it not been for that announcement, the conversation would have continued.

Sam departed, but an informal discussion continued for a few minutes longer until one by one the leaders filed out of the room and only three people remained. Bill and Susan stood by the door briefly, chatting about what had just happened while Jane packed up her computer and shut down the projector. She caught up with them on her way out. "Well, that was an interesting discussion,"

Jane said.

"Yes, it was," Bill responded with enthusiasm.

"I have to admit," Jane added, "I'm glad you asked your question." This was the first time Susan had seen Jane smile.

"So am I," replied Susan.

With that, the three of them said their goodbyes and headed out to their respective offices.

★ ★ ★

Two nights later, Susan and her husband Greg enjoyed a quiet dinner at home. Greg had been out of town since early Monday morning, and the two were glad to be back together. Susan found Greg to be a great listener and advisor when it came to thinking through the challenges she faced at work.

They finished the meal, cleared the dinner table, and began to clean up the kitchen. As they washed the dishes, Susan shared with Greg the events of the week. She picked up where their conversation had last ended as the two of them rushed out the door Monday morning prior to her meeting with Bill. She shared with him her discussion with Bill and how her question at the Monday morning staff meeting started a much-needed conversation among the leadership team. She also filled him in on the conversation she had the following day with Sam about his goals and how her team could help him achieve them.

"Did you tell him about Oliver and show him the *Perspective Matrix*?" Greg asked.

"No, I decided to hold off on that conversation until I had another chance to meet with Oliver and had learned some more."

"What made you decide to hold off on telling Sam?"

"I *do* feel that we can learn a lot from Oliver, but I don't want to get Sam's hopes up. I'd rather wait to see where things go and bring Sam up to speed when the timing seems right."

HIGHLIGHTS

Step 1: Gain Perspecitve

"Perspective is all about determining what matters to those who matter to you."

KEY POINTS:

Grand plans without funding and senior leadership support are hallucinations.

All organizations, divisions, teams, and individual employees exist to serve others.

Don't simply measure what can be measured, measure what is important.

Customers are often pleasantly surprised when you ask them what matters most to them.

Great questions generate great conversations.

LEADER CHECKLIST:

✔ Brainstorm list of customers

✔ Identify your top three customers

✔ Complete the Perspective Matrix Tool by answering the following:
   ● Who do we serve?
   ● What matters most to them?
   ● How are they performing on what matters most to them?
   ● Which areas that matter most can our team impact?

Step 2: Define Purpose

Chapter 10: New Student

When the time for Thursday morning meeting at Oliver's Spot arrived, the store's owner was surprised to see that a third student had joined the class. After the staff meeting, Michael Thomas had stopped by Susan's office to talk about the discussion and to inquire as to what had motivated her to ask Jane the question. Susan told Michael about the previous week's meeting that she and Bill had had with Oliver and briefly conveyed what they'd learned. Susan was shocked when Michael nearly insisted that he attend the next session. With that, the group of two grew to three, and Michael found himself wedged into a seat in Oliver's back room. Unlike the other students who seemed relatively comfortable in the surroundings, Michael was crammed into his space at the table. Nonetheless, he was seated and ready to start when Oliver made his way into the room.

"Before we start the next step, I'm curious how things went this past week. Were you able to look into the issue of perspective?" Oliver asked.

Bill and Susan provided Oliver a quick update of the week's events. They explained the progress they had made and some of the challenges they'd encountered. When the discussion turned to the weekly staff meeting, Michael added to the conversation by sharing that Susan's question about the twenty-four metrics truly ignited the leaders with an energy he had yet to see since Jane Hudson started to monitor performance. Michael stated, "At one point, it even felt as if Jane was on our team, helping us to figure out what truly mattered to Mr. Morgan. I, for one, started to see what really mattered to those above our boss. The complex metrics began to make sense to us."

Oliver was pleased with their progress, and after a ten-minute recap of the week's events, he worked his way to the old chalkboard. He erased the words "Your Team" from the middle circle and replaced them with "Step 2: Define Purpose."

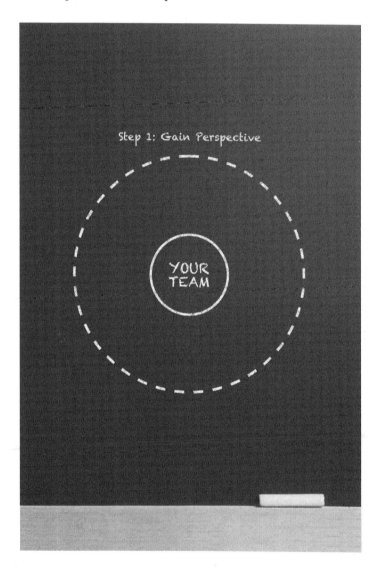

Oliver ran his hand through his hair, turned to face the team, and began his lesson. "I recognize that each of you has some work to accomplish in order to gain a true perspective, but you've made some great strides, and I trust that you'll continue your efforts." He made his way to the open seat at the table and said, "The second step is about defining the purpose for your team. That's articulating why your team exists, what you do, and who you serve—"

Michael interrupted, "Oliver, I have a quick question. Excuse me if I'm off base, but don't people already know why my team exists? After all, our group's title is pretty clear."

"That's a fair question," Oliver responded. "Indeed, most people think that everyone, both inside and outside the team, knows their team's purpose. After all, the team is listed on the organization chart, and as you said, the team title often conveys its function."

He paused for a moment to gather his thoughts before he continued. "Michael, let's take your team as an example. You said that you are in charge of sales. Is that correct?"

Michael nodded and responded with a short, "Yes."

"Would you agree with the statement that there have been times in the past when people have misunderstood the purpose of your team? This might have occurred when they expected your team to do something you believed was outside the scope of your team's role, such as handling shipping issues, or if they criticized your team for not accomplishing something that, in fact, you had little or no control of."

Now Oliver had Michael's attention. He sat up even straighter in his chair, making his already large frame appear bigger, and responded with a strong, "Yes, that happens all too often."

Oliver continued, "This type of situation occurs for a number of reasons. Sometimes it's simply people trying to get you and your teams to accomplish something they don't want to do. Other times, it's a new task that has no clear home within the organization and by default ends up on your team's plate. However, more often than not, people simply *aren't clear* on the purpose of your team. From my years of studying the subject and my own personal experience, I have observed that, left to their own devices, people will define the role your team to be *whatever* they want it to be. This can be a very dangerous situation. It can lead to all sorts of communication and performance breakdowns. These breakdowns are often the result of a lack of shared expectations. Clarifying your team's purpose is all about creating shared expectations both inside and outside your team."

Oliver observed the group's reaction. From the looks on their faces, all three seemed to agree with his comments. "Just between the four of us, on a scale of one to five, with one being low and five being high, how well would your team members agree with these three questions? First, what score would your team members give to the question, 'My team has a clearly defined purpose'?"

Oliver paused while everyone gathered their thoughts. Then he went around the table to get a sense of where each person stood. Sitting to Oliver's immediate left, Susan was the first to respond, admitting that she might struggle herself with clearly articulating her team's precise purpose, and that she imagined her team would do the same. She scored her team a three. Next was Bill. A man of few words, he simply said that his team was a four. Michael agreed with Bill's assessment and gave his team a four as well.

After going around the table, Oliver provided the second statement. "How well would your people score the statement, 'My team members know our team's purpose'?"

Another pass around the table revealed two three and a halves and one three.

"Now, the last statement," Oliver said. "Using the same one-to-five scale, how would your team members score the statement, 'Our stakeholders know our team's purpose'?" He wasn't surprised when all three ranked their teams below three on the one-to-five scale. "I applaud your honesty," Oliver said. "The reality is that most teams don't do the hard work of communicating their purpose and rarely take the time to assess how well others within and outside the team know the team's purpose."

Although quiet for most of the discussion, Bill took the pause in the conversation to add his thoughts. "I must admit, I had never really given this issue much consideration. I guess, I always figured that people knew what my team did, but I'm often surprised at how few people can distinguish the various roles we perform. In fact, my experience suggests that most people can't tell me the difference between accounting and budgeting. The reality is that it's all money to them, and as long as I help them get what they need, they're fine with me. If they don't like what I tell them, they just go around me." Susan and Michael both chuckled at this assessment. "I do think that it would be beneficial if everyone was clear on my team's purpose," Bill added.

"Bill's right," Susan said. "We run into the same problem. My question is, if defining the purpose of the team is so important, how does a team go about doing it? Is it something that I create and share with them, or do we do it together?"

"That's a great question," Oliver responded. "I have found, and the books I have on my shelves suggest, that the best way to define the team's purpose is for the leader to draft a statement, two or three sentences in length, and then share it with the team for them to provide feedback and to put their own touch on the purpose statement."

"Okay, that makes sense," Susan added. "So what goes into a good purpose statement?"

"Another great question," Oliver said. "Team purpose statements focus on why the work of the team matters. They help team members and external stakeholders understand how the team connects to what matters most to the organization and define the customer needs that the team addresses. Teams that explain these items in a few sentences and ensure that every team member can explain the team's purpose statement are in a far better place than those that can't.

"My suggestion to each of you is that you reflect on the purpose of your team, couple that with the information you gathered during the perspective step, and draft a statement. I've found that it takes a leader some time to draft the statement, followed by about an hour or so of reviewing it with his or her team to get feedback. Any more time spent than that becomes an argument over using the word 'happy' versus 'glad.' Let's face it, trying to write a few sentences by a committee can be painful. Just get your team's input based on your initial attempt at the statement. Then take all of their thoughts under consideration and finalize the statement. If you'd like, you can float the revised version past everyone one more time for comments before you accept the final version."

"That sounds like a pretty good plan," Susan replied. "But what do we do with the perspective information we have developed so far?" She rested her chin on her hands with her elbows on the table.

"What do you think?" Oliver asked.

"I guess, we share it with them to help them better see what's going on. I know that clarity helped me; it would probably be useful to them as well."

"Certainly," Oliver confirmed. "That's exactly what you need to do. I do have one last thought. You and Bill made great progress in one week with the perspective piece. I'm sure Michael will work hard to catch up with the two of you. Keep the momentum. Draft your statements today, if possible, and meet with your teams in the next few days. Teams that do well at implementing the five steps tend to be proactive."

The three agreed that they would follow the same schedule Bill and Susan established last week. They would work to draft their purpose statements and talk to their teams and then get together on Monday morning before the staff meeting to discuss their progress. They also agreed to meet with Oliver the following Thursday morning to discuss progress and to learn about step three.

Chapter 11: Bringing the Team on Board

Susan took Oliver's suggestion and set up a meeting for early Friday afternoon with her three direct reports. Before the meeting, she didn't give many details but simply explained that she wanted to spend some time together talking about the direction of the HR team and doing a little team building. With only minor resistance, each agreed that they could move a few things around on their calendars to accommodate the short-notice meeting.

All three respected Susan as a leader. Two of them, Kimberly and Chris, rarely second-guessed Susan's decisions. The third, Todd, seemed to push back on any and all requests he received from her or anyone else. Susan knew that he was competent in his role, but she had concerns about his attitude. She felt that, if they were going to really advance as a team, Todd's attitude would need to be addressed. At the time, she didn't realize that the five steps Oliver was taking her through would have such a dramatic impact on Todd's attitude and performance.

After setting up the meeting with her team, Susan spent half an hour late Thursday afternoon and another one that evening working on a draft purpose statement. Her husband, Greg, helped her put the finishing touches on it. Susan and Greg had been married for almost twenty years, and she always trusted his advice and counsel. As she got ready for bed, she felt good about what she had accomplished so far and looked forward to sharing with her team and gaining their input.

★ ★ ★

Friday morning quickly passed. When she arrived at work, two urgent voicemails awaited her, and she worked until noon putting out the proverbial fires that tend to creep up in the workplace. She was barely able to print out copies of the draft statement before meeting with her team.

When she arrived, all three of her team members were present. She grabbed the fourth and final chair in the small conference room and pulled it up to the table. Susan and her team members had worked together for the better part of the last three years. They had grown close and, for the most part, got along well with one another. Reflecting earlier that morning on the closeness of her team, she had decided to start the meeting with a little exercise.

"Thanks for dropping everything and meeting with me on such a short notice," Susan started.

"Did we have a choice?" Todd added, somewhat sarcastically. He saw that his comment wasn't well received and offered a quick, "Just kidding."

Susan shot him a glance and continued. "I'm hoping that each of you will find the next hour very interesting." She looked around the table at her three direct reports. Chris sat to her left. He was in charge of Outdoor Essentials' training and development initiatives. Chris was young and energetic. In his late twenties, the position was his first stop in what promised to be an outstanding career. Next was Kimberly. Kim, as everyone called her, was responsible for recruitment, hiring, and new employee orientation. With the introduction of JWL Adventures into the equation, her role would likely grow to include promotions into the larger corporate structure. To Susan's immediate right was Todd. He ran the company's award and recognition program, handled many of the general HR activities, and was actively engaged in a new initiative to integrate Outdoor Essentials existing performance management system into JWL Adventures program. Despite Todd's cynical nature, he appeared as eager as the others to hear what Susan had to say.

Susan passed out three blank pieces of paper. She explained the importance of a team purpose statement and told them that she had spent some time drafting one for the team; however, before she shared it with them, she wanted to see how they saw the HR team's purpose. She gave them fifteen minutes to draft a team purpose statement individually and asked that each of them be prepared to share their thoughts when the time expired. Susan kept track of the time, and everyone dove into their drafting.

When fifteen minutes had elapsed, Susan said with a grin, "Okay, time's up—pencils down please."

"What are we, back in school?" Todd joked.

Chris latched on to the humor. He looked down at his paper and added, "Based on what I wrote, I hope Susan is grading with a curve."

Everyone laughed.

Susan invited each person at the table to read what was written on their page. She was amazed at the differences in the three statements. While Chris's attempt was short and to the point, Todd's was much longer. He listed almost everything that the team did in every aspect of their roles. Kim's was somewhere in the middle in both length and detail. When all three finished reading, Susan passed out a copy of her take on their purpose statement. She admitted that she had taken longer than fifteen minutes to craft the statement, but she felt that their versions were as good as or better than what she'd put together.

Everyone took a moment to read Susan's attempt. Once they all had a chance to digest it, they launched into a conversation about how they might adjust Susan's example to include a few aspects of the other team members' versions. The next forty-five minutes flew by as they talked about, adjusted, and began to own their purpose statement. They then discussed how they could use the purpose statement to better explain to people their individual roles and how they function as a team to support the company and its employees. Susan found the conversation invigorating. It was filled with energy and passion she had not observed in her team in a long while. She was most amazed at how Todd joined in the discussion. Sure, he cracked a joke or two, but much of the cynicism that had been present was no longer there.

Wanting to avoid the concern Oliver mentioned about trying to write a sentence by committee, Susan looked for a pause in the discussion and brought the meeting to an end, saying, "I just looked at my watch and realized it was running late. I appreciate everybody's efforts and input. How about I take all of this information and come up with one last version for each of you to review?"

"That sounds great!" Kim said. Her colleagues nodded in agreement.

"One last thing before we finish. I'd like us to get together again next Friday to talk a bit further about our team and to build on today's efforts. Once I have something, I'll send out the statement we drafted today for everyone's review. So let's plan for the same time next week."

★ ★ ★

Susan Greg took a much-needed getaway over the weekend. The demands of their jobs created the need to reconnect. Normally, work was off-limits on these types of trips, but Susan was so excited about the progress she was making with her team that Greg agreed that they would make an exception, eager to listen to her talk about the exciting developments at work. They did agree, however, to limit work discussions to their time in the car. Thus, once they reached the hotel, work was off-limits.

Staying true to the agreement, Outdoor Essentials, Oliver's teaching, and the progress she was making with her team were not discussed after arriving at their hotel. However, as the car worked its way north along the winding road, the conversation covered little but Susan's work-related topics.

Greg found himself particularly interested in what she had to say, as he planned to apply what she was learning to his own team at work. They spent the drive up talking about what she had learned thus far and most of the drive back guessing what Oliver would teach the following Thursday. They figured that since *perspective* and *purpose* started with a P, there was a good chance that whatever the topic this week, step three would also start with a P. They were right.

Chapter 12: Progress Check

Five minutes before starting time, Susan and Michael were settled into their seats. Although the discussion hadn't officially begun, Bill and Oliver were already engaged in deep conversation about how things were going with Bill's team. Susan listened as the two men exchanged thoughts. Her ability to focus on their discussion was hampered by her interest in watching Michael fold himself into his seat. After working his way into his chair, he apparently decided to remove his coat. For some reason, he elected to accomplish this without standing back up and moving to where there was more space for him to maneuver out of the jacket. Susan laughed aloud as she watched him struggle with his jacket and nearly break his hand as he banged it against the back wall. He hit the wall so hard that Bill and Oliver stopped their discussion for a moment to see if he was okay. He assured them that he was fine, and the two continued. As he finally extracted himself from his coat, Michael caught Susan's eye, giving her a sheepish look.

Right on time, Oliver brought his conversation with Bill to a close and began the session. "All right," Oliver said, "I've had a bit of an update from Bill, and I'm encouraged by how things went with his team. I'm keen to hear about the progress the two of you made."

Michael responded, "I have to admit that I didn't cover as much ground as I'd hoped." Oliver listened intently as Michael continued. "Perhaps I had expected too much, but I had a hard time getting both *perspective* and *purpose* accomplished this week. Frankly, the problem wasn't with covering the two steps as much as it was with getting the right people together for a discussion."

Bill and Susan nodded in agreement.

"We're right in the middle of launching a new product line. Three of my sales people had to drop everything and take a quick trip to a customer in order to attend to some major issues. Consequently, I was without a few key people for our discussion. I really want to get their input before I finalize anything."

When Michael paused to catch his breath, Susan jumped in. "In addition, early Monday morning we learned that our staff meeting was canceled, as our boss, Sam, received notice of a last-minute meeting with his boss. Getting ready for the meeting required all of us to jump through hoops to pull reports together before he caught a flight out of town. So not only were we unable to learn more about the metrics, the three of us had no time to share our progress with one another."

Michael and Susan finished their updates, and Oliver responded to the situation. "You know, folks, I'm not at all surprised that you ran into some roadblocks this week. Day-to-day work often causes teams to have a hard time getting through the five steps. In fact, that's why so few of them do it. They either figure that it is too hard to accomplish from the start, or they hit a bunch of scheduling conflicts and decide to give up before they really start to gain traction."

"Well, I'm not going to give up," said Susan. "The last few days have been tough, and I missed having our Monday morning discussion. But I'm optimistic about the progress my team has made thus far, despite the challenges of the day-to-day work."

"Go on," Oliver encouraged her. "Tell us more."

Susan explained how her week progressed. She shared how she'd drafted a team purpose, brought it to her team, asked them create their own versions, and how they worked together to finalize the product. She also explained how she spent much of her weekend with her husband talking about the progress and about how having the discussion about purpose had allowed her team to start feeling a collective sense of direction. She ended by saying, "I don't mean to be too dramatic, but I really felt that all three of my people, including the person who has been driving me a bit crazy lately, seemed to enjoy the discussion."

"Thanks for the update Susan. Would you be willing to share the rest of the story?" Oliver asked.

"I'm not sure I know what you mean."

"May we hear your team purpose statement?"

Susan looked a bit surprised by the request. "Sure, I'll share, but I have to admit that it still needs some work. The latest version of the statement is currently with the team for feedback, and we're going to meet tomorrow to hopefully finalize it and get to work on the step three."

She opened her binder and took out a sheet of paper that was folded in half and tucked into a pocket inside the binder's front flap. Susan unfolded it, cleared her throat, and read from the paper, "The Human Resources team leads recruitment and on-boarding, provides training to our employees, and develops and sustains critical workforce development programs. We leverage our abilities to meet the ever-changing demands of Outdoor Essentials' leaders, employees, and customers. The skills, tools, and resources we provide allow everyone to focus on our mission of being the world's leading outdoor clothing and equipment company."

When she finished, Oliver, Bill, and Michael all applauded her efforts.

"That was great," Oliver said. "You should be very proud of your team's efforts. I think your write-up provides a clear picture of what your team does for the organization, who you do it for, and why it matters. I do have a couple of minor suggestions for you to consider."

Pen poised, Susan waited for his input.

"First, remember that less is more. You may want to remove any unnecessary words from the statement." He paused to look at the notes he'd jotted down as Susan had read her team's statement. "For example, as long as it doesn't lose the meaning of what you're trying to say, consider changing *provides training to the staff*, to *provides staff training*. It cuts out a couple of words and shortens the statement. Shorter statements are easier to remember."

Susan nodded in agreement. "That makes sense," she added.

Oliver continued, "I'd also suggest that you remove some of the jargon. You used the phrase *leverage our abilities to meet the demands*—that sounds like a lot of consultant double-talk. I'd just put it in plain English, saying something like *we work together to*. Well, those might not be the right words; thus consider my thoughts here, not my vocabulary."

He paused while Susan finished her notes. When she was done writing, she looked up at him.

"Susan," Oliver continued, "let me be clear. These are just minor suggestions to help you with the language. The most important thing is that you and your team put a stake in the ground and proclaim, 'This is what we do, who we do it for, and why it matters.' That's big stuff, and I can see why you were so excited."

Susan smiled at Oliver and her colleagues.

Oliver then turned to Bill. "You gave me a pretty good rundown of how things went for you and your team this week. Why don't you share with the group and, if you don't mind, read your team's purpose statement."

Bill provided the group an update on his team's progress. Just like Susan, he had met with his team and crafted a purpose statement. He admitted that he wished he had tried Susan's approach because, instead of giving them something to start with, he simply brought his team into a room and had them work together to create a statement.

"It was like writing a sentence by a committee, which was pretty painful at times," he explained. "It took twice as long as I had planned, but we did get through it, and in the end everyone seemed pleased, although exhausted, with the result of our efforts."

With that, he shared his team's purpose statement. Oliver provided him feedback, and Bill committed to working with his team to finalize it over the next week. Michael also agreed to spend time with his team finishing steps one and two. Oliver suggested postponing the discussion of step three for a week to allow all of them a chance to finish the work on the first two steps. Surprisingly, all three of his students firmly declined his offer, suggesting that Oliver move onto step three now and that they meet again in two weeks to share progress, agreeing that they would complete all three steps in that time.

Oliver agreed that the schedule made sense and prepared to launch into step three.

HIGHLIGHTS

Step 2: Define Purpose

"Purpose is articulating why your team exists, what you do, and who you serve."

KEY POINTS:

More often than not, people inside and outside the team aren't always clear on the team's purpose.

Clarifying a team's purpose is about creating shared expectations.

Team purpose statements focus on why the work of the team matters.

If a team's purpose is not clearly understood, people will define it to be whatever they want it to be.

Great team purpose statements avoid unnecessary words and jargon. They are clear and concise.

LEADER CHECKLIST:

✔ Draft your team's purpose statement on your own

✔ Meet with the team and share your draft statement with them

✔ Solicit team member input and adjust the statement to best reflect your team's purpose

✔ Distribute the statement to those who matter to you and your team

✔ Use the statement daily as a reminder of who your team serves and why your work matters

Step 3: Determine Priorities

Chapter 13: Defining the What

"Just like the first two steps," Oliver began, "Step three begins with the letter P. In fact, I'll go further and confirm that all five steps begin with the letter P. The third step focuses on defining your team's priorities."

Oliver paused as he watched Susan, Michael, and Bill jot down the word *priorities* in their notes. Returning to his trusty chalkboard, he added the words "Step 3: Determine Priorities" to the graph he'd started during the first session.

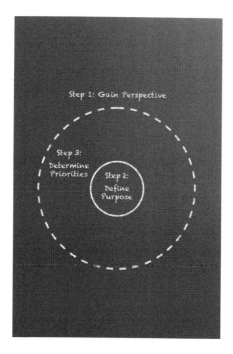

He waited for Susan, Bill, and Michael to add this to their graphs. When all three were ready, he said, "By priorities, I mean what are the key goals your team must accomplish to positively affect what matters most to those you serve, and to simultaneously affect your purpose. As you can see," he pointed to the board "determining priorities sits between the outer circle of perspective and the inner circle of purpose because your priorities are influenced by both. The challenge to step three is to identify these priorities."

Michael interjected, "I hear what you're saying, but the reality is that we have more things to work on—what you call priorities—than you can imagine. Every day, we seem to have new items handed to us by our customers or our parent company that we must prioritize into our daily work. Now you want me to capture *all* those things we need to do?"

Oliver replied, "That's a great question. I'm not talking about coming up with an exhaustive list of all the work you and your people need to do and calling those your priorities. I'm talking about determining, out of all the things you can do, which are most important. When I say most important, I mean those goals that will give the organization and the customers you serve the biggest bang for your buck, as the saying goes."

"I have to agree with Michael. We've gone through the prioritizing drill a hundred times, and it seems as if all we do is create a longer and longer list of tasks we must accomplish," Bill added.

"Let's try this," Oliver said, "instead of trying to explain to you what I mean by priorities, let's just do it. Would each of you please take a clean sheet of paper from the stack I put out this morning?"

He waited while Bill, Michael, and Susan each secured a fresh piece of paper from the pile on the table. When everyone had a sheet, Oliver continued. "Take five minutes on your own to brainstorm a list of all the possible goals you and your team could accomplish. You can include items that are already on your plate, those you've been thinking about in the back of your mind, and perhaps some tasks that you've yet to consider, but might make sense to visit." He paused for a moment to let each of them digest what he said, and then he added, "Any questions? No takers? Okay, start."

Susan, Bill, and Michael immediately began creating their lists. Susan seemed to have no problem creating a laundry list of possible goals. She began work at the word "start" and continued writing down items until Oliver told the group that the five minutes had lapsed. Bill and Michael started off more slowly; however, Michael picked up steam as time went on and created a fairly lengthy list. With less than ten items, Bill's list was the shortest.

After time had expired, Oliver said, "Okay, now that each of you has created your list, please take a moment and put a checkmark next to the items you believe will have the greatest impact on your customers' top priorities. Please limit yourself to no more than six checkmarks."

As he watched them work, Oliver reminded himself that this is where things would start to get interesting. For most people, all the items on their list represented important accomplishments of their team and were thus hard to discard. Susan, who was unwittingly prepared to prove his point, interrupted these thoughts.

"Why do we have to narrow the list to six?" she asked. "My paper is covered with priorities that I think are important for us to accomplish."

"Let me see if I understand you," Oliver replied. "As you look down your list, you see many items that would be good for your team to accomplish?"

"Absolutely!" she enthusiastically responded.

Oliver nodded in acknowledgement of her excitement. "The reality is that this is where the problem begins for many teams. No one wants to say no to a good idea. In all likelihood, accomplishing good ideas is what has made each of you so successful in your careers." All three seemed to agree with this statement. "Your accomplishments are what gets you promoted and increases your responsibilities. However, I'm trying to get you to separate the merely *good* ideas from the *truly great* ones. So as you look down your list, try to pick the six best possible ideas that you and your team can accomplish in the next twelve months or less."

His response seemed to satisfy Susan, and she returned to the task of placing a checkmark next to the top six items. As he watched her, Oliver chuckled to himself thinking, *Wait until I ask her to cut that list further.*

When they finished placing checkmarks next to the items, Oliver asked each person to take a moment to share the list they had created, placing special emphasis on the six items that received checkmarks. Each person went through their list and shared their ideas.

Everyone seemed to agree with the others' decisions. The only exception came when Michael explained that he had placed a checkmark next to the goal called "improve communication among sales team members."

Oliver stopped him, saying, "Michael, I totally agree that improving communication is very important, but I think you are going to find it hard to keep that as a goal for several reasons."

He paused and waited for Michael's response. Although Michael didn't verbalize his disbelief, it was evident in his facial expression that he questioned Oliver's comment.

By way of reassurance, Oliver said, "The problem with goals like communication, collaboration, trust, and so on is that they are hard to measure and often hard to impact in a way that doesn't distract from driving the organization forward. I can imagine that you can think of several ways to improve communication. However, I also believe that, in the end, you would find that they might result in too much busywork for your team. Don't get me wrong, I'm all about improving communication, collaboration, and trust. I'm just *not* all about making them one of your top goals.

"What I've found," Oliver continued, "is that when you create a compelling goal for your team to work on and they work together to accomplish it, the by-product of that effort is improved communication, collaboration, and trust."

Oliver leaned in closer to Michael and said, "You played basketball in college. Think about the difference between a winning and a losing basketball team. My bet is that teams that win also experience higher trust, collaboration, and communication both on and off the court." With that comment, Michael put a line through the communication goal— enough said.

Oliver went back to his trusty chalkboard. He turned the knobs on either side and rotated the entire surface to reveal the opposite side, on which he had pre-drawn instructions for the next step.

Pointing at the chart, Oliver explained, "You can use a chart like this one to help you finalize the six remaining ideas, to find which ones are truly the best."

"Hold on," Susan exclaimed. "Are you saying that we need to shorten the list more?"

"Yep, that's exactly what I'm saying," Oliver responded with a warm smile. "My view is that less is more here, and my research supports that. I'd recommend that you shorten the list to the three to five most important goals. Listen, I know that narrowing the list of goals is tough, but it's essential and it's what the most effective leaders and teams do."

"Alright," Susan stated. She continued hesitantly, "I'll give it a try. How do we use the chart?"

Prioritization Matrix

POTENTIAL GOAL	Feasible Can we get it done?	Measurable Can we tell if we won?	Meaningful Is it important?	Easy to Understand Does it make sense?	Effective Will it help our team fulfill its purpose?	Financially Doable Do we have or can we get needed funding?	TOTAL SCORE

SCORING SYSTEM

1	2	3	4	5
Absolutely Not		Maybe		Absolutely

"The first thing you do is list your six potential goals on the left side. Then going from left to right, score each of the potential goals based on how strongly you believe the possible goal is feasible, measurable, meaningful, easy to understand, effective, and financially doable on a scale of one to five, with five being high and one being low. Then tally the score for each potential and compare the scores. The form is pretty simple to follow. Let's take five minutes or so for each of you to complete it."

All three copied what was on the board and worked quickly to complete the *Prioritization Matrix*. They then shared the results with each other. As they shared their selected goals with their colleagues, they became more confident in the selections they had made and their rationale behind each decision. Oliver told them to hold on to that confidence, as it would be vital when discussing the goals with their teams and their boss.

Oliver's comment about sharing the goals with the teams raised a question in Bill's mind. "Oliver, when we work with our teams, should we simply walk in and say, 'Here are the goals, deal with them,' or should we ask for their input?"

"Yet another great question," Oliver said. "Both approaches have their pros and cons. Sharing the goal with the team and explaining that it is written in stone is certainly the fastest way to move through the process. It also allows you to provide clear direction about what you expect from them. The negative side to this approach is that you might lose buy-in from your team members if they feel this is *your* goal, rather than *theirs*. On the other hand, asking them to create the goals can often slow the process down and may take more than one meeting to solidify them. Of course, it's worth the investment of time if that is what it takes to get everybody's commitment to the right goal."

As his students finished their notes, he said, "Like everything else you approach in your job, it's about which approach is right for your situation. If you believe the goals are the right ones to tackle at this point, you may want to go in and say, 'Folks, I've been thinking about our priorities, and here are the five things I believe we need to accomplish.'"

"Ah, but won't that kill buy-in?" Michael asked.

"It could if you do it in a way that turns everyone off; however, as long as you can justify your selection, you will be fine. Moreover, when we get to the next step, you'll be asking them about how to accomplish the goals, and that's where the *real* buy-in takes place. Anyway, you know what I've found *really* kills a team buy-in?" Oliver asked.

"What?" Michael replied.

"When a leader acts as if he or she wants input, but in reality expects the team to simply accept the given priorities without any objections," Oliver explained.

"I've seen that on more than one occasion," Susan added. "You're right, people can't stand that. They like it much better when someone comes out and tells them what needs to be done."

Oliver glanced at his watch and noticed that they were way over time. "Although we're running late, I'd like to share with you one more thing before we call it a day." As there were no apparent objections, after a slight hesitation, he added, "A goal isn't a goal unless it is well stated. There are several different ways to do this, but you have to make sure that you make it very clear what needs to be done and when. Let me give you an illustration. Let's say that I told you my goal was to improve my health. What would you say to that?"

"Well, I'd probably say that improving your health is good, but what do you want to improve?" Susan asked.

"You hit the nail on the head. I'd need to tell you what measure I was going to use to determine if my health improved. I could reduce my weight, improve my cholesterol, decrease my body mass index, or any number of other possible measures. The key is that I need to pick one. So, Susan, how would you feel if I said that I was going to decrease my weight? How would that settle with you?"

Susan appeared excited to respond. "I would say that was better, but how much weight do you want to lose?"

"And when do you want to lose it by?" Bill added.

"That's exactly right. A well-stated goal needs to tell you the gap and when you want to close it by. More importantly, it needs to be realistic, and if you look at my waistline over the years, you will see that my commitment to accomplishing this goal is not very good."

Everyone laughed as Oliver patted his belly in jest.

They wrapped up the session by agreeing that each of them would meet with their teams to finalize their goals and to set up a meeting with their boss Sam to bring him up to speed on the work they had been doing with the process. Each felt confident that they would be ready to share with Sam by the following Wednesday, and if they could get time on his schedule, they were sure that he would be open to the conversation.

As they walked out the door, Oliver said, "Oh yes, one last thing—don't get caught up in the 'how discussion' when you talk to your teams."

"How discussion? What's that?" Bill asked.

"The priorities discussion is about *what* you want to accomplish, not *how* you are going to do it. Your people will want to figure out how they will do it. Ask them to hold off on that by saying that you will get to that in a week or so."

Chapter 14: Momentum

Early Friday afternoon, over lunch at her desk, Susan reflected on Todd's involvement during last Friday's session and his quick, positive feedback on the team purpose statement. She felt that his participation indicated that he valued the discussion and wanted the team to have clarity of purpose. Her excitement about Todd's involvement was somewhat muted as she reminded herself that new habits take time to form and that Todd's enthusiasm might turn out to be short-lived. As she finished her salad, she vowed to remain adherent to Oliver's process, in hope that it would continue to have positive impact on Todd and the team.

A couple of hours later, Susan's team was assembled for their second session. She looked around the table at her teammates. "Let's get started," she began with a warm smile. Being creatures of habit, all four of them sat in the same seats as the week prior.

"Thank you for your quick feedback on our purpose statement. I appreciated your input and believe that we created a statement that explains who we are, what we do, and who we do it for. If his schedule allows, I'm hoping to meet with Sam Finch next week and share with him our purpose statement and the result of today's meeting."

"So what are we going to talk about today?" Kim asked.

"We are going to talk about our priorities. These are the top goals we need to accomplish in the next year or less to fulfill our purpose and to maximize our impact on our customers," Susan explained.

Deciding to maintain the momentum with Todd, she turned to him and thoughtfully inquired, "Todd, are you ready for another exercise?"

"Sure, why not?" Todd's positive response brought a smile to Susan, Kim, and Chris. As an HR professional, Susan often wondered why some people started their careers with such passion and potential, only grow cynical, almost resentful, as time goes by. She had seen it several times and wondered if the process they were going through truly might help people like Todd return to an earlier enthusiasm about their jobs.

Pressing forward, Susan handed each of her team members a piece of blank paper. "Alright, I'm going to give each of you five minutes to complete our next activity." She paused for a moment, fully expecting Todd to object. As no complaints emerged, she continued, "I'd like each of you to write down a list of possible goals our team can tackle over the next twelve months. These can be projects we're already working on, tasks we have discussed but have yet to accomplish, or simply anything you think might be a good goal for us to accomplish."

She asked if everyone was clear on the task, to which all responded affirmatively. Susan glanced at her watch and waited for the second hand to tick into the twelve position. When it arrived, she announced, "Okay, begin."

Her team members jumped into the exercise with even more enthusiasm than the past week's activity. Time passed quickly as she watched their lists grow. After five minutes, Susan announced that it was time to stop. Following Oliver's lead, Susan asked each of them to place a checkmark next to the ideas they thought were the most important, limiting each of them to no more than six checkmarks. Todd, Kim, and Chris each selected six items from their lists. She then asked them to rank the six items using the criteria Oliver had shared with her the previous day and then narrow the list to the three to five most important goals. Not being an expert at the process, a couple of her instructions required clarification, but all three of her team members eventually completed the activity.

When everyone finished, Susan explained, "I would like each of you to share the goals that you ranked the highest. When you're done, I'll explain the items I selected when I did this activity yesterday. Chris, if you don't mind, will you please capture everyone's ideas on the board?"

"My handwriting isn't very good, but I'll give it a shot." He sprang to his feet and grabbed a marker to use on the dry-erase board.

Each team member explained their selected goals. Susan facilitated the discussion, asking the presenter to pause occasionally to ensure everyone understood what was being said and to ask for clarification where necessary. Susan went last, explaining her list. When everyone had finished, they looked at the board to survey the results. Their seventeen "best" ideas were listed in Chris's barely legible handwriting.

Susan thanked Chris for his excellent work as the group's scribe. She stood and walked to the board as Chris returned to his seat. "Alright, we have seventeen items listed on the board. Clearly, that's way too many," she explained. "We need to somehow narrow this list."

"I have a suggestion," Todd said, pointing to the board as he continued. "If you look, each of us talked about the need to improve training delivery. Those can probably be combined into one goal, don't you think?"

All agreed, and the four items were surmised into one concise goal statement. For the next half an hour, they continued to reduce the list. In the end, the team had five well-written goals listed on the board.

With their newly defined goals, Kim made the comment that Oliver had said was coming. "Susan, I think we can all agree that these are good goals for us to achieve, but I'm wondering how we're going to get these done. As we've been talking, I've created a lengthy list of all the things we need to do in order to accomplish each of these goals."

Susan's response would have made Oliver proud. "Kim, you raised an excellent point; however, our task today is to decide *what* we want to do, rather than *how* we are going to do it. When we get together next time, we'll discuss the *hows* for each of these goals." Kim's expression conveyed her willingness to follow Susan's lead. Susan continued, "So, I have two tasks for all of us. First, if you have ideas about how to accomplish these goals, please hang on to them for our next meeting. Second, as we discuss the *hows*, we need to be willing to adjust the goals to account for workload, available funding, and a number of other constraints. I want to ensure that when we finalize these goals and our plan for making them happen that we are all confident that we will be successful. Does that make sense?"

"Not only does it make sense," Todd declared, "it makes perfect sense. I feel as if we're often chasing our tails, responding to whatever new idea somebody else dreams up for us. But these goals," he said, gesturing toward the board, "these are the ones that really matter. If we can really figure out a way to make them happen, I'm fully on board."

The meeting ended a few minutes later, but Todd's comment stuck with Susan for the next several days. On a number of occasions, she caught herself thinking, *Oliver is really onto something here!*

Chapter 15: Status Meeting

Outdoor Essentials' interim president arrived in the upstairs conference room a few minutes before the meeting was scheduled to start. Sam wasn't exactly sure of the gathering's purpose, but after receiving the third of three invitations from members of his leadership team to attend a one-hour "Status Meeting," he knew a coordinated effort was underway. Typically, Sam would decline an invitation that didn't come along with an agenda. He learned this trick early in life, and he was confident that it had saved him hundreds of nonproductive hours over the course of his career. However, on this occasion, he was willing to make an exception because he valued Susan, Bill, and Michael. He was confident that they wouldn't ask for the meeting and violate his "no agenda, no meeting policy" if they didn't have a good reason.

He entered the room to see his three direct reports already seated around the table. Susan stood up and walked towards a screen with the words "Status Update" plastered across it. Sam grabbed his usual seat at the end of the table.

"Okay," Sam said. "I'm not exactly sure what this meeting is all about, but I learned a long time ago that when the three of you have something to say, it's always best to listen." His face brightened. "So what are we here to talk about?"

Without hesitation, Susan began. "Sam, first, I would like to thank you for taking the time to meet with us. We know that you have a busy schedule, but we think that you'll find what we are about to share with you interesting." She paused for a moment, watched her colleagues nod in agreement, and then continued. "Do you remember a couple of weeks ago when several of us went out to lunch at the sandwich shop across town?"

"Yep, I remember that day well," Sam said. "The food was good, and the conversation was certainly interesting. Why do you ask?"

"Well," Susan said, a smile emerging on her face, "after we finished our meal, I slipped into a nearby bookstore to look for inspiration. Frankly, the discussion had left me a bit drained, and I was hoping to find something in there that would help me better understand our current situation and how we might better perform on Alex Morgan's metrics. I believe that you would agree that we were all struggling that day as we grappled with how to meet his goals." She looked to Sam for a response.

"Yes, I'd agree. I guess you must have found a pretty interesting book, given the discussions we've had during our recent Monday morning staff meetings," Sam said, referring to the conversation that had started a couple of weeks earlier when Susan had asked Jane Hudson, Alex's surrogate, to identify which of the metrics mattered most. That one question had started the best dialogue to date on the subject, and it had seemed to change the relationship between Jane and the company's leadership.

The moment Susan asked the question, Jane had stopped her usual briefing and shared a draft of Alex's strategic vision for JWL Adventures. The sharing had continued during the most recent staff meetings when Jane presented a revised version of the metrics and provided further explanation. In the new presentation, the metrics were aligned to Alex's "Pillars of Success," and Jane had added a weighting system for the metrics. This allowed the Outdoor Essentials leaders to see which goals had the greatest influence on the pillars. At once, Sam Finch and his management team began to better understand where they should put their efforts.

Sam's thoughts returned to the room as Susan answered his question. "Actually, it wasn't a book. It was a person. To put it more accurately, it was a person who has read a lot of books."

"A person?"

"Yes, a person. Actually, he's the store's owner. His name is Oliver Stanton. I asked him to suggest some books that covered the topic of organizational performance. Instead, he invited me to meet with him, saying that he had read numerous books on the subject of management and leadership, and at their essence, most of them say the same thing." A grin appeared on Sam's face, indicating that he'd had the same thought himself. "Oliver explained to me that he had learned, both form theory and practice, that there were five steps every leader should follow in working with a team."

Sam's face turned from agreement to skepticism as he listened to her presentation. "Susan," he interrupted, "it's great that Mr. Stanton is well-read, and I'm interested in what you have to say, but does he have any practical experience?"

"The same question was running through my mind when I started talking to him," she answered. "Actually, he has a great deal of experience. Years ago he started, expanded, and then eventually sold a chain of bookstores called AC's."

"Oh yes, AC's, I remember that chain. I think it was a pretty big business at one point, before some other company came along and bought them."

"That's exactly right," Bill interjected. "But there's something else about this guy that makes him different. Beyond reading many books and growing a business of his own, he has an uncanny ability to teach business concepts in a way that really resonates with people. Plus, he really seems to have the desire to help our team. "

Susan nodded in agreement with her colleague. "Now, Oliver is back in the book business, but working with just the one small store.

He says that he's very content with keeping it that way and occasionally likes to share what he has learned with others."

"And you've been meeting with him?" Sam inquired.

"Yes, we've all been meeting with him." Susan motioned to her two colleagues.

Michael added, "I was the last to join the group, and I have to admit, Sam, it has been a very interesting and challenging experience."

Sam seemed to lose his skepticism as he listened to Michael. After a moment of reflection, he motioned for Susan to continue.

Susan used her presentation slides to prompt her efforts. With each click of the remote, a new slide appeared revealing another step. She briefly explained the three steps they had learned, the importance of each, and that Bill, Michael, and she had been working with their teams to complete each step.

Following the quick overview, Susan, Michael, and Bill shared their efforts to date with Sam. They then asked Sam for feedback on their work, explaining that they wanted to ensure that they were moving in the right direction before going on to steps four and five. They admitted that they weren't certain as to the last two steps but that they had a pretty good feeling what they might entail.

Sam was completely engaged in the conversation. He was amazed at the accuracy of their perspective assessment. Offering only a few minor suggestions, Sam believed their *Perspective Matrix* captured the most important points. "I have to admit," he said, narrowing his eyes as he concentrated on his thoughts, "I have been through many strategic planning sessions where experts have shared the results of lengthy external and internal studies, and I have yet to come across something as simple and straightforward as this."

When they presented their draft purpose statements, the trio explained that they had worked with their teams to craft and refine the statements. Susan highlighted that the discussion with her team was very positive and had helped all of them gain clarity. Michael added that his team members had already started posting the statement in their workspace as a reminder of what the organization wanted them to do.

"This last week," Bill began, "we started work on step three—determine priorities." He turned to face Sam. "I have to admit, this has been a challenging step for my team. Walking in the room, I assumed that we all knew the most important tasks to focus on. Boy, was I wrong! Everyone had a different opinion of what mattered the most."

"Different in what way?" Sam asked warmly.

"The first thing I did," Bill explained, "was to ask them to grab a blank piece of paper and write down their ideas for the top goals the finance team must accomplish in the next twelve months. The results were embarrassing." Bill paused to consider the fact that he had just told his boss that his team didn't agree on what was most important. His moment of concern quickly faded as he realized that Susan and Michael would likely reveal similar results. So he pressed on. "Keep in mind, there were four of them in the room, and I asked each of them to give me the top three to five priorities. I knew that in a worst case scenario, we would end up with twenty different goals; actually twenty five, including my own."

"Well," Sam asked excitedly, "what did you get?"

"I got twelve different answers. Honestly, they were all over the map. And you know what the most amazing thing was?"

"Go ahead," Sam prodded.

Sheepishly Bill continued. "As they went through the different priorities, all of them came from me. I was the source of all the ideas. I was the cause of much of the confusion on my own team."

Before Sam could say a word, Michael added, "Sam, I had the same experience on my team. There was much confusion about the top priorities. Don't get me wrong, the people could recite Outdoor

Essentials' mission statement from memory, but they were not in agreement about what we needed to accomplish in the short term to make everything else come together."

"Ditto," said Susan. "When I asked my people the same question, I was confident that they would come up with the same answers, but they didn't. It became clear that the daily work, ongoing meetings, shifting priorities, production schedule changes, and overall challenges of their jobs, and my own role, were causing confusion."

Susan clicked the remote, and the screen displayed, "Step 3: Determine Priorities."

As her colleagues turned to face her, Susan said, "With your permission, Sam, we'd like to share with you the top priorities each of our teams identified. Our hope is that you will provide us your feedback and direction to ensure that we're on the right track."

They followed the same format used for the first two steps. Susan went first and explained her team's priorities, followed by Michael and Bill. Susan presented four priorities, while Michael and Bill each presented five. On occasion, Sam would stop the presenter to clarify an item or to challenge their thinking. The discussion was collaborative, and Sam found little that wasn't in alignment with his understanding of the business. He was surprised that most of their priorities required very little, if any, funding. Of the fourteen items presented, only one had the potential to require funding beyond what was currently in the team's budget. At first, he considered rejecting the priority because of the financial requirements, but he agreed to let the team continue to work on it in order to identify exactly how much financing it would require. Then he would make a final decision about approving or disapproving the effort as stated.

Although the entire conversation was of great interest to Sam, it was the final slide that caught his full attention. Susan clicked the remote one last time, revealing a graph of how the three leaders' priorities tied to Alex's metrics. Two things became immediately clear. First, everything the teams had picked affected at least one, if not multiple metrics. Second, the bulk of the selected priorities connected *directly* to Mr. Morgan's top goals Jane shared with them.

Michael, Bill, and Susan had hoped that this final slide would "seal the deal." They wanted it to convince Sam to approve their teams' priorities and to encourage them to continue the process with Oliver. Sam didn't disappoint. "So what do you need from me?"

"Glad you asked," Susan said with a smile. "We'd like your approval on these goals, subject to the changes you provided today, of course. Also, we'd like to meet with you next week to share our progress."

Sam agreed to both requests, stating, "I had no idea what I was getting into when I walked into the room, but I'm glad that I came. Please send me a final copy of the last slide once you insert the changes we discussed today. Also, shoot me an invitation for our next meeting. I look forward to it."

"Our pleasure," Susan replied.

Sam thanked them for their time and was, as usual, on his way to another meeting.

Susan, Bill, and Michael spent a few minutes basking in the moment. "Well, I don't think that could have gone any better," Bill stated, delivering a rare high-five to his colleagues.

Chapter 16: Two Great Lessons

Oliver was deep in thought when his students arrived at the store. Even the jingle of the door's bell did not stir him. Susan's "Good afternoon, Oliver," startled him though. He looked up from his book to see Susan, Bill, and Michael standing at the counter. In his typical form, Oliver ran his hand through his disheveled hair and peered at them over his reading glasses.

"Well, hello there," Oliver said, clearing his throat. "I didn't hear the three of you enter the shop." Turning to Susan, he added, "I told you when we first met that I could get lost in a book." He glanced at the regulator clock hanging behind him to check the time. It indicated that it was fifteen minutes from their normal start time. "The three of you are early."

"We have lots to share," Susan responded enthusiastically.

Bill added, "It's been an interesting two weeks."

"You've piqued my curiosity," said Oliver as he walked from behind the counter. All three noted that he was dressed in his usual attire of starched khaki pants, blue button-down shirt and a smock. Per usual, everything was in place except the crop of hair perched like a nest on his head. "Let's get started."

As the four walked to the store's back room, Oliver stopped along the way to say something to his colleague who would watch the store in his absence. While Susan, Bill, and Michael secured their usual seats, Oliver poured himself a cup of tea. Always a gracious host, he offered tea, coffee, or water to his guests. All three declined.

The host interpreted their rejection of a beverage less an indication of how thirsty they were and more as a desire to get the discussion started. He was right.

As soon as he secured the last seat at the table, Michael began. "Each of us met with our teams over the last two weeks. Although bumpy at times, the discussions went well, and we were able to come to an agreement with our team members on our goals. After we solidified our goals, we then met with our boss to bring him up to speed on our efforts and gain his feedback."

Not one to let a question pass through his head without asking it, Oliver inquired, "I definitely want to hear about how the discussion went with your boss, but I'd first like to learn a bit more about your team meetings. May I ask a couple of questions?"

"Of course," Michael answered.

Oliver began questioning in his typical quizzical style. "When you say that the discussions were bumpy at times, what bumps did you run into?"

"I'd say we ran into two key issues, one of which came from the discussion I had with my people, whereas the other surfaced as Bill worked with his team." Michael explained as he turned to Bill and asked, "Would you prefer to go first?"

"You've got the floor," Bill replied. "Just keep going."

"Fair enough. My team had no difficulty coming up with possible goals. In fact, they came up with a very long list of ideas. At first, I was surprised by how many potential goals they listed. As they went through the list, though, I started to see that all of the ideas were well thought out and each of them could certainly make a difference. Thus, trying to narrow the list was painful to say the least."

"I see," Oliver said. "It sounds as if you were having a difficult time separating the good ideas from the great ones."

"Yes, that's exactly it," said Michael. "We have many great products to sell and a number of distribution methods to explore, all of which have the potential to make a big difference."

"So what did you do?"

"Well," Michael responded, "I did what you suggested. I remembered you saying that it's hard to say no to good ideas and that people who are high achievers typically take on many tasks. I explained this to the group, and they agreed. Nonetheless, we hit a stalemate. Sensing that we weren't going to make any more progress, I suggested we stop at seven goals, take a break, and reconvene after the weekend. I encouraged each person to truly consider what mattered the most and come back with the two items they would take off the list if they had to remove something."

"That sounds like a good approach," Oliver added. "How did that turn out?"

"We met on Monday, and everyone came with the two items they would remove. Guess what?" Before anyone could respond, Michael answered his own question. "With the exception of one person, everyone listed the same two items. The guy who didn't agree on both items did match on one, though. A brief discussion ensued. In the end he agreed with the group, and we shortened our list to the top five things."

"Michael, I have to tell you, this is excellent work; you learned a great lesson," said their instructor. "And you accomplished two goals that some leaders struggle their entire lives to achieve. First, you demonstrated to your team that they needed to make the hard decision in order to place their best energy on the most important things. Second, you allowed them to work together and *with* you to make that informed choice. That's great work." Oliver turned to Bill and asked, "What was the challenge you ran into with your team?"

"I have to admit," Bill replied, "it was almost as if my people were reading from a script, Oliver. They did exactly what you said they would do."

"And what was that?" Oliver asked.

"They kept getting into the weeds. Every one of them wanted to talk about how we would do this or how we would do that. Finally, in an effort to get them on track, I offered an analogy. Please forgive me if this was off target, but it seemed to work," Bill added sheepishly.

"No need to apologize," Oliver said. "We're in this together."

"Well, I told them that we were talking about finish lines, not how we were going to get there. I asked them to imagine that we were runners on a track team. Thus, if we were asked to run a relay race, our first questions would probably be, 'How far?' and 'How fast?' I told them that was the purpose of the prioritizing step."

"Yes, I like that. Go on," Oliver urged.

"I then said that a future discussion would be about arm swing, stride length, and baton handoffs. It took a few minutes to sink in, but they got it. From that point on, anytime someone started getting too far into the details, someone would say, 'That sounds like a baton handoff,' and like magic, the conversation would work its way to the right spot."

"Wow! That's a great lesson too," Oliver stated. He stood and began walking toward the chalkboard. He reached for a piece of chalk. After selecting one from the trough at the base of the board, he turned to the others, saying, "That's exactly what we are going to talk about. How you and your teams will accomplish these priorities. The baton handoffs, if you will." He flashed a smile at Bill.

Susan interrupted. "Oliver, hold on one second. We definitely want to learn about that, but we have yet to tell you the best part of the last two weeks."

She stopped him in his tracks. Oliver put the chalk down and retreated to his seat. "I'm sorry; I thought the three of you were finished. Please continue."

Over the next several minutes, Oliver learned about the meeting with Sam. They told their teacher about the decision to invite him to the status meeting and of how Sam reluctantly attended. They shared their approach to presenting the information, Sam's engagement in the discussion, and ultimately his approval, with slight modifications, to their priorities. Susan ended with, "And the best thing is that he wants us to continue to meet with him to discuss our progress." She looked Oliver directly in the eyes and with a slight smile added, "So… no pressure here, but we have to deliver."

HIGHLIGHTS

Step 3: Determine Priorities

"Priorities focus on identifying the key goals your team must accomplish to positively affect what matters most to those you serve and to simultaneously impact your team's purpose."

KEY POINTS:

No one wants to say 'no' to a good idea, but prioritization demands tough decisions.

Improved communication, collaboration, and trust are often the result of selecting and accomplishing an important goal.

When determining priorities, focus on what you want to accomplish, not on how you intend to do it.

LEADER CHECKLIST:

✔ Brainstorm a list of possible goals your team can accomplish

✔ Narrow the list to the top six goals

✔ Complete a Prioritization Matrix and select top goals by answering:
- Can we get it done?
- Can we tell if we won?
- Is it important?
- Does it make sense?
- Will it help our team fulfill its purpose?
- Do we have, or can we get, needed funding?

Step 4: Formulate Plan

Chapter 17: Listen to Your People

Oliver added the words "Step 4: Formulate Plan" to his evolving model on the chalkboard. In addition to the words, he added an arrow showing a connection between steps three and four.

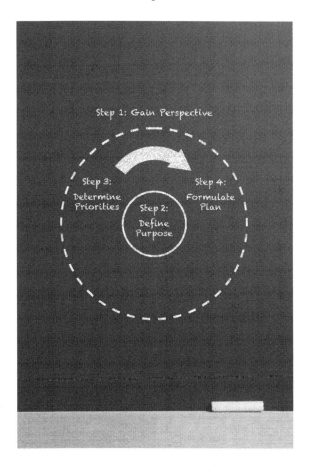

"The fourth step is to develop a plan for accomplishing each goal." As he spoke, he returned to the board and wrote, "Project or Process."

"To do so, you must determine if you are dealing with a project or a process goal. Project goals have a specific start and stop time-frame and involve a very specific deliverable. On the other hand, process goals deal with improving an existing process to reduce waste, improve up-time, and so on."

He waited a few minutes for Susan, Bill, and Michael to complete their notes and then continued. "I'm sure the three of you remember the example I gave the other day about setting a goal to lose weight." All three nodded. "Do you think that is a process or a project goal?"

After several silent moments, Susan decided to take a stab at the answer. "At first I thought it was a project goal, because you have a specific start and stop date and I could argue that your reduced weight was the deliverable. However, after thinking about it some more, I came to the conclusion that it's a process goal because there are things that you can do over and over to hit your target weight."

"That's exactly right," Oliver said enthusiastically. "To win on a process goal, you typically need someone to do something to some standard at some frequency. For example, to lose weight, I might need to run three miles at nine minutes each four times every week. Or I would have to eat no more than two thousand five hundred healthy calories per day. Does that make sense?"

"Yes, that makes perfect sense. How about a project-type goal?" Michael asked.

"Why don't you tell me?" Oliver responded.

"Always quick with the Socratic turn," Michael answered. He paused for a moment and responded, "Okay, I've got one. Let's say instead of setting a goal to lose weight, you set a goal to set up an exercise room in your home. In that situation, you would be dealing with a project where you wouldn't do the same things over and over."

"Yes, that's right; please continue," Oliver encouraged.

"If I were setting up a home gym, there'd be a list of things I would need to do, like design the layout, construct walls, pick out and install flooring, and purchase and set up the workout equipment."

"Right," Oliver interjected. "In the case of a project goal, you would need someone to do something by a certain date."

He returned to the board. Under the words "Project or Process," he drew two tables to capture the information they had just discussed. He then asked if Bill would be willing to help them complete the tables for each example goal. Bill rose from his seat and navigated his way to the board. Oliver handed him a piece of chalk and, with Michael's and Susan's input, he completed the matrices.

Process Goal Matrix

OVERALL GOAL: Lose 15 pounds by 12/31

Who?	Does What?	To What Standard?	How Often?
Oliver	Runs 3 miles	9-minute pace	3 times per week
Oliver	Eats	No more than 2,500 healthy calories	Each day

Project Goal Matrix

OVERALL GOAL: Set-up an exercise room in home by November 15

Who?	Does What?	By When?
Michael	Designs room and installs walls	September 30
Michael	Selects flooring and get them installed	October 15
Michael	Researches and purchases exercise equipment	October 21

"So here's the next step. Meet with your people and have them help you create a plan to realize your goals. As you do it, use your experience as a leader to determine if the plan is viable given the available resources and time required. I would suggest that you then take the plans to your boss to gain his input and support."

"That's exactly what we're going to do," Susan said. "Do you have any final words of advice?"

"I surely do," Oliver replied. "Work to create a plan that is *doable*, not too complicated, and captures the repetitive behaviors that will have the biggest impact on the goal, or in the case of project goals, identify the most important milestones that must be achieved. Finally, listen to your people. They often have the best ideas about how to accomplish goals; the problem is they're rarely asked."

Chapter 18: Developing Plans

Susan's Friday was a busy one. Typically, the end of the work week was a bit less hectic than the beginning. However, from the time she returned to the office on Thursday until the start of her team's session on Friday, she found herself running from one activity to the next, with barely enough time to squeeze in the requisite paperwork, e-mails, and phone calls.

She was disappointed when it dawned on her late Friday morning that she was going to have to postpone her team meeting by at least an hour to get her head above water and attend the last minute meetings added to her schedule. The last thing she wanted to do was send a message to her team that the process didn't matter, or that she would simply push it aside because of other demands. En route to a late morning discussion with a shift supervisor, Susan swung by her team's workspace to let them know of the delay. She found Kim, Chris, and Todd all at their desks.

"Folks, I hate to do this," Susan said with a slight grimace on her face, "but I need to postpone our afternoon meeting by an hour or so."

In typical form, Chris and Kim both said that the delay would be fine. Not surprising, Todd objected, "Do you really need to change the time?"

Susan felt herself stiffen as he asked the question. Over the past few weeks, Todd had become more positive about work and was starting to turn into the team player she'd envisioned. Trying to not be defensive, she said, "Yes, Todd. I'm sorry, but we will need to start an hour or so late. Will that be a problem?"

She braced for his response.

"It is not a problem per se," Todd answered. "It is just that we've made some great progress the last few weeks. I'd just hoped that we could roll our sleeves up this afternoon and start working on our plans. I, for one, find it very helpful to get our priorities straight, and I've been working on some ways for us to accomplish our goals."

Susan was speechless. She just stood there.

Todd filled the dead air. "Is it okay with you if the three of us meet at our scheduled time to get things started? You can join us as soon as your schedule allows."

Susan responded, "Um…sure, that would be fine. Let me take a few minutes to share with you what we were going to do today so that way you can get going on your own. I'll join you as quickly as I can."

Susan pulled out several sheets of paper that she had put together after her last session with Oliver. One side of each page showed a table labeled "Process Goal." The reverse side had one labeled "Project Goal." The tables had columns labeled as per Oliver's instructions. Susan quickly explained how to complete each table. After answering a few quick questions, she headed off to her meeting, promising to join them as soon as possible.

★ ★ ★

After her meeting, Susan hurried to meet her teammates. When she arrived, she found all three wrapped up in discussion. In less than an hour, they had managed to draft plans for each of the four HR priorities and were discussing how to present them to Susan. Her entrance brought the conversation to a close.

Obviously out of breath from her sprint across the facility, Susan announced her arrival. "Sorry for not being here earlier. I made the mad dash here as soon as the other meeting ended, but, as usual, couldn't make it across the production floor without a couple of questions along the way. How's it going?"

"Great," Kim replied.

"Absolutely," agreed Chris, with the enthusiasm Susan had grown to expect.

"It's going very well," Todd added. "In fact, if you'll allow us, we'd like to share with you our plans for making our goals happen."

"Sure, that would be great!" Susan exclaimed.

One by one, they addressed the goals. Using a sheet of large white flipchart paper with hand-drawn versions of the tables on them, Susan's three direct reports presented how the team would work towards accomplishing the three project goals and one process goal. She was amazed at their work! For each goal, they had set a clear plan for accomplishing it. The timelines were realistic, the distribution of tasks appropriate, and the budget requirements minimal. On a few occasions, she asked for a clarification and provided feedback as appropriate, but overall the plans were solid.

Oliver was right, Susan said to herself, *it is important to listen to your people.*

When they finished, Susan thanked them for their time and effort, adding, "Bill Engleman, Michael Thomas, and I are scheduled to meet with Sam Finch next Wednesday to provide him an update on our progress. Would one of you like to join me and present our plans?"

Todd chimed in immediately. "If it's okay with you, and if Kim and Chris don't mind, I'd like to volunteer."

With a smile, Susan replied, "That would be great!" Chris and Kim agreed.

★ ★ ★

That night Susan talked about the day's events over dinner with her husband. Greg listened with great interest. He then shared with her how well things were going with his team as he too applied Oliver's teachings. Both sat in amazement at the simplicity and power of the steps.

Chapter 19: An Unexpected Guest

Prior to the Monday morning staff meeting, Susan, Michael, and Bill conducted their weekly progress update, which also gave them a chance to help each other through any struggles or challenges.

All conveyed that they were surprised with how quickly the plans had come together. "It was interesting," Bill noted. "My team struggled with identifying the goals, but once we nailed those down, they were able to create plans fairly quickly. Oliver's right, teams do understand the details of how to get the work done...we just have to ask."

Michael agreed. "You're right, Bill, the plans did come together fairly well. One thing that stood out to me was that the goals that were deemed too tough by some people last week seemed doable to them this week once we started putting a plan together. To help them break out of their thinking on the subject, I built on Oliver's example. I explained to them that I was told to lose thirty pounds by my doctor."

"That's highly unlikely," Bill interjected. "I don't think you've put on a pound since your college playing days."

"That's very kind of you," Michael said with a grin. "Now where was I? Oh yes, thirty pounds. So if the doctor told you to lose thirty pounds, you might feel overwhelmed, but if I said for you to run three times a week and watch what you eat, you would probably say that you could do that."

"I really like that example," Susan said. "How did they react?"

"They liked it too," Michael said excitedly.

"I had an interesting experience too," Susan continued. "One of my team members volunteered to attend the review session with Sam this week. Actually, he did more than volunteer. He nearly insisted that he join."

"Who was that?" Bill asked.

"Todd," she replied.

"Really? I always thought he had a bit of a bad attitude. I'm surprised that he signed up for another meeting and face time with the boss," Michael said.

"Well, I won't talk specifics about his performance, but suffice it to say, he has been very enthusiastic lately."

Always the HR professional, Michael thought. *Susan would be the last person to talk about someone else's work performance without that person present.* He had always admired her for that.

The conversation came to a close as the start of the weekly staff meeting approached. Susan was the first to stand up from the table. She looked at her colleagues as they gathered their paperwork. "It's interesting," she said.

"What's interesting?" Bill asked.

"Not that long ago, I dreaded going to our staff meetings. Today, I see progress and a path we can take together. I'm actually looking forward to this morning's discussion."

★ ★ ★

On Wednesday afternoon, Susan, Todd, Bill, and Michael waited for Sam's arrival in the conference room. The words "Status Update – Part Two" appeared on the screen behind Susan. Sam arrived right on time. They were surprised to see that he wasn't alone. Most surprising to them was to see who he had brought with him.

"Please sit down," Sam said as he entered the room. "I hope you don't mind, but I decided to ask a guest to join us today." No one could miss Jane Hudson in her bright red pantsuit.

Sure, the last few Monday morning meetings have been going well, but did Sam have to invite Jane to attend our status meeting? Susan thought to herself.

"I know what you're thinking," Jane said. "I'm not here to present any slides or share anything on behalf of Alex. I'm simply here for my own education."

"Your own education?" Michael managed to ask.

"Yes, my own education," Jane replied. "During Alex's weekly conference call, I shared with him the improvements I've noticed at Outdoor Essentials. I then asked Sam what he thought was the source of the difference in attitude and focus of some of his leaders. He told me about the meeting he'd had with this group." She gestured to those in attendance. "I thought that it would be great if I could tag along to your next session so I could learn more about the process your teams are going through. In other words, I'm here to learn."

"Well, I don't know if we have much to teach you, but you're certainly welcome to join us," Susan said, and with that, she started the presentation.

For the better part of the next hour, Susan, Michael, and Bill shared their teams' efforts to date. They emphasized the work their team members had put into developing realistic and timely plans to make their priorities come to fruition. At one point, Todd joined the conversation, explaining how he found the process very helpful to him and his colleagues as they worked with Susan to better understand their customers, clarify their purpose, and establish top priorities, with a clear path to realizing them in practice. He added that he had already seen some positive changes in their team.

As the session drew to a close, Jane thanked everyone for allowing her to participate and said, "It's interesting…as part of my job, I read a lot of books and attend seminars on performance improvement, but what you presented here seems to cut to the essence of what all those writers and presenters are trying to explain. I, for one, am very impressed with your progress and can't wait to see your plans put into action."

Step 4: Formulate Plan

Leaders should listen to their people when formulating plans. Employees often have the best ideas about how to accomplish goals; the problem is they're rarely asked.

KEY POINTS:

Create plans that are doable, not too complicated, and capture the critical activities for success.

Ensure activities are assigned to specific individuals or roles. Assigning an activity to everyone is assigning the activity to no one.

Be realistic about timelines. People often have work responsibilities in addition to the goals. Don't lose sight of this.

LEADER CHECKLIST:

✔ Determine if the goal is a project or a process goal

✔ For project goals, complete a Project Goal Matrix to determine your plan by answering:
- Who?
- Does what?
- By when?

✔ For process goals, complete a Process Goal Matrix to determine your plan by answering:
- Who?
- Does what?
- To what standard?
- How often?

Step 5: Drive Performance

Chapter 20: It's More Than Flipcharts on Walls

As usual, Oliver started the session punctually. "Welcome back, folks. Today marks our last session together. I'm going to share the step five with you, but before we start to talk about the last step, let me give you a warning. This is the hardest step and is really what separates the excellent teams from the mediocre ones. When performed correctly, these teams truly embrace excellence."

Oliver returned to the trusty chalkboard and added the words "Step 5: Drive Performance" to his evolving image.

He paused and waited for his three students to write down the words. "The fifth step is where the rubber meets the road, or as I like to say, it's where teams realize that it's more than flipcharts on walls. What do you think I mean by that?" He waited a minute for a response. The blank stares around the table suggested that one wasn't coming, so he continued. "I bet over the course of your careers that each of you has spent much time in meetings, albeit in more appropriate surroundings than what I have to offer." He motioned to the cluttered back room in which they sat. "You're probably more accustomed to meeting rooms in a better looking facility. I also bet that in those meeting rooms, you sat with colleagues and came up with big plans that you wrote on flipchart paper and placed on the walls. The words on the sheets represented hours of discussion and debate. Does this sound familiar?"

"Absolutely," Bill replied, "that sounds exactly like our company's annual planning session."

"I agree," Michael confirmed.

"I *also* bet," Oliver continued, "that you can think of a time where six months after the planning meeting ended you found yourself wondering what happened to all the great ideas you discussed. Don't get me wrong, I'm not saying you weren't busy over the last several months. You were. However, you and your team simply lost sight of some of those goals due to the daily demands of your jobs. Does this sound familiar?"

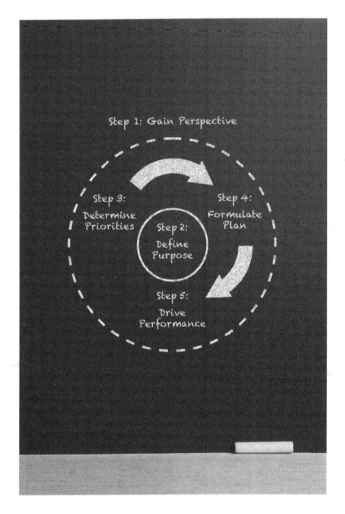

"Sadly, it does," Susan replied. "Okay, so we've all experienced something like this?" Oliver asked. All three nodded in agreement. "I have one last bet to make," Oliver said. "I bet that, at a later time, you found yourself in another conference room, filling out more sheets of paper, and that those papers contained many of the same items that you had previously discussed. But this time you vowed that things would be different. Am I off the mark?"

"Not at all," Bill answered. "I can't tell you how many times I've seen this type of scenario. We get excited about a goal and the plan to make it happen, but we quickly find ourselves losing sight of both."

"I had this type of conversation during our team meeting this past week!" Michael exclaimed. "We were talking about our goals, and one of my more seasoned salespeople challenged me, saying that we've talked about many of these ideas for years and never turned them into reality. He wanted to know what would be different this time."

"And what did you tell him?" Susan asked.

"I told him to give me a week to think about it. Then I prayed that Oliver would provide some insight that would help me answer his question."

Susan and Bill both let out a nervous laugh, suggesting that they shared Michael's sentiment.

Oliver said, "I'm going to use an illustration to explain what needs to happen for your team to accomplish your top priorities in the face of the day-to-day work. And I'm going to pick on you, Michael, to do so. Will that be okay?"

"Sure."

"Good. Now, pretend for a moment that you're ten years old again. You and three of your friends are shooting baskets in your driveway. You are just having fun, throwing up shots, acting silly, perhaps talking about a new song you heard or something you saw on television. Can you picture this?"

"Absolutely, that's how I spent most of my days as a kid."

"Okay, now after a while, one of your friends says something like, 'This is getting boring. Let's play a game.' He then points to one of the two other boys and says to you, 'He and I against the two of you.' The first team to score ten points gets a free ice cream from the losers.' Now, what happened to you at that very moment?" Oliver asked.

"A little switch in my head just flipped." Michael made a flipping a switch motion with his thumb and forefinger. "It went from *we're just playing around* to *game on, this really matters.*"

"That's exactly right. Immediately, the intensity goes up, your desire to score increases, you improve your shot selection, you start talking to your teammate, you come up with a game plan, and the list goes on. You simply become much more focused." Pointing to Michael, Oliver added, "Susan and Bill, look at Michael. Do you see a change in him right now as we talk about this?"

They both turned to look at their colleague. Oliver was right. Michael was now leaning forward in his seat, and he had become much more engaged in the conversation.

"That's the type of engagement teams need to achieve their best. Every person on the team needs to realize that the goal matters. Their individual contributions matter. We're keeping score, and they all have a role to play."

Oliver turned back to the board and drew two vertical lines making three columns. He labeled the columns "Individual," "Team," and "Leader." Under the word "Individual," he wrote, "Understand role and complete tasks." Below "Team," he wrote, "Discuss and track progress." In the "Leader" column, he listed "Facilitate process and assist team members."

INDIVIDUAL	TEAM	LEADER
Understand role and complete tasks	Discuss and track progress	Facilitate process and assist team member

"Just like the players on any sports team, the members of your team must understand their roles and complete critical tasks every week. This might sound easy, but it's not common practice."

The three students nodded in agreement.

"For example, my wife and I have two grown up sons," Oliver explained. "I remember that when they were school age, they would sometimes wait until the last minute to complete a class project. Even if the teacher assigned the work six weeks earlier, they would often be up the final night, trying to get the project done. They would be frustrated and so would my wife and I."

"That sounds familiar," Bill said.

"All *too* familiar, I'm sure," Oliver continued. "It wasn't because they were bad kids; it was just because their daily activities of school, friends, sports, and family kept their attention off the long-term goal of the course project. The only way to break this cycle was to get the boys to break the work up into segments and to complete the necessary daily and weekly tasks to get the project completed on time. My job as the parent was to make sure the process was moving along and that they had what they needed to succeed. This wasn't something I would do at the beginning of the assignment and then wait for the grade to show up on the project—it was something I would do every week."

"What do you mean, 'something you would *do* every week'?" Susan asked.

"I mean that every week, as the leader, I would have a huddle with my sons. We would discuss where things stood, how they were progressing, and what I could do to help. We'd talk about the good, the bad, and the ugly. What was and wasn't working well for them.

"To use another sports analogy," Oliver continued, "making this work for your teams is very similar to a football game. What happens after each play?"

"The team huddles," Michael answered.

"That's exactly right. In a huddle, they quickly discuss how the last play went. A player might say, 'Great catch,' or 'You missed that block.' Then they look at the scoreboard to see where things stand and decide what play to run next. They confirm each person's assignment, saying things like, 'Run this route,' or 'Make sure you block that guy.'"

"And this is similar to what we should do?" Susan asked.

"Yes, it's very similar. If you want to accomplish your goals without losing focus on everything else that needs to happen at work, you move with the speed and intensity of a football huddle. Once per week, you need to check in with your folks and see how things are going to ensure that the process and project goals are staying on track and that you are getting the expected results."

"So we need to add *another* meeting?" Bill groaned.

"Not another meeting, a football-type huddle. Make it quick, engaging, focused, and brief. A meeting like this is the only way to keep the goal moving and to not cause yourselves to sit back in another conference room a year from now talking about the same old goals you failed to accomplish this year."

"Okay, I get it," Bill said. "I'm the last guy who wants another meeting, but I agree." He glanced at his notes to ensure that he understood the key points. "If we really want to accomplish these priorities and move the metrics in the right direction, we have to make time for these huddles. I also agree that my job is to facilitate the process and to help my people win. Their jobs are to understand their roles and to perform them in the face of all the other tasks we need to accomplish. It won't be easy, but it does make sense to me."

"To help keep your teams focused," Oliver explained, "I suggest creating and using a goal tracking matrix. The simplest way to accomplish this is by building on the process and project goal matrices you completed during step four, planning."

Oliver rotated the chalkboard to reveal the back side of the surface. The information Bill had printed about losing weight and setting up a home gym during their last meeting remained. However, Oliver had some additional information to help with goal tracking.

"The first goal we talked about was a process goal," Oliver explained. "It focused on my losing fifteen pounds by December 31. I've added a couple of things to what Bill wrote down during our last meeting. First, I placed 'Where I should be' and 'Where I am' under the explanation of the goal. This allows people to see where we currently stand, compared to where we should be. This tells us if we are on or off track.

"Second, I added columns to the table for me to write down whether I met the daily or weekly requirements or not. I added four columns, because that's all I had room for on the board. You would need to put a column down for every week through the end of the goal. For this simple example, I put down a plus sign when I met the requirement and a minus sign when I didn't. It's quick and easy to read."

Process Goal Tracking Matrix
Overall Goal: Lose 15 pounds by December 31
Where I should be: Down 2.5 lbs (as of September 1)
Where I am: Lost 3 pounds

Who?	Does What?	To What Standard?	How Often?	Week			
				1	2	3	4
Oliver	Runs 3 miles	9-minute pace	3 times per week	+	-	+	+
Oliver	Eats	No more than 2,500 healthy calories	Each day	-	+	+	+

"Could we use something like a smiley face or a checkmark instead of the plus and minus symbols?" Susan asked.

"Absolutely!" Oliver responded. "I'm just showing the basic information. You can add whatever you want as long as it helps your team track progress. Now, let's take a look at the project goal."

Oliver pointed at the second table on the chalkboard and said, "The second goal dealt with setting up a home gym in Michael's house. Again, I kept this simple; and, as Susan pointed out, you can add other items to help your team stay focused. For this one, I included an 'as of date' under the goal and 'Status' and 'Notes' columns to the table. You can see that I added information about what has been completed, whether or not it was done on time, and activities that are currently under way."

Project Goal Tracking Matrix
Overall Goal: Set up an exercise room in home by November 15
Results as of: October 1

Bill, Michael, and Susan copied Oliver's additions to their notes from the previous session.

Who?	Does What?	By When?	Status	Notes
Michael	Designs room and installs walls	Sept 30	Done on time	Room designed and walls installed 1 week ahead of schedule
Michael	Selects flooring and get them installed	Oct 15	Working	Picked up samples and discussing with wife
Michael	Researches and purchases exercise equipment	Oct 21	Working	Talked to rep at fitness store and have websites to visit

"Along with conducting huddles and using a tracking tool," Oliver continued, "I suggest you pick a date in the future, say in three to six months, for your team to present their progress to your boss. Having this date on the calendar is similar to having to turn in the homework assignment. It provides another level of accountability and lets the team know that we are *not* going to forget about the goal."

"That makes sense to me. Is there anything else?" Susan asked.

"Yes, the three of you and your teams have put much time and energy into the last several weeks, and you've made great progress. As I look at each of you, I get the feeling that you are both encouraged and discouraged by this final step. I understand—there is no quick fix. You're going to have to do the hard work of carving out time to talk, holding yourselves and your teams accountable every week, and making decisions that move teams from mediocrity to excellence.

This might mean saying *no* to ideas you have said *yes* to in the past. This will also mean being a bit uncomfortable when someone misses a obligation and you have to address the situation. However, you will have the ability to celebrate successes like you have never celebrated before and to build a team that can accomplish anything they choose to tackle."

He returned one last time to the chalkboard and rotated it so his five steps model reappeared for the group. He then added an arrow that connected step five to step three.

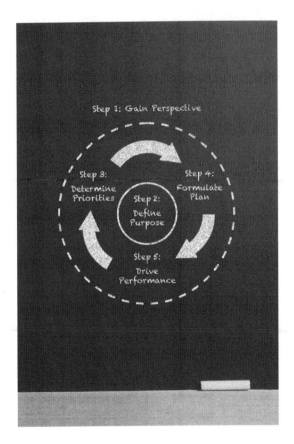

Oliver added, "As your teams accomplish their plans, each of you, as a leader, must ensure that the desired results are achieved, changes in the environment are considered, and new priorities are established to ensure ongoing success."

Oliver paused and looked each of his students directly in the eyes. "It has been an absolute pleasure getting to know each of you. Each week, I have looked forward to our meetings together and it has been thrilling to witness your accomplishments. Please promise me that at least one of you will stop by at some point in the future and give me an update on how things are going."

"Wait a second, Oliver," Susan interrupted. "When we first met, you asked me about our goals, then we met each week and discussed our progress, learned new information, and you helped us think through our challenges. Now you're asking us to come back in a few months and provide you an update on our progress. It sounds like you're using the five steps to teach us the five steps. Is that right?"

With a wink Oliver replied, "That sounds about right!"

Chapter 21: Getting Results

The door swung open, and the old bell rang once again. Susan recognized the familiar sound. Although she hadn't entered the store in over four months, the memorable noise transported her back to the first time she entered the store. The shop hadn't changed a bit. She glanced at the piles of books scattered throughout the store. Susan smiled to herself as she realized that the place she once viewed as a disorganized mess was now one of warmth and learning.

She saw Oliver sitting on the stool behind the counter. More accurately, she saw Oliver's full head of hair behind the counter. As always, he had his head down and his mind lost in the book that lay open before him.

Susan waited a few minutes before she let her presence be known, simply watching the man who had become her friend and teacher doing what he enjoyed most. When it became evident that he was not going to notice her, Susan made her way from the door to the counter. Her arrival occurred at the same moment as a particularly humorous part of Oliver's text. He lifted his head in laughter at the author's jest and caught a glimpse of Susan.

"Well, look who's here," Oliver said. "It's been way too long. How are you doing?"

Oliver sprang to his feet and worked his way out from behind the counter. His outfit didn't disappoint. The pressed khaki pants, blue button-down shirt, smock, and glasses were exactly the attire Susan expected. They gave each other a brief hug as Susan said, "I've been doing great. I'm just sorry I haven't stopped by sooner." She offered a warm smile.

"That's okay. I know you have a lot going on. What brings you by today?" he asked.

"Yes, I've been very busy, but before things get busier, I wanted to share with you what has happened since my last visit and our discussion about driving performance. Do you have a few minutes to talk?"

Not surprisingly, Oliver answered, "My time is your time."

Susan explained that a great deal had happened since the last time they met. She, Michael, and Bill met with their teams and discussed what it would take to perform at the highest level. The discussion with her team went well, and she received everyone's commitment to the process. From the very first huddle and a progress review, she saw a marked difference in the team's performance.

"As we've implemented the five steps, I've seen my team more engaged in this process than ever before. Sure, we have some challenges, and it's a bit uncomfortable when we get behind schedule on a project goal or fail to perform as agreed upon for a process goal, but we talk about, learn from it, and recommit to staying on track."

"That's wonderful," Oliver responded.

"It is indeed. In fact, one of my team members, who had the worst attitude and was on his way to losing his job, has really turned a corner over the last six months. He has gone from a person I was happy to avoid to someone I seek out when the toughest tasks come our way."

"Do you mind if I ask a question?" Oliver asked in his usual polite manner.

"I'd be surprised if you didn't," Susan replied.

Oliver smiled and said, "What do you think has caused him to change?"

"I asked him that exact question," Susan replied. "He told me that he changed when he saw that we were going to get clear on what mattered most to the team and that he and his colleagues had a voice in setting both the priorities and the plan to accomplish them. He said that, until that point, he was simply moving paperwork across his desk each day and it really didn't matter if he showed up for work or not. Now he tells me that he feels a sense of purpose in our work and knows how our team will drive the organization's results."

"Susan, that is wonderful. I'm so happy for you and your team. I bet you're also more fulfilled."

"Absolutely! I now look forward to the Monday morning meeting and seeing how we, as a company, are advancing on our goals."

"So is everyone at Outdoor Essentials on board with the five steps?" Oliver inquired.

"Not everyone," Susan answered, "Although they'll all be using them soon!"

"Tell me more," Oliver prodded.

"About four weeks after we finished our last session with you, my boss, Sam, said that he began to see a real separation between the teams that Michael, Bill, and I lead from other teams in the company. While everyone else was still operating under the old model of doing things, we were more focused and our teams were beginning to accomplish things no one thought possible. Old ideas that were discussed for years were starting to come to fruition. It was very exciting."

"I bet it was."

"So, Sam asked the three of us to share the process with our colleagues. We didn't do as good a job as you did, but we did manage to share the basics and get everyone started. It wasn't perfect, but the entire company started making positive strides, and the metrics began moving in the right direction."

She continued, "I just came from a half-day meeting with Sam, his boss who created the metrics, and all of my colleagues."

"How did that go?"

"All in all, I think it went very well. We've made some tremendous progress over the last several months, and those above us at JWL Adventures expressed their pleasure with our efforts. Don't get me wrong," she added, "we still have plenty of work to do if we are to accomplish all our goals, but we're seeing movement and the mood in the company seems different."

"That's wonderful, Susan. I'm so happy for you, Michael, Bill, and all of your people."

"Well, there *is* one more thing," she said.

"What's that?"

"My boss has asked me to put together a training program for the entire company to teach everyone the five steps and to provide them the tools they need to follow the process time and time again. I still have work to do, but I came up with the title for the process. I'm going to call it The Five Ps of Team Success."

"Wow! That's amazing," Oliver said, a huge smile appearing on his face. "Would you be willing to share the materials with me when you finish? I'd love to see them."

"Absolutely," Susan replied. "You will get the first copy off the printing press."

"I'm looking forward to it." He paused for a moment to gather his thoughts and continued. "Susan, I'm often delighted by the wonderful people who find their way into this old bookstore, but you, my friend, are a cut above my other customers. I've so enjoyed our time together and hope that you have learned as much from the experience as I have."

"I've learned so much more than you could imagine," Susan said.

The conversation continued for a few minutes until Susan excused herself to get back to the plant. She promised not to let so much time pass between her visits. They hugged goodbye, and she walked toward the entrance.

As she reached for the doorknob, Susan looked over her should to see Oliver buried back in his book. Susan shook her head in amusement. At that moment, the door opened and she nearly ran headfirst into a man in his thirties. They exchanged pleasantries as they passed one another. Just before the door closed behind her, she heard the man ask, "Excuse me sir, do you happen to have any books on employee engagement?"

"Certainly, we have a number of books that address employee engagement," the familiar response came. "But first, when you say employee engagement, what do you mean?"

HIGHLIGHTS

Step 5: Drive Performance

"Performance is the hardest step and is really what separates the excellent teams from the mediocre ones."

KEY POINTS:

It is critical to keep the goal in front of your team to ensure they don't lose sight of it.

Team members need to understand that the goal is there to stay and not simply a random or passing thought.

Everyone must understand the role of the individual, the team, and the leader when it comes to accomplishing goals.

Develop and utilize a Goal Tracking Tool to measure progress.

Don't be afraid to have the tough accountability discussions.

Teams must conduct huddles to stay on track. It is critical that they be consistent, focused, and fast.

LEADER CHECKLIST:

✔ Ensure every team member is clear on the priorities and the plan to make them happen

✔ Develop and use a tracking tool to measure progress

✔ Meet frequently to discuss progress and ensure everyone remains focused on the goal

✔ Set a date to review the results of the effort and celebrate successes

Author's Notes

For more than 20 years, I have had the pleasure to work with amazing colleagues, lead exiting and diverse projects that have taken me around the world, and partnered with clients who are true professionals in every sense of the word. Although my name is listed on the cover of this book, the text would not exist if it wasn't for the continual support of my wife and business partner, Jamie, our two children, Alex and Clay, and all of my colleagues. Jamie and I met in college, and she has been my best friend and the love of my life since our first conversation.

True, the characters depicted in this book are fictitious; however, the various concepts and processes outlined are very real. They represent a compilation of our efforts working with clients to help them maximize the passion and potential of their people and accomplish meaningful results. I appreciate each of my colleagues for the role they played in helping this book come to fruition.

The concepts outlined in this document stem from my time in the United States Army. As a young lieutenant completing infantry, ranger, and airborne schools, as well as leading an airborne platoon in the 82nd Airborne Division, I quickly learned the importance of understanding the situation, developing a clear mission, and executing with excellence.

The Five P's of Team Success

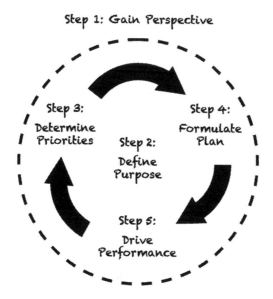

Step 1: Gain Perspective

Step 3: Determine Priorities

Step 2: Define Purpose

Step 4: Formulate Plan

Step 5: Drive Performance

Step 1: Gain Perspective
Determine what matters the most to those who matter to you

Step 2: Define Purpose
Articulate why your team exists, what you do, and who you serve

Step 3: Determine Priorities

Focus on identifying the key goals your team must accomplish to positively affect what matters the most to those you serve and simultaneously affect your team's purpose

Step 4: Formulate Plan

Listen to your team members when formulating plans; employees often have the best ideas about how to accomplish your priorities

Step 5: Drive Performance

Ensure that team members are clear on the priorities and plans towards accomplishing them; use a tracking tool to measure and discuss progress

Visit OliversSpot.com to read Oliver's insights, book reviews, and recommended reading lists. You can also ask Oliver a question and benefit from his wit and wisdom.

Advancing Knowledge in Service-Learning

Research to Transform the Field

a volume in
Advances in Service-Learning Research

Series Editor:
Shelley H. Billig
RMC Research Corporation

Advances in Service-Learning Research

Shelley H. Billig, Series Editor

Service Learning: The Essence of the Pedagogy (2002)
edited by Andrew Furco and Shelley H. Billig

Service Learning Through a Multidisciplinary Lens (2002)
edited by Shelley H. Billig and Andrew Furco

Deconstructing Service-Learning:
Research Exploring Context, Participation, and Impacts (2003)
edited by Shelley H. Billig and Janet Eyler

New Perspectives in Service Learning:
Research to Advance the Field (2004)
edited by Shelley H. Billig and Marshall Welch

Improving Service-Learning Practice:
Research on Models to Enhance Impacts (2005)
edited by Susan Root, Jane Callahan, and Shelley H. Billig

Advancing Knowledge in Service-Learning

Research to Transform the Field

Edited by

Karen McKnight Casey
Michigan State University

Georgia Davidson
Michigan State University

Shelley H. Billig
RMC Research Corporation

Nicole C. Springer
Michigan State University

INFORMATION AGE
PUBLISHING

Greenwich, Connecticut • www.infoagepub.com

Library of Congress Cataloging-in-Publication Data

International K-H Service-Learning Research Conference (5th : 2005 :
Michigan State University)
  Advancing knowledge in service-learning research to transform the
field / edited by Karen McKnight Casey ... [et al.].
    p. cm. — (Advances in service-learning research)
  Includes bibliographical references and index.
  ISBN-13: 978-1-59311-569-2 (hardcover)
  ISBN-13: 978-1-59311-568-5 (pbk.)
  1. Student service—Congresses. I. Casey, Karen McKnight. II. Title.
  LC220.5.I58 2005
  361.3'7—dc22

                                        2006026420

ISBN 13: 978-1-59311-568-5 (pbk.)
          978-1-59311-569-2 (hardcover)
ISBN 10:   1-59311-568-7 (pbk.)
            1-59311-569-5 (hardcover)

Printed in the United States of America

DEDICATION

This volume is dedicated to John Duley, professor emeritus, Justin Morrill College, Michigan State University, and a noted "pioneer" in the service-learning and civic engagement movement. John has retired from teaching, but continues to work as a scholar and advocate in the field. John's commitment to purposeful and reciprocal connections among faculty, students, and community has not waned. He inspires all around him to seek transformations and to serve as agents of social change.

CONTENTS

ACKNOWLEDGMENTS

We gratefully acknowledge the excellent detailed work of our editor, Mary Ann Strassner, and all of the scholars who wrote for this book and presented at the 5th Annual International K–H Service-Learning Research Conference. We are also very grateful to RMC Research Corporation and Michigan State University for the funding of this work.

INTRODUCTION

**Karen McKnight Casey, Nicole C. Springer,
Shelly H. Billig, and Georgia Davidson**

Service-learning is not simply a pedagogy. Rather, service-learning is a means to empower students and educational institutions to become more aware of the needs of the communities of which they are a part and to become engaged and civically active in mutually beneficial ways. Community-based service that relates to course and curricular content is becoming increasingly embedded in curriculum, kindergarten through higher education. Evidence is beginning to show that service-learning has not only begun to transform education, but it also has transformed the lives of many of the students involved.

Many prominent researchers in the field of service-learning gathered at Michigan State University in late fall 2005 at the 5th Annual International K-H Conference on Service-Learning Research. Those who presented at this conference were invited to submit their presentations to be considered for publication in this sixth volume of the *Advances in Service-Learning Research* book series. Presentations that received the highest ratings in a blind peer-review process are included in this volume.

This book is organized into five sections. It begins with a close examination of the connection between service-learning and civic engagement. In chapter 1, Rick Battistoni, one of two keynote speakers at the conference, discusses how civic engagement has become the buzzword in higher education. With all of the discussion and current research, he questions whether those involved in service-learning know what practices actually produce greater civic engagement. He makes a strong case for learning the skills of democratic civic engagement through practice, both inside and outside of the curriculum.

In chapter 2, Pritzker and McBride document the growth of service-learning as a civic intervention. They point out that multiple studies have identified positive civic outcomes for precollege students involved in service-learning activities, but that the rigor and generalizability of the studies is not as high as some researchers claim. They use their chapter to synthesize results in order to validate, and in some cases, invalidate claims. Billig and Root, in chapter 3, describe two case studies of high school classes that have demonstrated strong results of participation in service-learning on high school students' civic engagement. The case studies illustrate specific strategies in place that appear to be related to robust outcomes. These classes also serve to show that young people can be re-engaged in civic life through public education when teachers are flexible in the way they deliver curriculum.

The second section, International Perspectives on Service-Learning, brings in the voices of researchers from Argentina and Mexico, providing an international perspective of service-learning and civic engagement. In chapter 4, Tapia of the Latin American Center for Service-Learning and her coauthors, González and Elicegui, present readers with descriptive exploratory research on Argentina's K-12 community service-learning. The chapter provides statistical data on schools with students participating in service by geographic location, level, type of administration (state or private), and social context. This study is critical in showing how service-learning is implemented in other countries. Mexican authors Pacheco-Pinzón and Diáz Barriga A. examine the critical thinking process and how it manifests itself in the reflections of various higher education students at the Mérida Marist University in chapter 5. This qualitative study utilized a critical thinking questionnaire given to the entire student population of the school of psychology and documents the experiences of four students during a one-semester service-learning experience. The service-learning program is presented as a model experiential learning program for the professions that promotes socially responsible education committed to improving the quality of life for everyone, everywhere.

Section III contains studies that demonstrate the impacts of service-learning on its participants. Simons and Cleary present their evaluation of academic service-learning in chapter 6. Using a mixed-methods design, the differences between students in undergraduate psychology courses who participate in service-learning and those who do not were evaluated. The results show differences in attitudes and skills, and that service-learning influenced nearly every aspect of a student's development. The chapter concludes with a discussion of the ways in which service-learning can help teachers employ different pedagogical methods because of the additional community-based experts available to the students.

Chapters 7 and 8 address service-learning pedagogy in higher education and the increasingly important issue of faculty development. Chapter 7, written by Harwood, Fliss, and Gaulding from Western Washington University, presents an analysis of a 2-year Faculty Fellows Program that was designed to enhance the service-learning pedagogy and scholarship of faculty at their university. Participation in the Faculty Fellows cohort program provided a sense of campus community, led to professional and personal development, and improved community and student outcomes. The supportive culture created through the program was found to be central to its powerful impact. In a complementary fashion, Kecskes, Collier, and Balshem, from Portland State University, studied the scholarly application of pedagogies of engagement and note the importance of this application in advancing the practice of service-learning. The authors share the basic tenets of an innovative program model at Portland State University called the Scholarship of Teaching Resource Team. Their research on the program demonstrates its strong impact on faculty and on their scholarly production. The chapter helps the reader identify engaged scholarship and learn how an institution of higher education can support it.

The purpose of this series of books is to advance the knowledge in the service-learning research field. More importantly, this research is to be used to transform the field. This transformation will come from realizing both the history of service-learning and trying to imagine what the future may look like. In chapter 9, Shumer starts by identifying the most important research studies from the past 25 years and their influence on the evolution of the field. Using a Delphi study, he ranked the various types of influence and analyzes how and why these studies were important. In the final chapter of the book, Casey and Springer examine developing trends to institutionalize service-learning in higher education. The authors revisit the long-standing question as to whether institutionalization is preferable and provide supporting documentation that it is. Indicators, standards, and the growing momentum for service-learning implementation are examined.

The chapters in this book all demonstrate just how far service-learning research has come. Researchers, practitioners, and students alike have benefited from its dissemination and use the research to improve practice. The research does not simply inform educators how to create a better

pedagogy. Rather, it informs a service-learning practice that can transform both individuals and institutions.

Section I

SERVICE-LEARNING AND CIVIC EGAGEMENT

CHAPTER 1

APPROACHING DEMOCRATIC ENGAGEMENT

Research Findings on Civic Learning and Civic Practice

Rick Battistoni

ABSTRACT

The field of service-learning has come a long way in its efforts to understand and implement service-learning and its potential connection to education for democratic civic engagement. New and different ways of thinking are needed concerning the approach to what is currently one of the major outcomes for service-learning practice. Work and research in this area over the past few years has indicated that this paradigm shift must occur in 2 important ways. A shift in attention and focus is necessary, along with a need to explore/examine the "premises and assumptions" of the field (to borrow from the conference theme).

Advancing Knowledge in Service-Learning: Research to Transform the Field, 3–16
Copyright © 2006 by Information Age Publishing
All rights of reproduction in any form reserved.

3

EXAMINING THE APPROACH

The amount of institutional infrastructure and the number of quality programs have increased dramatically over the past 16 years. In addition, the research base has grown exponentially and internationally. Researchers are now providing vast amounts of information about the conditions in which service-learning works best and also the impact of service-learning on students, and to a lesser degree, on schools, educational institutions, and communities. In terms of "civic engagement" outcomes, there has also been progress. In 1993, shortly after the passage and signing of the National and Community Service Trust Act of 1993, a meeting at Wingspread was convened at which leading higher education practitioners heard from governmentally funded researchers for Learn & Serve America that they planned to study the civic responsibility outcomes for participants through the use of a single question: "Are you registered to vote?" The field has come a long way from this one-dimensional measure of civic engagement.

Civic Learning

Educators and practitioners who chronicle the history of this field in the United States talk about the shift in the field's framing language and underlying premises. Earlier concerns, especially during the period in which Campus Outreach Opportunity League and Campus Compact (the late 1980s), focused on advancing community service and volunteerism. The current emphasis is now on civic engagement as the ultimate outcome or goal of our work. With the first shift from community service to service-learning, a great deal of definitional and programmatic precision was gained so that today, there is a general agreement about what constitutes *real* service-learning, as opposed to community service or volunteerism. There is even an emerging consensus among researchers about what quality factors are most crucial in achieving certain kinds of outcomes, at least for students. Some contention and confusion still remain, however, and when it comes to practical implementation and research on impacts, a great deal of variation exists between programs or courses that call themselves service-learning.

This more recent shift to civic engagement has not brought the same kind of precision. Historically, civic has meant belonging to or of a city, relating to citizenship. From its Latin origins, the word civic was also used to describe a public realm that was distinguished from the military or ecclesiastical realms of a community. In this sense, the civic was the realm of politics and public life, the place where citizens heard about, discussed, debated, and even decided upon issues of public concern. During the French Revolution, in a democratic move, the title "citizen" replaced "*monsieur*" as the preferred mode of address between people, and people took a civic oath of allegiance to the new order of the Revolution. Therefore, it is important to remember that the words citizen or civic have public, even political and potentially revolutionary origins.

In the United States, something occurred to blunt the edges of the words civic and citizenship and leave them less than inspirational. It may have been the practice of civics as the dry and boring teaching of institutional facts and memorization of bites about government or the Constitution that took away some of the original revolutionary emphasis. Perhaps it was the common practice of giving schoolgirls and boys grades for citizenship along with marks for subject matter, to reward obedience to the teacher. The concept of citizenship at that time emphasized overall conformity, easing citizenship away from its political nature.

The result is a word that produces a problematic framework for practice and research. In the United States, civic engagement and citizenship are amorphous and contested terms. For a number of years now, at service-learning workshops, in AmeriCorps and other service-learning participant trainings, and with students in a number of his classes, this author has been doing an introductory exercise that asks participants to rank order a list of 15 items—ranging from "voting" to "tutoring in a local elementary school" to "organizing a campaign against domestic violence"—in light of their own understanding/philosophy of civic engagement or good citizenship. More than anything else, this exercise demonstrates the very different, often antithetical, ways that people conceive of exemplary civic engagement. Some people rank voting at the top; others give priority to service-oriented items; still others prefer activist items. When words are so amorphous that they can be filled with very different content or meaning even when it seems that the use of these words is intentional as opposed to using other terms which may convey a particular direction, they lose their precision in both programming and in research.

There are other complications with the terms civic or citizenship. Citizenship is conceived as a status, one that endows certain individuals with rights or other legal entitlements. This promotes exclusivity, particularly in any society rich with immigrants who are alienated based either on their status as noncitizens, or regardless of their status, are regarded as outsiders. In the United Kingdom, researchers distinguish between conceptions of citizenship based upon *status* and those premised upon a *practice*. The latter notion conceives of citizens as individuals possessing a common identity who have responsibilities to work together to achieve common purposes (Nelson & Kerr, 2005).

Complications with the terms civic or citizenship are magnified by the fact that good citizenship has traditionally conveyed a sense of conformity to rules, obedience, or complete integration/assimilation into a dominant culture, or do-goodism. As such, the very conception of citizenship or civic naturally links to thin notions of community service volunteerism. At the 2005 Association of American Colleges and Universities conference on civic engagement, Cruz reminded us that those engaged in collective action to change conditions in the world rarely call what they do civic engagement, or even service.[1] Even with the language shift from service-learning to civic engagement in recent years, many schools and colleges that talk about civic engagement are not doing anything different than when they used service-learning as their framing language. In fact, they may not be doing things in a different manner than when community service was the operating framework.

This is why I prefer more overtly political understandings at the foundation of conceptions of civic engagement. Democracy needs to be explicitly and overtly referenced in the field's pedagogy, so education for citizenship in a democracy seems a more appropriate framework. An aversion to using more political language exists, especially in this country, given the association between politics and partisanship, the increasing youth and adult turnoff from politics as popularly understood, and given the prohibitions in the United States on political activity in the legislation authorizing governmentally supported service and service-learning. Some research, including the oft-cited Center for Information & Research on Civic Learning and Engagement (CIRCLE) study by Keeter, Zukin, Andolina, and Jenkins (2002), even distinguishes between civic engagement and political engagement. There is a need to connect understanding of engagement to participation in public life, and for precision in understanding exactly what this civic goal or outcome entails. What it is called is actually less important than the precision with which it is framed.

Here is one area where people in the United States have much to learn from our international colleagues. In the United Kingdom, educators use the term "active citizenship" to describe the goals of their new national curriculum. The development of a statutory national curriculum in citizenship in the United Kingdom was begun as a recommendation of an advisory group chaired by Sir Bernard Crick in 1998, which followed the shift in emphasis that came with the new Labour government in 1997. In fact, a key line from the Crick Report (Qualifications and Curriculum Authority, 1998) stated the primary goal was to create a "change in the political culture" (p. 7). A follow-up report from the British Home Office on post-16 education added this to the following concept. Active citizenship can be defined as "citizens taking opportunities to become actively involved in defining and tackling ... the problems of their communities and improving their quality of life" (Firm Foundations, 2004). The report wanted to emphasize the point that by relying on indirect methods, such as voting, many individuals miss the real opportunity to "[create] a better society through a direct and positive contribution to their communities."[2] All through this curricular reform, the effort in the United Kingdom has been focused on involving young people in active citizenship, enabling them to make decisions and take action, both in schools and other learning organizations and in the wider community.

"Active citizenship," the goal of this national curriculum, contains the following 6 dimensions:

1. **Awareness** of issues beyond the individual self, at the community, national, global level (a twist on the **knowledge** component of citizenship education, with the understanding that knowledge goes beyond institutions and historical "facts" and must encompass knowledge of public policy issues).

2. Desire to address issues and act upon them. A genuine interest in being involved, having influence or taking action to promote change, or the **motivational** dimension of civic/political involvement.

3. Ability to make judgments and decisions, based on ability to balance evidence and use this ability to take action in an informed manner (the **skills** component to citizenship education).

4. Taking direct peaceful action in the organization, community, national or international arena (the **action** component to citizenship education).

5. Combining with others to address commonly defined problems and to improve services, affect change or enhance the political process (the **coalition or community building** component).

6. **Reflecting** upon decisions, actions and work undertaken, in order to understand, assess, and review their quality and outcomes (the important but often neglected **reflection** component) (Qualifications and Curriculum Authority, 2004).

In addition to specifying the dimensions of active citizenship, leaders in the citizenship education movement in the United Kingdom have also said what active citizenship should not be. That is, volunteering or community service devoid of any underpinning knowledge and understanding or decision-making opportunities and devoid of a desire to instigate change or reflect upon what was learned through the experience. With all the fine tuning of the definition, curriculum development, and evaluation, including an inspection system for the citizenship curriculum, huge challenges still remain. These challenges arise not only in understanding what is meant by active citizenship, and not confusing it with volunteering or community service, but also in implementation of the practices associated with active citizenship outcomes. Studies in England suggest that about 25% of English schools are deemed well on the road to offering holistic citizenship programs that include the "3 Cs of citizenship": citizenship education in the curriculum or classroom; citizenship in school culture and governance; and citizenship in the wider community (Kerr, 2004). Schools in Scotland and Wales are a bit behind the English in implementing a citizenship curriculum, and the curriculum in Northern Ireland is just being put in place now.

The reason for emphasizing what is happening in the United Kingdom, and primarily in England, is because education for citizenship is driven by similar concerns that people in the United States have about the growing disengagement among the citizenry from public life, particularly among young people. In fact, in the two most recent national elections in the United States and the United Kingdom, electoral statistics for voters overall and for young people's participation are eerily similar.

Furthermore, research suggests that having this conceptual framework, and a national curriculum that follows it, not only makes for outcome-based evaluation and an inspection system to evaluate the progress in achieving outcomes and implementation, but also makes for clarity in research. Every recent research study on civic engagement in the United Kingdom references a common set of goals and definitions and looks at the impact of different curricular and cocurricular programs on these defined citizenship outcomes. Moreover, based on this set of common understandings, an 8-year longitudinal study of citizenship education (Kerr, Ireland, Lopes, & Craig, 2004) was undertaken involving students, teachers, and school leaders. It is much easier to identify variables and to operationalize them when you are working from a precise conceptual framework.

In some ways, the approach in the United Kingdom is not a whole lot different from definitions of citizenship outcomes in *The Civic Mission of Schools* report (Carnegie Corporation & CIRCLE, 2003), which emphasized civic skills, values, civic knowledge, and the ability and inclination to act politically. The approach also bears similarities to the constructs emerging from the Carnegie Foundation for the Advancement of Teaching's Political Engagement Project[3] in higher education and can also be compared to recent work of Saltmarsh (2005), who offered a way of thinking about civic learning, as opposed to civic engagement, framed in terms of the development of civic knowledge, skills, and values/attitudes/dispositions. Our conceptual framework must have greater precision about ends and outcomes, specifically defining what is meant by education for civic engagement in a democracy, and more explicitly, connecting this to active participation in public life, or politics.

Active Citizenship

Besides a clear conceptual framework for thinking about civic engagement, I want to urge a different way of thinking about educating for democracy and democratic civic engagement. This is an area in which little progress has been made. With all of the new experiments in teaching and learning, the question can still be posed, as it was by Dewey 80 years ago (1916/1944, p. 38): "Why is it, in spite of the fact that teaching by pouring in, learning by a passive absorption, are universally condemned, that they are still entrenched in practice?" The way citizenship education is measured and taught is still dominated by an approach based on the acquisition of civic knowledge. It is fueled by the mistaken belief that knowledge about political institutions alone will translate into civic capacities and action. Knowledge is one small component of a child's political education; greater attention needs to be placed on other components, such as his/her capacities, dispositions, attitudes, and values, as well as addressing the key question of motivation and opportunity for political participation. In England, these components are called the desire and action components of active citizenship. Students need to see a reason for engaging in the public realm that is connected to their desires or passions around issues that matter to them. They also need practice in the processes of democracy, democratic organizing, and democratic government. Educational institutions can be effective practice grounds for citizenship education, just as they provide practice grounds and spaces for musicians or athletes.

Students, especially those of immediate postsecondary age, come to college campuses with few experiences of lived democracy, let alone respect for their autonomy or voice, either in their schools or in their daily lives outside of school. This has clear implications for the work in service-learning. After all the years of educational reform and all the research that informs the field about how students learn, educational institutions still promote a fairly traditional approach to teaching and learning. With few exceptions, students complete secondary education in an environment that is dominated by knowledge transmission and recall, where the product—be it a grade, a high test score, or even a diploma—always seems to trump the learning process, and certainly the process of democratic deliberation and action. The process and its outcomes are dictated by those adults who are in charge, not by the students in collaboration with their teachers or educational policymakers.

The history of successful democratic communities shows that their approach to educating for public life was experiential, cultural, and practice-oriented, not formal and institutional. Athenian democracy was bolstered by and sustained by an education that came from extensive participation in public life itself and from public exposure to the culture makers of the society, the poets, and the playwrights. Early American democratic institutions, especially those in New England, were supported by young people's participation in voluntary associations (as de Tocqueville [1848/1969] noted in *Democracy in America*) and in the democratic life of congregational churches. These examples are of exclusive democracies, where vast numbers of people were not considered citizens. For a more inclusive vision of democratic civic education through practice and culture one need only look to earlier Americans, the Haudenausaunee (Iroquois). Young men and women in Iroquois communities learned alongside their elders by participating in longhouse decision making and in the rituals and activities associated with tribal councils. These are traditions of democratic institutions informed by a more practice-based, rather than knowledge- or transmission-based education, traditions that have been neglected for too long.

The importance of practice-oriented approaches to citizenship education becomes even clearer when thinking about the long-term civic disengagement that has occurred over the past few decades and the socializing role of popular culture in contributing to it. It takes a lot of effort to fight back the forces of socialization that mitigate against the formation of active citizenship, and only through sustained practice is there hope to overcome these centrifugal forces.

Recalling the study by Stanton, Giles, and Cruz (1999) on the pioneers of service-learning, it is well to remember that the aim of many of the founders of the movement was just this practice-oriented revolution in the approach to thinking about education. This is echoed in a recent article by Gorham (2005) who discussed the kind of political knowledge and skills that come from service-learning.

Democratic Practice

There is a growing body of research literature that points in the direction of democratic practice. The most recent 28-country International Association for the Evaluation of Educational Achievement (IEA) study demonstrated unmistakably the importance of both democratic classroom climate and democratic student governance to student civic/political learning outcomes. In their IEA study report, Torney-Purta, Lehmann, Oswald, and Schultz (2001) wrote:

Schools that model democratic values by ... inviting students to take part in shaping school life are most effective in promoting civic knowledge and engagement ... and they are more likely to produce students that expect to vote as adults than other schools.

Case studies in Finland and Norway, and preliminary data from the English longitudinal study, suggest a strong, positive link between student opportunities to participate in school both in lessons and in governance and citizenship education outcomes. The work of Hannam (2005) in England goes beyond civic education impact. His research on a group of selected participative schools found levels of achievement and attendance that were higher than expected when compared with similar schools in England, and the overall rate of permanent exclusions (suspensions/expulsions) was significantly lower than for schools in similar circumstances that were not participative. His study also reported that 82% of students in these select schools felt that there has been significant improvement in their relations with teachers, and 84% felt significantly more motivated or interested in school through their participation.

Project 540, a major national high school initiative funded by The Pew Charitable Trusts, was based on an alternative, practice-oriented conception of civic education in which young people participate in public life by direct involvement in the public life of their schools and communities. Over a 2-year span, more than 270 urban, suburban, and rural high schools across the country, and a diverse group of over 150,000 students, participated in the project in some way. Over 10,000 students were involved fairly extensively. Project 540 gave students the opportunity to identify the issues that mattered to them and to work together to address those issues. The students then began working with the adults in their schools to change the policies and issues they cared about. The process included deliberative dialogue, agenda setting, action recommendations, and implementation of an action plan. Project 540's program evaluation, which employed extensive site visits and interviews with students, teachers, and administrators, showed that Project 540 changed a number of things, both in terms of school culture and student learning. Some of the most commonly mentioned things that students and their teachers said students learned from Project 540 were:

- Increased understanding of the complexity of issues, and that the history, regulations, different opinions and perspectives, and the knowledge of what others are doing about the issue all need to be considered in making decisions;
- Public communications skills, including the ability to speak up and in front of peers and adults, and to listen to and accept everyone's voices and opinions, no matter what you think of them;

- Public problem solving; how to prioritize, strategize, and make decisions regarding a problem, along with the ability to compromise and accept compromise;
- Increased understanding of how systems work, where the "levers of power" are in schools and communities;
- Understanding of and respect for diversity/differences among students;
- Understanding the difference between complaining about and changing policies;
- Patience, and the knowledge that change takes time;
- Teamwork;
- Group facilitation;
- The art of constructive criticism ("You learn to get 'shot down' in a constructive way"); and
- The attitude that you really can make a difference if you try, and not to give up on the things you want.

The Pew Charitable Trusts also supported an extensive research study on Project 540, conducted by Borgida and Farr (2005) at the University of Minnesota. The most interesting results came from their 1,500 student two-wave survey panel. They found a generalized effect of the project on all students, from those who participated the most to those who did not participate at all. These students came to have a greater sense of identification with their fellow students and with their schools—what the researchers called an important precondition of civic and political engagement. Before individuals come to think of themselves as democratic citizens, much less take civic actions, they must identify with a larger community whole. Beyond this generalized effect, the research study showed that the most active participants witnessed significant increases in their beliefs and attitudes about:

- Community participation;
- Volunteering and service;
- Having a sense of worth and accomplishment;
- The value of deliberation; and
- Their expectations to participate in political life in the future.

They also reported that they expressed themselves by engaging in politically related actions and that their interpersonal and civic skill set was enhanced over the course of the year.

We have the beginnings, then, of a research base to support this alternative, experiential or practice-based approach to educating for civic engagement, the second element of "approaching" civic engagement.

Implications for Research

The change in these two dimensions of approaching civic engagement will impact programs, practices, and research. The shift in democratic citizen involvement might impact research in service-learning in the areas of:

- Longitudinal research;
- Understanding the importance of teachers;
- Comparing the impact of service-learning to other active pedagogies; and
- More qualitative research work.

Properly Funded Longitudinal Research

The potential importance of the longitudinal study in England cannot be minimized, and the United States can learn much from it. Good examples from this conference of the type of longitudinal research that need funding are:

- The work of Vogelgesang (2005) of the Higher Education Research Institute at UCLA.
- Keen and Hall's (2005) study of the Bonner Scholars Program.

The Importance of Teachers in Civic Education

What I have said about our approach to civic engagement speaks to the importance of teachers, how they frame their work, their understanding of and experience with it, and how they see their role in citizen education and engagement. There is a need to further study teachers' intentions and understandings. The English longitudinal study coordinated by Kerr and colleagues (2004), which surveyed the same teachers and school administrators over time, as well as a panel of students, offered insights in this area.

A recent study by Billig, Root, and Jesse (2005) for CIRCLE on the civic impact of participation in service-learning also looked at some of these factors. So, too, did studies involving interviews with teachers by Kahne and Westheimer (2006). Research needs to explore how teachers are framing their work in service-learning and civic engagement, and the connections between teacher intentionality and educational outcomes for students.

Research on the Comparative Impact of Service-Learning and Other Active Pedagogies

This is an area that needs to be expanded. As the Carnegie Foundation's Political Engagement Project research and a recent study by Billig and colleagues (2005) showed it is often not a simple choice for the educator or practitioner between service-learning and a traditional, lecture-style or "banking" model of educational delivery. A twofold approach to civic engagement would indicate that service-learning is only one of a number of potential vehicles to greater civic engagement, and research is needed to show when and whether other pedagogies can lead to better outcomes, as well as under what conditions a service-learning approach confers "additional benefits over other active pedagogies" (Billig et al., 2005, p. 1)

More and Better Qualitative Research

More research is being conducted involving experimental and quasi-experimental designs. But better qualitative work is also needed, especially studies that evaluate student and teacher understandings of what they are doing and how they conceive of civic or political engagement. This research might offer insight into the how—as opposed to the whether or why—of service-learning's impact on learning and citizenship outcomes. Survey research has a place, but can be supplemented with more qualitative approaches. John Tukey, the man who introduced the words "software" and "bit" into our vocabulary, is quoted as saying: "Far better an approximate answer to the right question than a precise answer to the wrong question." Qualitative techniques are not at all at odds with experimental or quasi-experimental design and can complement them in this field.

CONCLUSION

There is a growing interest in civic engagement in this country. By using service-learning as the framing terminology are researchers constraining this field's influence and potential? Could a broader perspective better position this work to influence institutional and social change? The three strategic strands of K-12, higher education, and teacher education have traditionally been the focus areas. Can something broader and more internationally connected better do what is needed and move the agenda forward? It is time those invested in service-learning research start looking more closely at the concepts of civic engagement, education for citizenship, political or community involvement, public work, and most importantly social sustainability. Perhaps a new language is needed beyond service-learning to rally the troops and move the agenda forward.

NOTES

1. N. Cruz (2005, November), Plenary address, Association of American Colleges and Universities' conference on The Civic Engagement Imperative: Student Learning and the Public Good, Providence, RI.
2. Active Citizenship Centre, http://www.active-citizen.org.uk/active.asp
3. For information on the The Political Engagement Project, see The Carnegie Foundation for the Advancement of Teaching Web site. Retrieved June 1, 2006, from http://www.carnegiefoundation.org/programs/index.asp?key=25

REFERENCES

Billig, S., Root, S., & Jesse, D. (2005). *The impact of participation in service-learning on high school students' civic engagement* (CIRCLE Working Paper 33). College Park, MD: University of Maryland, The Center for Information & Research on Civic Learning & Engagement. Retrieved August 23, 2005, from http://www.civicyouth.org/PopUps/WorkingPapers/WP33Billig.pdf

Borgida, E., & Farr, J.(2005). *Final report to Pew Trusts: University of Minnesota research findings on Project 540*. Minneapolis: University of Minnesota.

Carnegie Corporation of New York and the Center for Information and Research on Civic Learning and Engagement. (2003). *The civic mission of schools*. New York: Carnegie Corporation of New York and CIRCLE.

de Tocqueville, A. (1848/1969). *Democracy in America* (J. P. Mayer, Ed., G. Lawrence, Trans.). Garden City, NY: Doubleday.

Dewey, J. (1944). *Democracy and education*. New York: MacMillan. (Original work published in 1916)

Firm Foundations. (2004). The government's framework for community capacity building. London: Home Office's Communities Group, Civil Renewal Unit. Retrieved June 12, 2006, from http://www.bswn.org.uk/BSWN%20Resource%20Library/Change%20Up/ho_firm_foundations0812.pdf

Gorham, E. (2005, September-December). Service-learning and political knowledge. *Journal of Political Science Education*, *1*(3), 345–366.

Kahne, J., & Westheimer, J. (2006, April). The limits of political efficacy: educating citizens for a democratic society. *PS: Political Science & Politics*, *XXXIX*(2), 289–301.

Hannam, D. (2005). *Education for democracy and education through democracy*. London: National Foundation for Educational Research, Department for Education and Skills.

Keen, C., & Hall, K. (2005, November). *The Bonner Program: Student impact survey report*. Presented at the International Service-Learning Research Conference. East Lansing, MI.

Keeter, S., Zukin, C., Andolina, M., & Jenkins, K. (2002, September). *The civic and political health of the nation: A generational portrait*. College Park, MD: The Center for Information & Research on Civic Learning and Engagement.

Kerr, D. (2004). Western Europe regional synthesis. In C. Birzea, D. Kerr, R. Mikkelsen, I. Froumin, B. Losito, M. Pol, & M. Sardoc (Eds.), *All-European study on education for democratic citizenship policies* (pp. 54–60). Strasbourg, France: Council of Europe.

Kerr, D., Ireland, E., Lopes, E., & Craig, R. (with Cleaver, E.). (2004). *Citizenship education longitudinal study: Second annual report. First longitudinal study: Making citizenship education real* (Research report No. 531). London: National Foundation for Educational Research, Department for Education and Skills.

National and Community Service Trust Act of 1993. H.R. 2010, P.L. 103–82; 107 Stat. 785, 103rd Cong. (1993) (enacted). Retrieved August 8, 2006, from http://frwebgate.access.gpo.gov/cgi-bin/getdoc.cgi?dbname=103_cong_bill& docid=f:h2010eh.pdf

Nelson, J., & Kerr, D. (2005, September). *International review of curriculum and assessment frameworks. Active citizenship: Definitions, goals, and practices*. Slough, Berkshire, UK: National Foundation for Educational Research.

Qualifications and Curriculum Authority. (1998, September). *Education for citizenship and the teaching of democracy in schools: Final report of the Advisory Group on Citizenship*. London: Author. Retrieved June 12, 2006, from http://www.qca.org.uk/downloads/6123_crick_report_1998.pdf

Qualifications and Curriculum Authority. (2004). *Play your part: Post-16 citizenship*. London: Author.

Saltmarsh, J. (2005, Spring). The civic promise of service-learning. *Liberal Education, 91*(2), 50–55. Retrieved June 1, 2006, from http://www.aacu.org/liberaleducation/le-sp05/le-sp05perspective2.cfm

Stanton, T. K., Giles, D. E., Jr., & Cruz, N. I. (1999). *Service-learning: A movement's pioneers reflect on its origins, practice, and future*. San Francisco: Jossey-Bass.

Torney-Purta, J., Lehmann, R., Oswald, H., & Schultz, W. (2001). *Citizenship and education in twenty-eight countries: Civic knowledge and engagement at age fourteen*. Amsterdam: International Association for the Evaluation of Educational Achievement.

Vogelgesang, L. (2005, November). *Understanding the post-college impacts of service-learning*. Presentation at the International Service-Learning Research Conference, East Lansing, MI.

CHAPTER 2

SERVICE-LEARNING AND CIVIC OUTCOMES

From Suggestive Research to Program Models

Suzanne Pritzker and Amanda Moore McBride

ABSTRACT

Service-learning has been identified as an intervention that may address low levels of youth civic engagement. Service-learning is compared to 2 other interventions that have been associated with civic outcomes: community service and civic education curricula. Studies of these 3 types of interventions are systematically reviewed and compared, taking into account rigor of designs and methods. Across a range of civic indicators, no clear pattern was found regarding the main effect of each intervention. This chapter highlights the need for increased rigor and sensitivity of measurement in future research on civic development among school-age students.

Advancing Knowledge in Service-Learning: Research to Transform the Field, 17–43
Copyright © 2006 by Information Age Publishing
All rights of reproduction in any form reserved.

THE NEED FOR CIVIC INTERVENTIONS

Low levels of civic engagement among youth have been identified as problematic. Youth in the United States exhibit low levels of knowledge about politics and government and are less likely than adults to be involved in various political activities (Center for Information and Research on Civic Learning and Engagement, CIRCLE, 2003; Olander, 2003). Although voting among youth aged 18 to 24 increased by 4.6 million between the 2000 and 2004 presidential elections, it declined significantly between 1972 and 2000, and remains lower than any other voting age cohort (CIRCLE, 2005; Gibson, 2001; Levine & Lopez, 2002). More promising trends are evident in terms of social action. For example, youth in the United States between the ages of 15 and 25 have been found to volunteer at higher rates than older age cohorts (Keeter, Andolina, Jenkins, & Zukin, 2002). However, major concerns about low levels of youth civic engagement exist among both scholars and public officials.

The lack of youth engagement in political and community-based activities raises significant social justice concerns about whose voices, interests, and needs are heard by those in power. In particular, political as well as social forms of civic engagement are lower among low-income and minority youth (CIRCLE, 2003; Flanagan & Faison, 2001; Torney-Purta, 2001). Finn and Checkoway (1998) suggested that youth are resources whose active community participation can help address social issues and improve the well-being of their communities. Moreover, Youniss, McLellan, and Yates (1997) have linked active civic participation during one's youth with continued engagement as an adult, thus increasing civic outcomes among youth is essential for the individual youth, their communities, and for socially just government policies and services.

In light of compelling concerns about the state of youth civic engagement today, it is increasingly important that we identify and replicate interventions that positively impact youth civic outcomes, particularly in the political sphere. Service-learning has gained a reputation in the practice community for successfully influencing civic attitudes, knowledge, and skills of K-12 students. Service-learning enables students to transfer knowledge and experience between the classroom and a real-world setting. Positive civic impacts are expected because students are able to become involved in addressing community problems in a structured environment. By connecting their volunteer activity to a curriculum, students have the opportunity to reflect on their experiences, thus translating their experiences into civically oriented attitudes and skills. As noted by Billig (2000), multiple studies support this assertion; however, because the rigor of the designs and methods of some studies can be considered low, definitive claims of service-learning's success as a civic intervention are tenuous.

Moreover, it is unknown whether service-learning is more effective at increasing particular civic outcomes among school-age children and youth than other interventions. In fact, studies of community service programs and civic education curricula also claim positive civic outcomes for K-12 students.

Is service-learning "uniquely poised to teach ... civic virtues," as the National Commission on Service-Learning (2002, p. 39) suggested? We conducted a systematic analysis of research on the civic outcomes of service-learning and compared these findings with those from studies of other interventions. Given concerns among leading service-learning scholars about the low levels of rigorous designs and methods in service-learning studies, only the most rigorous studies were selected for this analysis. Presented are inclusionary criteria for the studies reviewed here, as well as the methods used to review each study. Studies were then reviewed to determine whether particular interventions are more effective at, and provide clear evidence for, increasing specific civic outcomes among K-12 students, and to identify strengths and weaknesses of the designs and methods used in current civic development research.

TYPES OF CIVIC INTERVENTIONS: FORMS AND OUTCOMES

A wide variety of civic outcomes have been measured in service-learning research. Across studies of K-12 service-learning, Billig (2000) identified multiple outcomes related to civic responsibility, including commitment to service, sense of civic responsibility, understanding of how government works, desire to become politically active, and engagement in community organizations. Although positive civic outcomes have been identified for service-learning in some studies, the results overall appear to be mixed (Billig & Furco, 2002b; Galston, 2001). This may be due in part to a range in the quality of service-learning programs, as well as to whether civic engagement is an intentional goal of the service-learning programs that have been studied (Billig, 2004).

Mixed outcomes and the lack of definitive assessments that can be made about possible associations between service-learning and civic outcomes also may be attributable to insufficient rigor of methods. In recent years, leading service-learning scholars have called for increased rigor in service-learning research (Billig, 2003, 2004; Billig & Eyler, 2003; Billig & Furco, 2002a, 2002b; Bringle, 2003; Eyler, 2002; Furco, 2003). While service-learning has grown in implementation—at least 28% of public schools offer service-learning (Scales & Roehlkepartain, 2004)—research that is rigorous and replicable is still rare (Billig, 2003).

Billig (2003) suggested that research on service-learning for K-12 students can be strengthened with more robust study designs. Experimental designs with randomization of groups are extremely rare. Because studies build upon each other infrequently, they are, as Furco (2003) pointed out, "a mass of disconnected investigations" (p. 15). Utilization of designs that compare service-learning to a control or matched comparison group and studies that build upon each other will increase generalizability of service-learning research findings.

Replication can be increased through theory-based research that leads to findings with broader implications beyond a given study sample. Currently, service-learning research rarely tests theory or competing hypotheses (Billig, 2003; Billig & Eyler, 2003; Bringle, 2003; Eyler, 2002). Additionally, although longitudinal studies have been identified as essential for moving the field forward (Billig & Furco, 2002b), few studies provide insight into long-term impacts (Eyler, 2002; Furco, 2003).

Service-learning research also can be strengthened by better defining service-learning as a construct with requisite independent variables. Components of service-learning such as intensity, duration, and degree of reflection should be clearly specified and measured when study findings are reported (Billig & Furco, 2002a; Eyler, 2002). A need for multisite studies; increased use of reliable and valid psychometric measures; and triangulation of data, rather than reliance on self-report measures, have also been identified in reviews of service-learning research (Billig & Eyler, 2003; Billig & Furco, 2002b; Eyler, 2002; Furco, 2003).

Leading service-learning scholars have advocated for increased rigor not only in service-learning research in general, but specifically in research measuring civic outcomes. In proposing a research agenda for K-12 service-learning, Billig and Furco (2002a) called for strengthening the quality of service-learning research as it pertains to civic outcomes. Billig and Furco also proposed several research questions to strengthen the base of research evidence related to developing civic engagement; among these is to assess how service-learning compares to other models that aim to develop the civic capacities and actions of students.

Consistent with this proposed line of research, two additional interventions for civic development have been identified in this chapter to enable comparison with service-learning: community service programs and civic education curricula. Studies of both intervention types have also measured civic engagement outcomes. The three interventions vary widely from each other in design, incorporating different degrees of classroom instruction, explicit civic content, and facilitated discussions or reflection about program activities. The degree to which community service is incorporated also varies among the three intervention types.

Community service programs tend to focus on volunteering activity. Community service participation among students is widespread, with community service opportunities offered to students by 64% of public schools in the United States (Skinner & Chapman, 1999). Like service-learning, community service programs vary widely in practice in terms of type of service, scope of student responsibility, duration, intensity, and their voluntary or mandatory nature. Reviews of the effects of community service on civic outcomes have tended to include service-learning studies (e.g., Perry & Katula, 2001; Walker, 2002); accordingly, it has been difficult to differentiate the effects of community service from service-learning.

Formal civic education in K-12 schools has long been a priority of American public education. Thirteen states identify the promotion of good citizenship as a primary purpose of the state's educational system (CIRCLE, 2003). In public schools, civic education curricula have often been the method used to develop citizenship among students. A number of formal courses or supplementary curricular units have been developed in recent years that focus on skills for political knowledge and involvement. Such units may incorporate community service or service-learning components. These interventions tend to be more standardized than other civic development interventions, with established curricula that can be used at multiple sites.

METHODS

Studies included in this review were chosen based on five criteria, including measures of rigor.

1. Studies were limited to those that integrated either a control or comparison group as a "no treatment" condition;
2. Quantitative measures had to be utilized to assess change in civic outcomes;
3. Only studies published since 1995 were included, in order to focus on the most recent research in the field;
4. All reviewed studies were limited to the United States; and
5. Studies were limited to those published in peer-reviewed journals or reported by nationally recognized research institutes, and accessible to the general public, either on the Internet or through university library systems.

Several of the more rigorous studies of youth civic engagement have been reported in evaluation reports by research centers, in dissertations, or in papers presented at conferences, limiting accessibility to the general public. As a result, some studies that met the other four criteria were not included in this review based on their lack of accessibility (e.g., Bailis & Melchior, 1998; Melchior & Orr, 1995).

To locate studies that met the inclusion criteria, an extensive search was conducted. First, seven electronic databases (Education Resources Information Center [ERIC]), PsycINFO, Social Science Abstracts, Social Science Citation Index, Article First, Sociological Abstracts, and Public Affairs Information Service [PAIS] International) were searched using combinations of the following keywords:

- Civic;
- Youth;
- Adolescent;
- Youth development;
- Political socialization;
- Community service;
- Service-learning;
- Extracurricular;
- Volunteer; and
- Civic education.

Second, reference lists on four major Web sites in the field related to service-learning, civic engagement, and youth development were searched.[1] In addition, reference lists from review articles related to civic education, civic engagement, community service, and service-learning were manually searched (Michelsen, Zaff, & Hair, 2002; Perry & Katula, 2001; Walker, 2002; Zaff & Michelsen, 2001).

Based on these criteria and search procedures, 18 studies were selected for inclusion in this review. Based on program design, these studies fall into three categories of interventions:

1. **Service-learning programs** (Billig, Root, & Jesse, 2005; Covitt, 2002; Furco, 2002; Leming, 2001; Melchior, 1999; RMC Research Corporation, 2002; Scales, Blyth, Berkas, & Kielsmeier, 2000; Stafford, Boyd, & Lindner, 2003; Switzer, Simmons, Dew, Regalski, & Wang, 1995; Yamauchi, Billig, Meyer, & Hofschire, 2006);
2. **Community service programs** (Furco, 2002; Metz, McLellan, & Youniss, 2003; Metz & Youniss, 2003, 2005; Waldstein & Reiher, 2001); and

3. **Civic education curricula** (Hartry & Porter, 2004; Kahne, Chi, & Middaugh, in press; McDevitt & Chaffee, 2000; McDevitt, Kiousis, Wu, Losch, & Ripley, 2003).

Previous reviews of models for youth civic engagement have focused on fewer categories of interventions or have not systematically assessed the rigor of the research designs and methods (e.g., Billig, 2000; Harvard Family Research Project, 2003; Perry & Katula, 2001; Walker, 2002; Zaff & Michelsen, 2001). This chapter evaluates the effectiveness of service-learning on civic outcomes among students by comparing significant impacts across the three types of interventions and by assessing the rigor of each study's design and methods.

The rigor of the design and methods used in each study was evaluated following an adaptation of the Methodological Quality Rating Scale (MQRS) model established by Miller et al. (1995). The MQRS was developed for use in the alcohol treatment outcome literature. It evaluates studies along 12 different criteria and provides a useful model for systematically comparing methodological strengths and weaknesses across studies. Because the alcohol treatment field is older, more methodologically advanced, and receives more funding and policy support than the service-learning and youth civic engagement fields, the scale was modified to allow for meaningful comparisons across the studies examined here. For example, the scale was modified to allow for comparisons of whether key methodological data, such as reliability and validity, were reported and whether components of the intervention, such as duration and intensity, were specified. It is worthy to note that we selected the MQRS rating scale for review rather than other scales commonly used in the education field such as the one used by the What Works Clearinghouse (n.d.). The MQRS is particularly well-suited for comparison across studies. It enables assignment of an individual score to each study, allowing for calculation of a mean score. Accordingly, studies can be compared and differentiated; in contrast, the What Works Clearinghouse categorized studies based on their standard of evidence into groups such as "Meets Evidence Standards" or "Meets Evidence Standards with Reservations."

The 12 criteria in the adapted MQRS, shown in Exhibit 2.1, are consistent with the elements of rigor called for by service-learning scholars and described in the review of literature above.[2] Each study could receive a maximum of 2 points for each criterion based on information provided in the write-up of the study,[3] with a possible range along a continuum from 0 to 24.

These ratings were divided into two groups along the mean (12.22): "more rigorous" methodology and "less rigorous" methodology. Group assignment was then combined with findings of statistical significance and

Exhibit 2.1.   Methodological Quality Rating Scale

Criteria	Rating (Points)
1. Study design	0 = Posttest only design 1 = Pretest/posttest (with comparison group) 2 = Pretest/posttest (with equivalent control group)
2. Subject selection	0 = Subjects self-selected for intervention condition, or unclear selection process 2 = Subjects assigned without self-selection
3. Theoretical foundation	0 = Theoretical basis for intervention or hypotheses unclear or not stated 1 = Hypotheses to be tested clearly stated 2 = Theoretical basis for intervention clearly stated
4. Standardization of intervention	0 = Guidelines for consistent administration of intervention not evident 1 = Specific manual/guidelines/training exists; however, variation exists among program sites 2 = Intervention is standardized
5. Specification of independent variable	0 = Components of the intervention (e.g. duration, type of activity, extent of reflection) not clearly described 1 = Multiple components of the intervention clearly described; analysis of specific components not conducted 2 = Statistical analysis conducted of component(s) effects on outcomes
6. Follow up	0 = No follow-up measurement 2 = Follow-up measurement
7. Triangulation	0 = No verification of participant self-report on outcome measures 2 = Verification of participant self-report using additional measures
8. Dropouts/attrition	0 = Dropouts/response rate neither discussed nor accounted for 1 = Intervention dropouts/response rate discussed and/or enumerated 2 = Statistical analysis of attrition conducted
9. Measures	0 = Reliability/validity of measures not reported 2 = Reliability/validity of measures reported
10. Analyses	0 = Differences between groups not analyzed 1 = Analysis solely controls for demographic differences between groups 2 = Analysis controls for baseline pre-test differences between groups
11. Multisite	0 = Single site, or comparison of sites with different interventions 2 = Interventions at multiple sites
12. Reporting of findings	0 = Not reported in peer-reviewed journal 2 = Reported in peer-reviewed journal

Note: The MQRS is adapted from Miller et al. (1995). Rating (points) ranged from 0 (low) to 24 (high).

Exhibit 2.2. Outcome Attainment Index

2 = Significant; more rigorous methodology (MQRS > 12.22)
1 = Significant; less rigorous methodology (MQRS < = 12.22)
−1 = Not significant; less rigorous methodology (MQRS < = 12.22)
−2 = Not significant; more rigorous methodology (MQRS > 12.22)

Source: Outcome Attainment Index adapted from Rhee and Auslander (2002).

nonsignificance to create a categorical outcome attainment score (−2, −1, 1, 2), based on an adaptation of Rhee and Auslander's (2002) Outcome Attainment Index (OAI). Thus, the claim of effect for a study with "more rigorous" methodology is indicated by either a "−2" if findings were not statistically significant or a "2" if findings were statistically significant. Likewise, a study with "less rigorous" methodology could receive either a "−1" if findings were not statistically significant or a "1" if findings were statistically significant. The adapted OAI is shown in Exhibit 2.2.

Outcome attainment scores were assigned for each of the 18 studies reviewed here along six categories of outcomes. The lack of consistency among the studies in terms of specific outcomes and the measures used for conceptually similar outcomes provided an impediment to comparing the effectiveness of each intervention type in impacting civic outcomes; therefore, we divided the outcomes into six conceptual categories. Civic engagement can be understood in terms of either social or political action (McBride, 2003), although conceptual distinctions are rarely made between service and advocacy-oriented activities in the community service literature (Walker, 2002). Civic engagement can be measured in terms of attitudes toward engaging, intended, or actual engagement behavior, and the skills and knowledge necessary for engagement. Thus, the various civic outcomes were divided into the following six categories, which are listed below. The numbers in parentheses refer to the number of distinct measures used within each group of conceptually similar outcomes (i.e., demonstrating a lack of consistency in measures).

1. Social knowledge and skills (8);
2. Social attitudes (25);
3. Social behavior (15);
4. Political knowledge and skills (7);
5. Political attitudes (10); and
6. Political behavior (21).

Exhibit 2.3 shows these six outcome categories as well as the array of distinct measures used in the reviewed studies.

Exhibit 2.3. Grouping of Outcomes Across Studies

Social Knowledge and Skills	Social Attitudes	Social Behavior/ Intended Behavior	Political Skills and Knowledge	Political Attitudes	Political behavior/ intended behavior
Community Understanding • Knowledge of social networks • Understand issues that affect the well-being of the community *Ethical Skills* • Ethical domain • Personal ethical agency *Leadership* • Civic skills • Have leadership skills • Personal leadership development subscale • Service leadership	*Altruism* • Altruistic self-image • Concern for social issues scale • Like to help other people • Like to help others even if they are not willing to help themselves • Social welfare subscale (concern for others' welfare) • Willing to take risks for the sake of doing what is right *Community Membership* • Belong to the community • Community attachment • Community engagement scale (feel proud of community) • Connection to community • Have pride in community • Viewed by community members as valued part of the community	*Current Behavior* • Commitment (to school and community) • Contribute to the community • Estimated hours of volunteer service in past 6 months • Involved in activities that will make peoples' lives better • Involvement in any volunteer activity in past 6 months • Personally responsible citizenship • Support for unconventional activism (confronting police, boycotting, buycotting) • Take action and make changes in community	• Civic knowledge (factual questions about government and civics) • Election knowledge • Integration of new information • Knowledge scale • Political knowledge • Salience of key state issue • Self assessment of civic knowledge	*Attitudes Toward Institutions of Government* • Appreciation of democracy • Assessment of government impact • Evaluation of government • Social trust *Efficacy* • Political efficacy *Interest in Politics* • Holding opinions • Interest and understanding (of politics) • Partisanship • Strongly held views *Political Responsibility* • Citizens responsibilities (importance of voting, protesting, campaigning)	*Current Behavior* • Attention to a key state election issue • Attention to election news • Attention to news (political news) • Attention to politics • Civic engagement activities (discussing politics, participating in rallies, following the news) • Frequency of election discussion with friends • Frequency of election discussion with parents • Frequency of reading newspaper (news) • Frequency of student-parent discussion (of campaign, election) • Participation in student government • Political participation • TV news viewing • Use of information

Efficacy
- Civic efficacy
- Efficacy subscale

Social Responsibility
- Citizen obligations (importance of serving)
- Civic dispositions
- Civic responsibility
- Community responsibility (importance of being publicly active)
- Duty subscale (responsibility to help others)
- Have a responsibility for the welfare of the community
- Importance of service (environmental, community, to persons)
- Personal and social responsibility

Multiple Domains
- Civic attitudes combined scale
- Contributor to community subscale (mostly attitudinal items)
- Social relatedness

Future Intentions
- Civic participation domain
- Commitment to help others in future
- Future service (intent to perform future voluntary service)
- Index of intentions to help Bay (to help environmental cause)
- Likelihood of future service (environmental, community, to persons)
- Moral-political awareness (anticipated future participation in community affairs)
- Would like to take action and make community changes

Current Behavior
- Willingness to express views (at a public meeting)
- Willingness to listen to opposing views
- Willingness to openly disagree with others about politics

Future Intentions
- Future unconventional civic intentions (boycott, demonstrate, work for future political campaigns)
- Future voting
- Justice-oriented citizenship
- Participatory citizenship
- Support for conventional politics (voting and contributing money)

In several of the reviewed studies, multiple individual outcomes with different findings of statistical significance were measured within one of the six outcome categories. When this was the case, determination of statistical significance or nonsignficance for the category was based on the majority of findings within the category (i.e., if a study found significance for three different outcomes within the category of "political attitudes" and nonsignificance for two different outcomes, the study was rated as having statistical significance for that category). However, if findings within a particular outcome category were evenly split between statistical significance and nonsignificance, a conservative decision was made to assign the outcome a score reflecting statistical nonsignificance. Cross-hatch shadings are used in Figures 2.1 and 2.2 to indicate such split scores.

Determinations of statistical significance and outcome attainment scores for each outcome category are based only on the main effect of the intervention. It should be noted that this is an important limitation to this analysis; recent research in the field (e.g., Billig et al., 2005; Melchior & Bailis, 2002) suggested that the relationship between service-learning and civic outcomes is moderated by the quality of the service-learning experience. Despite increased attention to moderating variables in the research, comparison across studies of the effect of moderating variables is limited. Although four studies reviewed here measure the effects of moderating variables, such as quality, the moderating variables identified by each study and their measurement vary.

RESULTS

Up to 2 points were assigned to a study for each of the 12 items on the MQRS, for a total of 24 possible points. Based on the information provided in the public write-up of each study, scores for the 18 studies reviewed here ranged from 7 to 18, with a mean score of 12.22. Studies with MQRS scores above this mean were considered to have more rigorous designs and methods; studies with MQRS scores below this mean had less rigorous designs and methods.

Social Outcomes

No consistent theme emerged across studies regarding the main effect of civic development interventions on social knowledge and skills. This category of outcomes measures skills such as ethical capacity and leadership. While multiple service-learning studies measure social knowledge and skills, only one study each of the community service programs and of civic education curricula measures this outcome. Among studies of service-learning, most find no significance, including two with more rigorous designs and methods (Billig et al., 2005; Leming, 2001, without an ethical reasoning component). Only three service-learning studies of social knowledge and skills clearly have statistically significant findings, as indicated in Figure 2.1 (Furco, 2002; Leming, 2001, for the ethical reasoning condition; Melchior, 1999, for high school students at the short-term and follow-up dates).

The social attitudes category includes a wide variety of civic outcomes related to how youth view themselves as part of a community and the importance they attribute to community service. Seven of the 10 service-learning studies measure social attitudes, but only two have significant findings, as shown in Figure 2.1 (RMC Research Corporation, 2002; Stafford et al., 2003). Most service-learning interventions show no statistically significant difference in social attitudes between participants and nonparticipants. Moreover, all service-learning studies with more rigorous designs and methods find no impact from service-learning on social attitudes. Although fewer studies have been conducted of the impact on social attitudes of community service (Metz et al., 2003; Waldstein & Reiher, 2001) and curricula (Hartry & Porter, 2004), each of these studies has statistically significant findings.

Social behavioral outcomes measure current or intended behavior by youth in community affairs. This is a common category of outcomes measured by both community service and service-learning studies. All five studies of community service programs and 6 of the 10 studies on service-learning measure social behavior outcomes. Overall, findings are mixed for all three interventions, suggesting that without moderators, these interventions have not yet demonstrated effectiveness for impacting civic behavior in the social arena. Three of the service-learning studies, including two with more rigorous designs and methods, have statistically significant findings, as indicated in Figure 2.1 (Leming, 2001, for the ethical reasoning condition; Melchior, 1999, for high school students at the follow up; Switzer et al., 1995).

Political Outcomes

Few civic development intervention studies measure political knowledge and skills. This outcome category measures knowledge of politics, elections, and issues relating to government. Only curricular interventions have statistically significant findings. In particular, as Figure 2.2 shows, two different more rigorous studies of the Kids Voting curriculum

Figure 2.1. Civic intervention studies by civic outcome: social outcomes.

Notes. -2 = Not statistically significant; more rigorous methodology; -1 = Not statistically significant; less rigorous methodology; 1 = Statistically significant; less rigorous methodology; 2 = Statistically significant; more rigorous methodology

In several studies, multiple intervention conditions were compared to a "no treatment" condition; in such cases, each separate condition is listed individually.

Shading reflects results for all studies measuring any effects in this outcome category. If no shading is shown for a study or condition, the study did not assess any effects in this outcome category. Cross-hatch shadings are used to indicate findings that were evenly split between statistical significance and nonsignificance.

Outcome categories (columns): Social Knowledge and Skills; Social Attitudes; Social Behavior — each subdivided into Not Statistically Significant (-2, -1) and Statistically Significant (1, 2).

Service
- Furco (2002)
- Metz et al. (2003) - with social cause orientation
- Metz & Youniss (2003) - mandatory; students "less inclined" to service
- Metz & Youniss (2003) - mandatory; students "more inclined" to service
- Metz & Youniss (2005) - mandatory; students "less inclined" to service
- Metz & Youniss (2005) - mandatory; students "more inclined" to service
- Waldstein & Reiher (2001) - varied service experiences

Service-Learning
- Billig et al. (2005)
- Covitt (2002) - standardized environmental service-learning
- Covitt (2002) - nonstandardized environmental service-learning
- Furco (2002)
- Leming (2001) - without ethical reasoning component
- Leming (2001) - with ethical reasoning component
- Melchior (1999) - middle school youth
- Melchior (1999) - high school youth
- Melchior (1999) - high school follow up
- Melchior (1999) - middle school follow up
- RMC Research Corporation (2002) - students Grade 6 and above
- RMC Research Corporation (2002) - students Grade 5 and below
- Scales et al. (2000)
- Stafford et al. (2003) - with immediate reflection period
- Switzer et al. (1995) - mandatory

Curricular
- Yamauchi et al. (2006) - with cultural curriculum
- Hartry & Porter (2004) - We the People curriculum
- Kahne et al. (forthcoming) - City Works curriculum
- McDevitt & Chaffee (2000) - Kids Voting curriculum
- McDevitt et al. (2003) - Kids Voting curriculum

have significant findings (McDevitt & Chaffee, 2000; McDevitt et al., 2003). The only service-learning study measuring this outcome finds no statistical significance, using more rigorous designs and methods.

Political attitudes, including such outcomes as feelings of civic obligation and opinions about politics, are measured primarily by the curricular intervention studies. As indicated in Figure 2.2, the three curricular studies measuring this outcome show mixed results. One study with more rigor finds statistical significance (McDevitt et al., 2003), while the other finds no statistically significant impact (Kahne et al., in press). Few other studies and no service-learning study reviewed here measure political attitudes.

Current political behaviors, as well as future intentions to participate in political activities, are also measured primarily by curricular interventions. As Figure 2.2 shows, four curricular studies measure this outcome, all with statistically significant findings (Hartry & Porter, 2004; Kahne et al., in press; McDevitt & Chaffee, 2000; McDevitt et al., 2003). Three of the four studies fall into the statistically significant, more rigorous category. There is no clear evidence of a statistically significant impact on political behavior from either community service or service-learning.

DISCUSSION

The comparative analysis suggests that service-learning may be less successful at impacting student civic outcomes than anticipated, particularly if moderating variables, such as the Essential Elements of Service-Learning (e.g., Billig et al., 2005) are not present. However, it cannot be concluded at this point that service-learning interventions do not increase civic outcomes. In order to determine whether service-learning has a comparative advantage over other civic development interventions for school-age children and youth, more attention should be paid to the specification and sensitivity of measurement of both the independent variable and the dependent variable, as well as improved rigor of designs and methods.

Support for Outcomes

One study among all three interventions had both rigor and statistical significance in terms of measuring impacts on social knowledge and skills. This is a service-learning study (Leming, 2001, with an ethical reasoning component); however, overall findings for the main effect of service-learning on social knowledge and skills are mixed. As is the case for all

Figure 2.2. Civic intervention studies by civic outcome: political outcomes.

	Political Knowledge and Skills				Political Attitudes				Political Behavior			
	Not Statistically Significant		Statistically Significant		Not Statistically Significant		Statistically Significant		Not Statistically Significant		Statistically Significant	
	-2	-1	1	2	-2	-1	1	2	-2	-1	1	2
Service												
Furco (2002)												
Metz et al. (2003) - with social cause orientation												
Metz & Youniss (2003) - mandatory; students "less inclined" to service										▓		
Metz & Youniss (2003) - mandatory; students "more inclined" to service												
Metz & Youniss (2005) - mandatory; students "less inclined" to service										▓		
Metz & Youniss (2005) - mandatory; students "more inclined" to service										▓		
Waldstein & Reiher (2001) - varied service experiences												
Service-learning												
Billig et al. (2005)	▓								▓			
Covitt (2002) - standardized environmental service-learning												
Covitt (2002) - nonstandardized environmental service-learning												
Furco (2002)						▓						
Leming (2001) - without ethical reasoning component							▓					
Leming (2001) - with ethical reasoning component												
Melchior (1999) - middle school youth												
Melchior (1999) - high school youth												
Melchior (1999) - high school follow up												
Melchior (1999) - middle school follow up												
RMC Research Corporation (2002) - students Grade 6 and above												
RMC Research Corporation (2002) - students Grade 5 and below												
Scales et al. (2000)												
Curricular												
Stafford et al. (2003) - with immediate reflection period												
Switzer et al. (1995) - mandatory												
Yamauchi et al. (2006) - with cultural curriculum												
Harty & Porter (2004) - We the People curriculum			▓			▓					▓	
Kahne et al. (forthcoming) - City Works curriculum												▓
McDevitt & Chaffee (2000) - Kids Voting curriculum				▓								▓
McDevitt et al. (2003) - Kids Voting curriculum				▓								

Notes. -2 = Not statistically significant; more rigorous methodology; -1 = Not statistically significant; less rigorous methodology; 1 = Statistically significant; less rigorous methodology; 2 = Statistically significant; more rigorous methodology.

In several studies, multiple intervention conditions were compared to a "no treatment" condition; in such cases, each separate condition is listed individually. Shading reflects results for all studies measuring any effects in this outcome category. If no shading is shown for a study or condition, the study did not assess any effects in this outcome category.

social outcomes, more studies of service-learning find statistical nonsignificance than significance. None of the intervention types show strong evidence of effectiveness in increasing social knowledge and skills.

Based on the frequency with which social attitudes are measured by studies of service-learning, service-learning appears to be commonly used as a means to increase youth social attitudes. However, it is possible that service-learning may not be the most effective method to increase social attitudes. Little support was found for service-learning along these outcomes; in fact, the four studies of service-learning with more rigor found no statistical difference between service-learning participants and nonparticipants in terms of social attitudes.

Evidence for the effect of service-learning on social behavior is mixed as well. Two studies with more rigor had statistically significant findings, but the majority of service-learning studies showed nonsignificance along this outcome. This may mean that service-learning is not particularly effective at impacting student behavior; however, across all six outcome categories, more service-learning studies with more rigor had significant findings for this outcome. Accordingly, in terms of civic outcomes, service-learning may be most successful at impacting student involvement within communities beyond the program experience. No conclusions for impacts on social behavior emerge from the other civic development interventions. The support for community service and civic education curricula is mixed.

Only one service-learning study measured any outcomes in the political sphere, with statistically nonsignificant findings for both political behavior and political knowledge and skills (Billig et al., 2005). Curricular interventions appear to be most concerned with political outcomes, although two community service studies measured political outcomes as well. Among the curricular interventions, studies of the Kids Voting curriculum (McDevitt & Chaffee, 2000; McDevitt et al., 2003) showed support for all three political outcomes. Each curricular study measuring political behavior or political skills and knowledge suggests a statistically significant impact on these outcomes. Two community service studies examined political behavior, yet no convincing statistically significant relationship was identified. Overall, curricular interventions appear to be the strongest for political aspects of civic engagement; however, it is difficult to draw definitive conclusions about the comparative effectiveness of this intervention because few of the other types of studies measure political impacts.

Although there is evidence that curricular interventions may be more effective at increasing political outcomes, few clear patterns of support exist within the social outcome categories. Certain types of interventions are more commonly studied in connection with certain outcomes, thus limiting our ability to compare the effectiveness of interventions. In particular, political outcomes tend to be measured by curricular interventions, while social outcomes tend to be measured by community service and service-learning interventions. Among civic outcomes, service-learning appears to be studied most in conjunction with social attitudes. Perhaps these delineations are attributable to conceptual differences in the purposes associated with the use of these different interventions (e.g., that service-learning may not be intended to impact political outcomes, while civic education curricula are). Further work in the field of civic engagement should explore whether such delineations are appropriate. For example, previous studies have suggested that service-learning can increase political engagement (Billig, 2000; Morgan & Streb, 2001); yet, only one service-learning study reviewed here measured any political outcomes. Given the current scholarly and public concern over the lack of political engagement among youth, it is important to ask why the most rigorous service-learning studies do not measure political effects.

Intervention Specification

It is worth emphasizing again that moderators are not included in the model for evaluating and comparing studies; only main effects are evaluated. While findings indicate that the mere adoption of service-learning or other civic development interventions may not result in positive civic outcomes, taking into account moderating variables, such as program quality, may result in greater findings of significance. Recent research associates quality service-learning with positive outcomes (e.g., Billig et al., 2005). For example, Morgan and Streb (2001) found more positive outcomes for service-learning when student voice was incorporated into the analysis. Duration, type of activity, and degree of reflection in service-learning programs also have been associated with positive outcomes (Eyler & Giles, 1997; Melchior & Bailis, 2002; Moore & Sandholz, 1999).

To determine how effective *quality* service-learning is in comparison with other interventions, improved specification and measurement of moderators is necessary. Moderating variables vary across the studies reviewed here and are analyzed only by a few of the researchers. Six studies provide little information about components of the intervention such as duration, type of activity, and the extent of reflection. Only five studies conducted statistical analyses based on variations in the independent variable. Exhibit 2.4 lists the moderator variables measured and analyzed among the service-learning studies. Further rigorous evaluation and comparison of civic interventions should take moderating variables into

Exhibit 2.4. Moderators Analyzed by Service-Learning Studies

Service-Learning Study	Moderator Variables
Billig et al. (2005)	• Student ratings of their experience (e.g., responsibilities, made contribution, discussion with adults) • Student engagement with service-learning project (e.g., worked hard, paid attention) • Type and nature of service activity • Duration (length of class time spent) • Quality (teacher score based on Essential Elements of Service-Learning) • Linkage between service and curricular content • Teacher characteristics • Instructional strategy
Covitt (2002)	(no statistical analysis)
Furco (2002)	(no statistical analysis; qualitative discussion)
Leming (2001)	• Structured ethical reflection
Melchior (1998)	(no statistical analysis; descriptive data)
RMC Research Corporation (2002)	• Quality (teacher score based on Essential Elements of Service-Learning)
Scales et al. (2000)	• Duration (hours of service-learning) • Degree of reflection • Motivational impact of service-learning
Stafford et al. (2003)	(no statistical analysis)
Switzer et al. (1995)	(no statistical analysis)
Yamauchi et al. (2006)	(no statistical analysis)

account; greater attention to consistency in identification and measurement can facilitate this.

Moreover, many of the community service and service-learning interventions involve students participating in an array of service activities. While some studies indicate the actual domains of service activity in which students participated, this is not the case for all studies. For the most part, differing forms of activities appear to be treated as comparable. In this review, the studies that identify various domains of service activities are grouped together with other studies of the same intervention because there are too few studies of each type of activity to allow meaningful comparison. However, variations in service type are indicated in Figures 2.1 and 2.2 when they have been specifically identified and measured by study author(s). If as Metz et al. (2003) hypothesized, the type or orientation of the service activity influences student outcomes, then specification of the domains of service activity is essential for determining whether some forms of service are more effective in bringing about positive outcomes than others.

Specification and Measurement of Outcomes

As Exhibit 2.3 illustrates, there is little consistency or precision across studies in terms of the measures used to study youth civic development outcomes. For example, outcomes categorized within the social attitude subgroup are measured by 25 different scales, indices, and single-item measures. Although there is great overlap in many of the measures, each is distinct. Moreover, few of the measures are explicitly linked to or derived from standardized measures.

The inconsistency across measures used by different studies makes comparison across interventions difficult. In order to strengthen consistency and precision of measures, clear operational distinctions need to be made between the different concepts measured in these studies. For example, an examination of the different measures presented in Exhibit 2.3 suggests that there are several distinct operational concepts within each outcome category. Within the social attitude category, we suggest that four main concepts emerge: social responsibility, altruism, community membership, and efficacy. Within the social skills and knowledge category, three main concepts are identified: community understanding, ethical skills, and leadership. Likewise, the social and political behavior categories can be further divided in terms of current behavior and intent to participate in the future. We also suggest four main concepts within the political attitude category: attitudes toward institutions of government, interest in politics, efficacy, and interest in politics. Research in this field would be strengthened by identifying and operationalizing these concepts and designing corresponding measures for use across studies.

Conceptual ambiguity about civic engagement (Walker, 2002) may be to blame for the wide variety of outcome measures in the civic development literature. However, more clearly defined and consistent measures would promote knowledge of how effective each of these interventions is in achieving desired outcomes. If studies consistently find statistical insignificance for a particular measure, it could be determined more easily whether this is due to poor validity of the outcome measure, or to current interventions not appropriately targeting that outcome. Thus, consistency across dependent variable measures could result in strengthened models for civic development programs.

Rigor of Design and Methods

Service-learning scholars, such as Billig, Eyler, and Furco, have raised concerns about the level of rigor in service-learning research. Based on the studies reviewed for this chapter, we identified strengths and potential weaknesses in both the service-learning research and civic development intervention research in general. Consistent with calls by scholars for triangulation of data, use of reliable and valid measures, and multisite studies (Billig & Eyler, 2003; Billig & Furco, 2002a; Eyler, 2002; Furco, 2003), eight of the reviewed studies triangulated participant self-report questionnaires with methods such as observation and focus groups. Fifteen studies provided reliability coefficients for outcome measures, although few measures exhibited reliability coefficients at accepted levels. Eleven studies were conducted at multiple sites, strengthening generalizability.

However, social scientific research faces challenges in conducting studies with randomized experimental research designs, and service-learning, in particular, is constrained by the lack of funding to support rigorous—and thus expensive—studies (Billig & Furco, 2002b). Without rigorous designs and methods, readers are left unable to make definitive claims about comparative impacts of civic development interventions. The field will benefit from increased attention to isolating the effectiveness of interventions so that causation can be better approximated. Although all studies that incorporated pretests into their design controlled for baseline pretest differences between groups; the use of posttest only designs (five studies) and self selection into study conditions (five studies) either allowed subjects to self-select or did not clarify the selection process) are still too common. Only one study conducted statistical analyses of attrition, while nine did not discuss nor report attrition or response rates.

Greater inclusion of follow-up measurements will move the field forward in identifying whether these interventions have long-term effects on students. While Hartry and Porter (2004) planned to use the data from their pilot study to develop a longitudinal study, and Billig et al. (2005) planned a second year of data collection, only one study reviewed here (Melchior, 1999) included follow-up measures.

Attention to design, methods, and substantive elements of reporting will increase the possibility for replication. Replication is a major component of the scientific method, essential for improving both civic development scholarship and practice. Replication also can be strengthened by increased reporting of study findings in peer-reviewed journals. Eleven of the 18 reviewed studies (5 of the 10 service-learning studies) have been published or are currently in press in peer-reviewed journals. Service-learning studies, in particular, appear to be published regularly in the form of research center evaluation reports or in book chapters. Submitting such studies to the peer review process and reporting findings in journals is likely to enhance both the quality of reporting and the audience for study findings, although it is acknowledged that there are few journals dedicated to service, which limits publication outlets (McBride & Sherraden, 2004).

CONCLUSION

This systematic assessment of the rigor of designs and methods of these studies suggests directions for future service-learning research that can inform strengthened program models. The knowledge base is growing, the field is indeed moving beyond descriptive research, but what more can be done? It is widely expected that the opportunities service-learning provides for youth to engage with their communities, to connect their experiences with their classroom learning, and to reflect on their experiences in a structured environment positively impact civic outcomes. Yet, with the caveats and substantial limitations of this analysis, comparative study of the main effects of civic development interventions raise significant questions regarding the effectiveness of service-learning as an intervention to increase youth outcomes across all civic categories.

More promising is the growing body of research that suggests that service-learning can positively impact civic outcomes when it is of high quality (e.g., Billig et al., 2005; Melchior & Bailis, 2002; Scales et al., 2000). This comparative analysis facilitates identification of the strengths and weaknesses of the current research base and highlights directions for future research that takes moderating variables such as quality into account. Improved operationalization and measurement of both independent and dependent variables and more rigorous designs and methods that isolate the effect of the intervention may well show service-learning to be the most effective civic intervention and result in the identification of effective models for replication.

This analysis also calls attention to the lack of consistency across studies in terms of the specific civic outcomes that are currently measured. Improved consistency of measures can facilitate comparison across studies, and it can increase the likelihood of positive civic impacts resulting from service-learning participation. If we want service-learning experiences to help students develop civic knowledge, attitudes, and/or behavior, we need to be more deliberate in selecting civic outcomes and in designing service-learning experiences that specifically target these outcomes (Melchior & Bailis, 2002). Through greater specificity of civic outcomes, we can better design—and test—interventions to help students become civically engaged.

NOTES

1.   The searched bibliographies were found on the following organizations' Web sites: the National Service-Learning Clearinghouse (http://www .servicelearning.org/), the Center for Information and Research on Civic Learning and Engagement (http://www.civicyouth.org), Learning In Deed

(http://learningindeed.org/index.html), and the Harvard Family Research Project Out-of -School Time Program (http://www.gse.harvard.edu/hfrp/ projects/afterschool/bibliography/index.html).

2. It is hoped that the methodological rigor of service-learning studies and other civic development interventions will continue to strengthen. As research develops, future reviewers may wish to hold studies to higher standards, similar to those of the original MQRS. For example, the internal reliability coefficients of outcome measures used in the literature appear to vary widely; future analyses may find it worthwhile to evaluate studies based on the reliability of measures used.

3. It is possible that additional criteria were met in conducting the study beyond the information provided in the write-up; however, exclusion of such study elements from the broader researcher and practitioner audience provides a significant impediment to expansion and replication of research.

REFERENCES

Bailis, L., & Melchior, A. (1998). *Evaluation of the active citizenship today (ACT) program: Final report.* Prepared for the Close Up Foundation and the Constitutional Rights Foundation. Waltham, MA: Brandeis University, Center for Human Resources.

Billig, S. H. (2000). Research on K-12 school-based service-learning: The evidence builds. *Phi Delta Kappan, 81*, 658–664.

Billig, S. H. (2003). Introduction. In S. H. Billig & A. S. Waterman (Eds.), *Studying service-learning: Innovations in education research methodology* (pp. vii–xiv). Mahwah, NJ: Erlbaum.

Billig, S. H. (2004). Heads, hearts, and hands: The research on K-12 service-learning. In J. Kielsmeier, M. Neal, & M. McKinnon (Eds.), *Growing to greatness (G2G): The state of service-learning project* (pp. 12–25). St. Paul, MN: National Youth Leadership Council.

Billig, S. H., & Eyler, J. (Eds.). (2003). The state of service-learning and service-learning research. In *Advances in service-learning research: Vol. 3. Deconstructing service-learning: Research exploring context, participation, and impacts* (pp. 253–264). Greenwich, CT: Information Age.

Billig, S. H., & Furco, A. (2002a). Research agenda for K-12 service-learning: A proposal to the field. In A. Furco & S. H. Billig (Eds.), *Advances in service-learning research: Vol. 1. Service-learning: The essence of the pedagogy* (pp. 271–280). Greenwich, CT: Information Age.

Billig, S. H., & Furco, A. (Eds.). (2002b). Supporting a strategic service-learning research plan. In *Advances in service-learning research: Vol. 2. Service-learning through a multidisciplinary lens* (pp. 217–230). Greenwich, CT: Information Age.

Billig, S. H., Root, S., & Jesse, D. (2005). *The impact of participation in service-learning on high school students' civic engagement* (CIRCLE Working Paper 33). College Park: University of Maryland, Center for Information and Research on Civic Learning and Engagement.

Bringle, R. (2003). Enhancing theory-based research on service-learning. In S. H. Billig & J. Eyler (Eds.), *Advances in service-learning research: Vol. 3. Deconstructing service-learning: Research exploring context, participation, and impacts* (pp. 3–21). Greenwich, CT: Information Age.

Center for Information and Research on Civic Learning and Engagement. (2003). *The civic mission of schools.* College Park, MD: Center for Information and Research on Civic Learning and Engagement and The Carnegie Corporation.

Center for Information and Research on Civic Learning and Engagement. (2005). *Census data shows youth voter turnout surged more than any other age group.* College Park, MD: Author. Retrieved May 22, 2006, from http://www.civicyouth.org/PopUps/ReleaseCPS04_Youth.pdf

Covitt, B. A. (2002). Motivating environmentally responsible behaviors through service-learning. In S. H. Billig & A. Furco (Eds.), *Advances in service-learning research: Vol. 2. Service-learning through a multidisciplinary lens* (pp. 177–198). Greenwich, CT: Information Age.

Eyler, J. (2002). Stretching to meet the challenge: Improving the quality of research to improve the quality of service-learning. In S. H. Billig & A. Furco (Eds.), *Advances in service-learning research: Vol. 2. Service-learning through a multidisciplinary lens* (pp. 3–14). Greenwich, CT: Information Age.

Eyler, J., & Giles, D. (1997). The importance of program quality in service-learning. In A. S. Waterman (Ed.), *Service-learning: Applications from the research* (pp. 57–76). Mahwah, NJ: Erlbaum.

Finn, J. L., & Checkoway, B. (1998). Young people as competent community builders: A challenge to social work. *Social Work, 43,* 335–346.

Flanagan, C. A., & Faison, N. (2001). Youth civic development: Implications of research for social policy and programs. *Social Policy Report, XV*(1), 3–14.

Furco, A. (2002). Is service learning really better than community service? A study of high school service program outcomes. In A. Furco & S. H. Billig (Eds.), *Advances in service-learning research: Vol. 1. Service-learning: The essence of the pedagogy* (pp. 23–50). Greenwich, CT: Information Age.

Furco, A. (2003). Issues of definition and program diversity in the study of service-learning. In S. H. Billig & A. S. Waterman (Eds.), *Studying service-learning: Innovations in education research methodology* (pp. 13–33). Mahwah, NJ: Erlbaum.

Galston, W. A. (2001). Political knowledge, political engagement, and civic engagement. *Annual Review of Political Science, 4,* 217–231.

Gibson, C. (2001, November). *From inspiration to participation: A review of perspectives on youth civic engagement.* Berkeley, CA: The Grantmaker Forum on Community and National Service.

Hartry, A., & Porter, K. (2004, July). *We the People curriculum: Results of pilot test.* A report to the Center for Civic Education. Calabassas, CA: Center for Civic Education. Retrieved October 7, 2005, from www.civiced.org/research/pdfs/pilot2.pdf.

Harvard Family Research Project. (2003). *Out-of-school time evaluation snapshot. A review of out-of-school time program quasi-experimental and experimental evaluation results.* Boston: Harvard Graduate School of Education.

Kahne, J., Chi, B., & Middaugh, E. (in press). Building social capital for civic and political engagement: The potential of high school government courses. *Canadian Journal of Education*.

Keeter, S., Andolina, M., Jenkins, K., Zukin, C. (2002, August-September). *Schooling and civic engagement in the U.S.* Paper presented at the annual meeting of the American Political Science Association, Boston, MA.

Leming, J. (2001). Integrating a structured ethical reflection curriculum into high school community service experiences: Impact on students' sociomoral development. *Adolescence, 36*(141), 33–45.

Levine, P., & Lopez, M. H. (2002, September). *Youth voter turnout has declined, by any measure* (fact sheet). College Park, MD: The Center for Information and Research on Civic Learning and Engagement.

McBride, A. M. (2003). Asset ownership among low-income and low-wealth individuals: Opportunity, asset ownership, and civic engagement (Doctoral dissertation, Washington University, 2003). *Dissertation Abstracts International, 64,* 3483.

McBride, A. M., & Sherraden, M. (2004). Toward a global research agenda on civic service: Editors' introduction to this special issue. *Nonprofit and Voluntary Sector Quarterly, 33,* 3S–7S.

McDevitt, M., & Chaffee, S. (2000). Closing gaps in political communication and knowledge: Effects of a school intervention. *Communication Research, 27,* 259–292.

McDevitt, M., Kiousis, S., Wu, X., Losch, M. & Ripley, T. (2003). *The civic bonding of school and family: How Kids Voting students enliven the domestic sphere* (Working Paper 07). College Park, MD: Center for Information and Research on Civic Learning and Engagement.

Melchior, A. (1999). *Summary report: National evaluation of Learn and Serve America* Waltham, MA: Brandeis University, Center for Human Resources.

Melchior, A., & Bailis, L. N. (2002). Impact of service-learning on civic attitudes and behaviors of middle and high school youth: Findings from three national evaluations. In A. Furco & S. H. Billig (Eds.), *Advances in service-learning research: Vol. 1. Service-learning: The essence of the pedagogy* (pp. 201–222). Greenwich, CT: Information Age.

Melchior, A., & Orr, L. (1995). *Final Report: National Evaluation of Serve America.* Cambridge, MA: ABT Associates.

Metz, E., McLellan, J., & Youniss, J. (2003). Types of voluntary service and adolescents' civic development. *Journal of Adolescent Research, 18,* 188–203.

Metz, E., & Youniss, J. (2003). A demonstration that school-based required service does not deter—but heightens—volunteerism. *PS Political Science & Politics, 36,* 281–286.

Metz, E., & Youniss, J. (2005). Longitudinal gains in civic development through school-based required service. *Political Psychology, 26,* 413–437.

Michelsen, E., Zaff, J. F., & Hair, E. C. (2002, May). *Civic engagement programs and youth development: A synthesis.* Washington, DC: Child Trends.

Miller, W. R., Brown, J. M., Simpson, T. L., Handmaker, N. S., Bien, T. H., Luckie, L. H., et al. (1995). What works? A methodological analysis of the alcohol treatment outcome literature. In R. K. Hester & W. R. Miller (Eds.), *Handbook of alcoholism treatment approaches: Effective alternatives* (2nd ed., pp. 12–44). Needham Heights, MA: Allyn & Bacon.

Moore, K. P., & Sandholtz, J. H. (1999). Designing successful service learning projects for urban schools. *Urban Education, 34*, 480–498.

Morgan, W., & Streb, M. (2001). Building citizenship: How student voice in service-learning develops civic values. *Social Science Quarterly, 82*, 154–169.

National Commission on Service Learning. (2002). *Learning in deed: The power of service-learning for American schools.* Newton, MA: W.K. Kellogg Foundation.

Olander, M. (2003, July). *How young people express their political views* (fact sheet). College Park, MD: The Center for Information and Research on Civic Learning and Engagement.

Perry, J., & Katula, M. (2001). Does service affect citizenship? *Administration & Society, 33*, 330–365.

Rhee, C. W., & Auslander, W. (2002, January). *Outcomes of psychosocial interventions for children with chronic illness: A critique of treatment effectiveness.* Paper presented at the Society for Social Work Research, San Diego, CA.

RMC Research Corporation. (2002, November). *Colorado Department of Education Service-Learning evaluation report.* Denver, CO: Author.

Scales, P., Blyth, D., Berkas, T., & Kielsmeier, J. (2000). The effects of service-learning on middle school students' social responsibility and academic success. *Journal of Early Adolescence, 20*, 332–358.

Scales, P. C., & Roehlkepartain, E. C. (2004). *Community service and service-learning in U.S. public schools, 2004: Findings from a national survey.* St. Paul, MN: National Youth Leadership Council.

Skinner, R., & Chapman, C. (1999, September). *Service-learning and community service in K-12 public schools.* U.S. Department of Education Statistics in Brief (NCES 1999-043). Washington, DC: U.S. Department of Education.

Stafford, J., Boyd, B., & Lindner, J. (2003). The effects of service learning on leadership life skills of 4-H members. *Journal of Agricultural Education, 44*, 10–21.

Switzer, G. E., Simmons, R. G., Dew, M. A., Regalski, J. M., & Wang, C. (1995). The effect of a school-based helper program on adolescent self-image, attitudes, and behavior. *Journal of Early Adolescence, 15*, 429–455.

Torney-Purta, J. (2001). What adolescents know about citizenship and democracy. *Educational Leadership, 59*(4), 45–50.

Waldstein, F. A., & Reiher, T. C. (2001). Service-learning and students' personal and civic development. *The Journal of Experiential Education, 24*, 7–13.

Walker, T. (2002). Service as a pathway to political participation: What research tells us. *Applied Developmental Science, 6*(4), 183–188.

What Works Clearinghouse. (n.d.). *WWC study review standards.* U.S. Department of Education: What Works Clearinghouse. Retrieved March 23, 2006, from http://www.whatworks.ed.gov/reviewprocess/study_standards_final.pdf

Yamauchi, L., Billig, S., Meyer, S., & Hofschire, L. (2006). Student outcomes associated with service-learning in a culturally relevant high school program. *Journal of Prevention and Intervention in the Community, 32*(1/2), 149–164.

Youniss, J., McLellan, J. A., & Yates, M. (1997). What we know about engendering civic identity. *American Behavioral Scientist, 40*, 620–631.

Zaff, J., & Michelsen, E. (2001, December). *Background for community-level work on positive citizenship in adolescence: Reviewing the literature on contributing factors.* Washington, DC: Child Trends.

CHAPTER 3

MAXIMIZING CIVIC COMMITMENT THROUGH SERVICE-LEARNING

Case Studies of Effective High School Classrooms

Shelley H. Billig and Susan Root

ABSTRACT

Civic engagement among high school students is particularly low and very challenging. For democracy to thrive, it is important for young people to form a social contract in which they feel responsible for the future and committed to civic participation. This chapter describes 2 case studies of high school classrooms where civic engagement was particularly strong. Students in these classrooms participated in high quality service-learning projects that were tightly connected to meeting community needs and in which students had significant discretion in choosing projects. Students engaged in research, action, and advocacy that resulted in acquisition of civic knowledge, skills, and dispositions at levels higher than their

Advancing Knowledge in Service-Learning: Research to Transform the Field, 45–63
Copyright © 2006 by Information Age Publishing
All rights of reproduction in any form reserved.

45

nonparticipating peers. The studies describe the service-learning approach and activities, and participants' perceived attributes of effectiveness.

INTRODUCTION

An informed, involved citizenry is necessary to the sustainability of democratic societies. Citizens must have sufficient knowledge of democratic principles, institutions, and issues to act on their own and their society's behalf (Patrick, 2003). Competent democratic citizenship requires three types of prerequisites:

1. *Skills*, such as the ability to analyze and critique alternative positions, engage in judicious deliberation, and use civic discourse to promote their own and the greater good (Patrick, 2003);
2. *Values and attitudes* needed for constructive engagement in the political system and community affairs; and
3. *Intentions and actions* such as following the news, monitoring public officials, taking a stand on issues of concern, or serving as community activists (Carnegie Corporation of New York and the Center for Information and Research on Civic Learning and Engagement, 2003).

According to Niemi and Junn (1998), "Schools along with their teachers and curricula have long been identified as the critical link between education and citizenship" (p. 3). However, numerous indicators in recent years suggest that schools are not doing well in this area. On the 1998 NAEP Civics Report Card for the Nation, for example, 35% of 12th graders failed to demonstrate even "basic" knowledge of civics and 39% scored at the basic level (Lutkus, Weiss, Campbell, Mazzeo, & Lazer, 1999). Only 28% of entering college freshmen in the fall of 2000 reported an interest in "keeping up-to-date on political affairs," down from 60% in 1966 (Galston, 2003). Research further shows that compared to older generations, young people express less trust in the political system, are less apt to discuss current affairs, and are less likely to follow politics in the news (Keeter, Zukin, Andolina, & Jenkins, 2002; Rahm & Transue, 1998).

Young people's limited civic engagement has been attributed to various factors, including reduced requirements for civics and government coursework, disillusionment with federal policies, and generational differences. However, several researchers, notably Flanagan and colleagues (1999), argued that the primary cause of civic and political disconnection among youth is a breakdown in the "social contract"; that is, the "set of mutual rights and obligations binding citizens with their polity" (p. 135).

These researchers posit that schools and other institutions should guide young people to form a social contract by engaging in activities that nurture a "civic commitment," defined as dedication to serving society and working toward democratic principles, such as equal rights, as personally important goals.

Studies have begun to identify factors associated with the development of a social contract. The motivation to do good and help others, the sense of efficacy that comes from having an impact on the community, and the desire to shape societal values "so that one feels at home rather than out of place" in one's society (Sherrod, Flanagan, & Youniss, 2002) have been found to help young people become more civically engaged. Civic commitment is also greater when young people come from families that:

- Demonstrate an ethic of social responsibility (Flanagan, Bowes, Johnsson, Csapo, & Sheblanova, 1998);
- Engage in frequent political discussion (Keeter et al., 2002); and
- Have greater educational attainment (Nolin, Chaney, Chapman, & Chandler, 1997).

Schools can play an important role in promoting civic commitment by providing youth with opportunities for meaningful civic participation, including exposure to the patterns of interaction and policy decisions that are characteristic of their societies. Schools that provide opportunities to discuss political issues in an atmosphere of respect for differences have students who are more willing to take on civic responsibility and involvement, such as belonging to organizations outside of school, following politics in the news, and signing petitions (Keeter et al., 2002; Torney-Purta & Amadeo, 2003). Membership in groups characterized by horizontal relationships (those that involve equitable distribution of power and responsibility) also appears to promote the understanding of the balance between rights and obligations and tolerance toward diversity that are essential in a democratic society (Flanagan & Faison, 2001). The knowledge, skills, and attitudes that are the goals of citizenship education are the "product, not the precursor" (Flanagan & Faison, 2001, p. 35) of these opportunities.

Service-learning is an approach to teaching and learning that incorporates many of the factors that researchers have found to be associated with civic commitment and the formation of a social contract. In typical high school classes that implement service-learning, students perform community service to meet a need as a way of learning important curricular objectives. Service-learning typically requires students to engage in *preparation* through conducting community needs assessments and/or research to uncover key challenges that the community faces and brainstorming strategies for addressing needs, and to *provide service* to the community, often in ways that directly engage them with the recipients of service. Preparation and provision of service serve to prompt awareness and knowledge of civic issues and acquisition of civic skills, such as how to gather information and develop strategies to meet community needs and how to access key decision makers. Young people often organize themselves to perform the service and thereby learn interdependence and project planning/time management skills. Preparation and provision of service often gives students exposure to role models and leaders of government or other institutions in situations where students are not simply observers but active participants in the democratic process.

Service-learning also typically includes *reflection* and often includes demonstration of learning. Students' reflections normally involve discussion and writing, and in the best situations, ask students to apply what they have learned to novel situations. Public demonstration of knowledge serves to elevate the importance of the work; to help students to develop deep understandings so that they can convey what they learn; and to assist students with acquiring public speaking, information organizing, and other skills associated with summarizing one's work, perspective-taking, and persuading others.

In this context, service-learning can be understood as a task structure that blends elements of formal and informal learning to provide opportunities for legitimate peripheral participation in democratic work. As such, service-learning has the potential both to impart civic/political concepts and skills and to provide situated information about the environments, roles, and practices within which those concepts and skills have meaning.

Recent research on the impacts of participation in service-learning demonstrates its promise as a vehicle to promote civic commitment. Studies have shown that service-learning participation is related to:

- Increased concern for social issues (Metz, McLellan, & Youniss, 2000; Yamauchi, Billig, Meyer, & Hofschire, 2006);
- Increased concern for others' welfare (Billig, 2000; Scales, Blyth, Berkas, & Kielsmeier, 2000); and
- Increased commitment to service in the future (Billig, 2000; Melchior, 1999).

However, research also shows that service-learning is not consistently associated with gains in political competence or engagement (Carnegie Corporation of New York and the Center for Information and Research on Civic Learning and Engagement, 2003; Kahne & Westheimer, 2003). One explanation for this finding may lie in the tendency of service-learning programs to emphasize a conception of the "citizen as helper" (Walker,

2002). Underlying this conception is the assumption that students will develop a general sense of social responsibility and civic commitment through meeting individuals' needs. However, helper-oriented programs have been criticized for their "decidedly nonpolitical, possibly even anti-political" stance (Niemi, 2000). As Kahne and Westheimer (2003) pointed out, helper-oriented programs may even interfere with civic development by failing to provide youth with an understanding of the structural sources of individual distress or the role of "collective efforts to improve policies and institutions" (p. 36).

What are the characteristics of service-learning programs that strengthen civic commitment and promote young people's attachment to democratic institutions and processes? The purpose of this chapter is to describe two case studies of high school service-learning programs that have made statistically significant impacts on the students in terms of their acquisition of civic knowledge, skills, and dispositions.

METHODOLOGY

The case study data were collected as part of a larger 3-year research project that examined the impact of participation in service-learning on high school students' civic and academic engagement. Sites in the larger study included high school classrooms that participated in service-learning matched with those that did not. The matched classrooms had similar demographic and achievement profiles, and were located in Anoka, Minnesota; Fort Myers and Miami, Florida; Humble, Texas; Menasha, Wisconsin; and Tillamook, Oregon.

Sites were identified by nomination from state Learn and Serve directors, civic organizations, and literature reviews. Screening criteria were applied, and the sample was selected based on answers to questions about:

- The focus of the service-learning approach (civic purpose);
- Early indicators of quality (presence of elements such as linkage to state content standards, regular reflection activities, student voice in the selection and implementation of the projects); and
- Availability of a matched comparison site.

A total of 27 matched pairs of classrooms with 2,424 students comprised the sample. The study employed multiple methods of data collection including surveys as well as qualitative approaches. Quantitative data were used to identify overall impact; results are presented elsewhere (Billig, Root, & Jesse, 2005). The larger study showed that students who participated in classrooms that featured high quality service-learning approaches had statistically significantly higher scores on several measures of civic knowledge, skills, and dispositions than their nonparticipating peers. High quality was associated with factors such as duration, teacher experience, linkage to standards, cognitive challenging tasks, and engagement in civic or political action (Billig et al., 2005, 2006).

Two of the 27 classrooms emerged as having the strongest civic impacts as measured by subscales on surveys rating objective knowledge, self-reported knowledge, and skills and dispositions. The qualitative data from these two sites are presented here.

Methods of qualitative data collection included observations, student focus groups, teacher interviews, and document analysis. During the spring, researchers observed an activity related to a project in each of the service-learning classrooms. Observations were for an entire class period. Student focus groups were moderated at each service-learning school. A convenience sample of 6 to 12 students was identified by the teachers and facilitated by researchers at each site. Focus groups followed a standard format and typically lasted for 45 to 60 minutes, covering a range of topics that paralleled those on the survey.

Interviews were conducted with service-learning teachers and school and district administrators at each site. The primary purpose of the interviews was to substantiate the information teachers provided in the surveys and to gain more information about the service-learning activities. Interviews followed a standard format and had multiple probes. Documents about the program or used as part of the service-learning approach were analyzed.

RESULTS

Quest High School

Quest High School is a magnet school of choice, located in the Humble School District, just outside of Houston. With an enrollment of 222 students, the student body is 90% White, 5% African American, 4% Hispanic, and 1% Asian American.

The mission of Quest High School is to provide "a personalized learning experience in a working partnership with the community to create lifelong learners and successful members of society" (Quest High School Mission, n.d., p. 1). This mission is grounded in a set of well-articulated beliefs that recognize the abilities of all students to learn given the right conditions, motivation, and guidance. Students are viewed as being at the center of the learning process, displaying a wide range of abilities, talents, and personalities that should be accommodated. The teaching and learning process is seen as collaborative, interactive, and flexible, and there is explicit recognition of the need for learning to be relevant to students' lives. Responsibility for learning is shared by students and teachers.

The Quest High School curriculum emphasizes the application of knowledge. Guided by three sets of standards, students learn how to learn; become academically prepared for postsecondary education, the workplace, or the military; and learn how to interact with the community.

Quest educators have been implementing service-learning for about 10 years. When service-learning was initiated, students provided tutoring to elementary school students and later, to middle school students.

> We have a mission in this district to have an entire education of a child to be holistic, and not just learning the core subjects, but going out into the field and applying that with what they learn in the classroom into the civic mission area. (Administrator)

All of the service-learning objectives and activities are strongly tied to state content standards. Many of the standards that are addressed are in the realm of Learner Behaviors, such as "evaluates the effectiveness of own action" and "examines critically and establishes a value system of right and wrong that promotes good citizenship, team effort, a cooperative work ethic, honesty, common courtesy, respect for others, and safety." Other standards are in the areas of Workplace Tools and Career Education and promote exploration of various career pathways.

Students perform service activities every Wednesday morning at over 40 sites in the local area. They are required to complete at least 30 hours of service per semester. Students choose sites and engage in projects that address diverse needs such as:

- Providing wellness information for Early Head Start and Head Start programs;
- Teaching English and foreign languages to participants of various literacy programs;
- Re-enacting historical events at a local homestead;
- Working with the elderly at local assisted living centers; and
- Engaging in microtechnology and chemistry projects with local colleges.

All students enroll in the Senior Seminar course that serves as a culminating experience for humanities coursework. In self-selected work groups, students develop sustainable action plans that meet community needs identified by these same students in previous years. The social action plan must build awareness for the topic, include research, address a community need, and have a lasting impact. Students use a process for social inquiry that encourages them to communicate effectively, interpret their ideas and feelings, participate in group work, contribute to a sense of community, and address a real-world issue. Designs must include project descriptions, need, a description of tasks, a list of needed resources, and criteria for success. Within the Senior Seminar, students also learn about implications of social issues; conflict resolution; research process, with an emphasis on source identification and citations; interview techniques; data analysis; and group dynamics. The course requires an exhibition of the work, presented in multimedia form and as a student portfolio.

Seniors also enroll in a course titled Senior Exploratory Foundations. This fall semester course precedes the Senior Seminar and focuses on facilitating students' understanding of general international issues and the role of the United States in global issues. Seniors study world economies and fiction and nonfiction that raise global issues. Writing assignments focus on a critical examination of the literature. Students also participate in activities that require them to work in groups, speak in public, use technology, and apply knowledge and skills in real world issues and situations. The students assume individual internships and work in groups to identify and address a social problem. Students themselves decide which group they will join. Groups develop a division of labor and self-regulate.

Exhibit 3.1 provides a description of a service-learning activity observed at Quest High School in the spring of 2004. Teachers implemented service-learning because they believed it was a good strategy for engaging students in content and in civic and workplace life. Teachers reported that students learned interpersonal skills, acquired knowledge about specific content areas, gained confidence in public speaking, engaged in more interactions with peers and adults outside their previous circles of friends and relations; and understood society and social issues to a much greater extent.

> I think it's powerful because it's all about people ... I think that's what is so cool about service-learning is that you really do raise the bar for kids to learn on a deeper level . . . When people come to our school, they always talk about ... your high schoolers are so comfortable with adults and they are so articulate. How do you teach that? I thought about it and I thought, we really don't teach it, we just allow them to have lots of interaction with those people so it becomes natural for them. There's a lot of things that service-learning does for kids as far as the whole child concept goes. (Teacher)

Exhibit 3.1. Service-Learning at Quest High School

After welcoming the 35 students, one of the four teachers in the room instructed the students to convene in their groups to continue discussion of their social action plans (SAPs). Students received written instructions that directed them to verbalize the activities contained within their SAP and receive input from another group that might help them improve the plan. A set of interview questions was included to help the students shape the conversations and conduct a gap analysis. Groups were assigned to interview each other, and students were reminded to select a recorder to note answers to the questions on the worksheet. Each group was working on a different project.

One group of students working on tolerance issues discussed the fact that they had changed their strategy from mailing a letter to middle school students to arranging for face-to-face meetings. The group was constructing a Web site that was intended to connect users to potential solutions to challenges associated with promoting tolerance. The group was engaged in organizing the information on the Web site so that it was user friendly. Another group, which was planning a fundraising event to build a health facility, had a discussion with their partners about whether the annual run that they had planned to raise funds and awareness was sustainable. Students responded that the YMCA helped to write the grant for the facilities and would likely sustain the effort in the future.

Another group discussed the difficulty of getting the community involved in their project. While the students felt there was common ground, they noted that partners often had their own agendas. Students worried that resources would be appropriated for other purposes. The students decided that this group had a "tight" plan that was well articulated and conceived. The only task that they felt was unfinished was the need to organize their written work in binders.

After about 45 minutes, one of the teachers got the attention of all of the groups. She pointed out that it was important for students to hear about what others were doing so that they could "see the kinds of actions that were being proposed." She asked, "What is the one thing that you are taking away from this activity?" One student pointed out that discussion illuminated missing steps in the action plan; another pointed out that the conversation showed them how little time they had left to implement the plan. A third student remarked that there was a need to make more people aware of their project, while another said that an exhibition of the work needed to be everyone's main focus. Three students pointed out that there was some urgency to take action with one discussing the need for motivation and another saying that there should be fewer meetings. This student said, "These meetings get in the way of action. It's hard to get people to realize what a complex issue this is. We need buy-in from our stakeholders. It's easy to convince district people but more difficult to get kids to understand that they can change policies." Other comments included the need to address breakdowns in communication, a need for more 'outside volunteers' to staff the project, and perhaps a need to change the overall concept so that exhibitions took place in the fall.

Service-learning was viewed as being more encompassing and comprehensive than typical instructional strategies, but also less predictable and more time-consuming. Teachers noted that service-learning required more flexibility and confidence in handling the unknown. Teachers felt that they had to be sensitive to "teachable moments" that are constantly being presented to them in order to capitalize on the experience. By being familiar with the content standards to be covered, the teachers reported that they were able to address content standards as the opportunity arose. Any standards that were not addressed were taught at another time, typically during in-class lectures or activities. Thus, there was no scope and sequence that was followed, but rather expectations of what was to be learned over the course of the year.

> You become much more of a risk-taker because you don't have total control over the information (the students) get.... You have to give up some of your power because it's real and you can't contrive everything about things. Sometimes things come up that are totally unexpected and you have to be flexible enough to deal with that and to allow that to be part of the learning process. That's really uncomfortable for some people. (Teacher)

Students from Quest did not master a specific set of facts about civics, but rather learned the ways in which decisions are made in a democratic society, the effects of those decisions on individuals and communities, and the interrelationships between institutions, including the relationship between schooling and work. They researched specific issues in order to plan their service.

> Because we deal with the actual society a lot in our service-learning ... and all of our topics. We don't do ... chapter by chapter in the book. We pick a topic and we research it for sometimes weeks, sometimes months at a time, and we look at every aspect of it. We look at their strengths and we look at their weaknesses and different time periods, and we look at what they've done and what they've accomplished and where their weaknesses fall and then we look at the past, present, and future and how society works and its strengths and faults.... In our social action plans and all of our service-learning right now, we look at society here today and we can tell you where there's strengths and where there's faults. (Student)

Students reported that they acquired stronger interpersonal skills and became better problem solvers through their service-learning experiences. Teachers believed that students demonstrated remarkable growth in terms of their understanding of civic life, including knowledge of how democracy works and their roles within society.

> It was really, really neat to hear kids ... so passionate about that (saying to other students) ... if we're not active as citizens in a democracy and we don't value free speech and we all sit back and we don't vote, then, you know, it's going to become something we have no control over because we haven't taken the control that we're offered. I mean, I'm just sitting there thinking, they got it, they got it, because they are so passionate about it, they're trying to get other kids to get it and that's a huge thing. (Teacher)

In focus groups, students tended to discuss the changes they experienced in terms of social responsibility, efficacy, and understanding of social issues.

> I think I've changed a lot. Like before, I didn't really, I don't know, I cared, but not enough to do something about current legislation and the current situation. And now not only do I care about it, but I want to like shout it from the rooftops, you know? I want to tell everybody. I guess that's because I know more now. (Student)

Many students reported that they formed networks with each other and with adults outside of the schools that they would never have contacted before these projects. They noted that many of the adults they met served as positive role models for them in terms of the way these adults dedicated their lives. They also felt that they had better relationships with each other and supported the members of their classrooms in positive ways. They were able to resolve conflicts and solve problems as they encountered them. Finally, they gained a respect for diverse opinions and circumstances.

Several students mentioned that they did not necessarily embrace service-learning before they participated in it, but that their participation was worthwhile. None of the students wished they had made different choices.

> Yes, I love it, I love doing (service-learning), but before I experienced it, I probably wouldn't have wanted to do it. Like I said, I didn't like the whole idea of service-learning. It was all right, but it wasn't something that really interested me. Now that I've done it, it is very exciting and especially the projects, you know, the independent projects are exciting to me. I just wish it could have been a year long. (Student)

Anoka High School

Anoka High School is located in Anoka, Minnesota, a medium-sized city 20 miles northwest of Minneapolis. The school is part of the Anoka-Hennepin school district, one of the most rapidly growing in the country. Anoka High School enrolls 2,052 students, 92% of whom are White; 2.8% Asian/Pacific Islander; 1.9%, American Indian; 1.7%, African American; and 1.4% Hispanic. Fourteen percent of Anoka students are eligible for free or reduced price lunch.

Anoka High School's service-learning program has been in existence for 13 years. Its founder and champion was a social studies teacher who established the program in association with a citywide improvement effort titled, Total Quality Community. This effort was launched in 1990 when civic leaders conducted an assessment of citizens' hopes and fears for the city in 2010. Anoka High School students helped summarize the results into a community vision that identified goals for preserving and improving community resources in several categories: history, culture, business, service, and natural environment. The result was a list of needs or targets in each area of community life. These targets are still being used by the social studies department and service-learning program at Anoka High School in planning student projects. The Total Quality Community vision is currently a responsibility of the 2020 Task Force, on which Anoka students sit earning service-learning credit for their participation.

From its inception, Total Quality Community has emphasized youth civic development as an essential building block of a quality community. Community leaders and Anoka High School staff work jointly to engage students as important players in community government and improvement.

> Everyone is on the team in our community, kids, adults, and senior citizens support shared action ... American communities are built on a sense of public teamwork. In an era of electronic entertainment, it is possible that no one will show up to do the public's work...., To generate more focused, creative, and committed workers and citizens, we need to share an understanding of the role of service in adolescent development. Through service, students learn that their personal problems are not the only drama in town.... Through organized learning activities, developed ... with help from ... community partners, the identity of students grows in strength and clarity. (Skogquist & Mittlefehldt, 2001, pp. 5, 8).

In 2003-2004, the projects completed by Anoka students included developing a proposal to bring a rail system to North Minneapolis and presenting it to the state legislature, working on a project to reseed the prairie, and initiating a water conservation project. Exhibit 3.2 provides a description of one classroom period in which students discussed their projects.

Anoka teachers were initially attracted to service-learning because it provided an authentic, motivating learning experience. One teacher was seriously concerned about the impacts of young people's current disengagement from civic life, and viewed service-learning as a vehicle for reversing this trend.

> I realized that the kids would learn more and have a richer, fuller experience if their learning were grounded in the community. Social studies can be boring, but it can be exciting if it involves autonomous learning in the community. Kids are falling into an abyss. They don't realize America is built on common ground, shared assumptions, and community action. And service to the republic. There's so many things disconnecting our kids from

Exhibit 3.2.   Service-Learning at Anoka High School

Class began at 9:12 a.m. with the teacher and 19 students present. The teacher asked students to describe any project that they were doing "that's connected to the community." One student started the discussion by reporting that his psychology class engaged in a drug prevention project. He said that students talked with police, the health department and schools, and reported that 50 people attended. Another student volunteered that he also was implementing a project on teens and drugs and had made a presentation at a nearby juvenile detention center. A third student added that he was working on a transportation project and had met with state legislators.

The teacher then asked the students to recall their last classroom discussion that focused on cultural conflicts. A student reminded the group that they talked about Aboriginals in Australia and dangers to indigenous peoples. The teacher asked why students might have an interest in these indigenous people. Students responded, "They may have cures for diseases," and "their language." The teacher asked, "How about food? All right, food, fiber, pharmaceuticals. Now, who can explain this diagram? (There is a graph on board with two lines, one at a sharper incline than the others.) We're having an explosion of what? Population. And we're limited in our learning. We have reason to think that problems in the future are coming our way, because our learning is not keeping up with change. So we had an idea to study indigenous populations on the edge of survival to see what we could learn from them. Who has a group that has achieved some integration?" Students replied, "The Aboriginals in Australia." The teacher explained that the Aboriginals are currently using the laws of the dominant culture to try to get their land back. He continued, "But it will be a struggle. Now, one of the things you had to do was find the Web address of a group that might care about these issues." Students give Web addresses of groups. The teacher continued, "(One student) and her team studied the Basque. What's interesting about their use of technology?" Students discussed the fact that the Basque have made effective use of the Internet to publicize Basque issues and culture. The teacher then summarized. Last week, we found an organization connected with an indigenous group. Next week we will write a letter to them."

the community that it actually takes effort and energy to build bridges. We've noticed that the kids develop a natural excitedness when people listen to them. (Teacher)

Teachers acknowledged challenges associated with using service-learning including the complexity of managing projects and the need to give over control of the learning experience to students.

Instructors who are control freaks, organization, and detail people can't use this approach. (Teacher)

Teachers also reported that service-learning provided students with first-hand knowledge of government and its operations.

I think they learn so much about how government works, about how open government offices are to citizens, the complexity of what government deals with. They learn what level of government deals with things. (Teacher)

All respondents, including administrators, teachers, and students believed that the service-learning program had positive impacts on students' civic knowledge.

> I think that service-learning has had an effect in terms of students' knowing and feeling what it means to be a good citizen and a good person. It has probably helped the climate of the school. They are continually doing things to make the world better, and they feel better about themselves. (Administrator)

Students who participated in the focus group affirmed the perception that service-learning positively affected their civic knowledge. Members of the group that had presented their proposal for an extended rail system commented that they gained a greater understanding of the workings of democracy. Students involved in other service-learning projects reported becoming more knowledgeable about state and local political leaders and local government. Focus group students also unanimously agreed that their projects increased their awareness of controversial political issues and alternative perspectives on those issues as well as problems in their society and community and activities citizens could undertake to address them.

Teachers noted that students' civic skills, such as project management and discourse skills, improved as a result of participation in service-learning. One teacher observed particular impacts on students' abilities to present information about a public issue.

> I know that I have lots of students who have presented at adult venues, such as the City Council or the school board, who feel very excited and very proud of themselves for addressing adults about an adult issue. (Teacher)

According to their teacher, students were treated as legitimate and valued members of the community in these venues. Adults responded constructively to the students' proposals, and treated them the same way they treated respected adults. The responses prompted a process of continuous skills improvement.

> One of the things I have appreciated ... is that they treat them as adult citizens, and ask the tough questions and point out weaknesses in their arguments.... And they (the students) go back and realize that maybe the people they are talking to have already thought about their idea, and they need to do some more thinking about it. And that's power and good for a learner to have. It's like a continuum of skills and information, and they realize at the next venue—I have to add information. (Teacher)

In addition, teachers reported that students gained problem-solving skills from their participation in the service-learning projects.

> It's a beautiful part of independent projects. I can't tell them what they're going to run into, but they're going to have to solve it. They have to work with their teammates in their group ... selecting topics, finding research, dividing up tasks. They problem solve from day one. (Teacher)

Students remarked that they learned "a lot" about gathering information, stating their opinions in a discussion and giving reasons for this opinion, listening to others even if they disagreed with them, making presentations, and creating a product their community could use. They gained a great deal of understanding about deliberative democratic dialogue and decision making.

> You can't be disrespectful and you can't say bad things. You have a right to your opinion, and they have a right to theirs. You have to respect that. (Student)

The teachers observed that students became more civically responsible and that this sense of responsibility did not develop from outside in, but from the opportunity to address a social problem that aroused students' deep concern. With this responsibility, students began to develop a sense of civic identity.

> One of the things that I have noticed is that they don't feel their responsibility until they feel their freedom. It's that freedom to select an object for their passion that makes them start feeling a sense of responsibility. You have to confront them with the challenge and then step back and say which part of the American dream do you want to take on.... They start to feel like, "This is my place; this is where my people are, and I'm doing the work of my people." (Teacher)

Most students said that participating in service-learning improved their sense of civic efficacy. They became both more optimistic and more committed to active civic engagement in the future.

> There's more hope for our society, because there's more chance for problems to be solved. (Student)

DISCUSSION

Service-learning at Quest High School was a primary vehicle for students to learn about themselves and society. By placing responsibility on the students for determining community needs, selecting societal challenges to address, and implementing service that attempted to meet the authentic need, students learned about a world much larger than the one they experience in the high school setting alone. They came to understand that they could contribute in positive ways to the betterment of their surrounding community, but that to be effective, they needed to develop a concrete set of skills, such as understanding how to research an issue, how to build a persuasive argument, and how to relate to adults and peers to accomplish a meaningful task within a specific timeframe.

Students also came to understand that they could not solve all of the problems they identified, so they became more realistic about what they could do and the conditions that would facilitate their success. Most students became more knowledgeable about potential careers and career paths and more cognizant of their own strengths and desires for the future. They generally came to see the value of interdependence and the need for leadership. They formed social networks and saw value in other students with whom they would not have associated before the experience. Finally, the students realized how important it was to have many ideas and to have respect for those who held different points of view. They felt that brainstorming and listening led to better decision making.

All of the areas of learning identified by students are related to the formation of a strong civic identity and the desire to contribute in the future as a participatory citizen. These students said they would not be passive observers in the future, but hoped to continue to actively engage to the betterment of their communities.

At Anoka High School, students who participated in service-learning addressed a community need related to a larger citywide initiative. They researched issues, presented propositions to adult decision makers and peers, and participated in deliberate democratic dialogue.

Students at Anoka High School felt that it was their civic duty to engage in improving their community. They uniformly felt that young people were important resources for change in the world, and that with the proper knowledge, skills, and opportunities, young people had both the capability and responsibility to contribute to the betterment of both the local community and to the larger society. Students felt a sense of being part of a global interdependent system. They were unafraid to tackle large issues, and in fact, felt it was their responsibility to do so. Their sense was that the world had multiple problems and that youth should be mobilized to help solve them.

The two case studies presented here illustrate the ways in which service-learning can be designed to address civic disaffection and promote the acquisition of knowledge, skills, and dispositions critical for fostering and sustaining young peoples' commitment to the polity. In both of these cases, *knowledge* acquisition was fostered by asking young people to research and choose the service issues that they believed were important. The learning was self-directed. Students accessed many sources of information, both through their formal research projects and by gathering information in interactions with others. They learned content and specific subject matters by studying the service topic. They learned research and writing skills, oral presentation skills, formulation of persuasive strategies, and how decisions on issues are made in communities and through government.

Students acquired a range of *skills* as they became involved in service-learning, interacting with community agencies and community decision makers, engaging in deliberations and dialogues with the purpose of choosing what actions they should take, and implementing a series of action steps to address societal issues. They learned how to come to consensus in the face of divergent opinions; interact with peers and adults in reciprocal, constructive, and respectful ways; and plan and implement service projects to benefit the local community.

Students acquired intentions to act as citizens and engaged in civic actions through their preparation and implementation of service activities and the reflections that occurred after the activities. They developed a sense that they personally, and youth more generally, could make a difference. As such, the students formed a social contract and civic commitment that went well beyond helping behaviors. They felt it was both their right and their responsibility to engage in social action. These actions were part of the students' notions of what democracy requires and their conceptions of citizenship. The community service they provided served to illuminate a social ill and the types of strategies needed to address the challenge.

These case studies show that service-learning can promote civic engagement and commitment. However, as the larger body of research on service-learning demonstrates, unless specific components are in place, service-learning will not realize its potential. What is needed is intentional instructional design to promote the internalization of the social contract by allowing students to research and choose issues, design action steps for service, tackle meaningful social issues, and advocate for their beliefs.

The classroom teachers in these case studies recognized the benefit of having students engaged in service-learning and found ways to maximize outcomes, both academic and civic. These teachers believed that any educator could implement service-learning and cover standards well as long as the teacher was willing to be flexible in terms of the timing during which standards were addressed. They felt it was best for students to learn as many of the content standards as possible in an authentic and embedded way. The standards that were not addressed within the service-learning approach were covered at another time. The teachers featured here were particularly adept at capitalizing on "teachable moments" as they naturally occurred. This took them time to master, and they noted that letting go of the scope and sequence normally found in classrooms was not easy. However, as each respondent group noted, the effort was well worth the time spent. These classrooms transformed their students into caring, connected citizens.

REFERENCES

Billig, S. H. (2000, May). Research on K–12 school-based service-learning: The evidence builds. *Phi Delta Kappan, 81*(9), 658–664.

Billig, S. H., Root, S., & Jesse, D. (2005). The relationship between the quality indicators of service-learning and student outcomes: In S. Root, J. Callahan, & S. H. Billig (Eds.), *Advances in service-learning research: Vol. 5. Improving service-learning practice: Research on models to enhance impacts* (pp. 97–115). Greenwich, CT: Information Age.

Billig, S. H., Root, S. & Jesse, D. (2006). *The impact of high school students' participation in service-learning on academic and civic engagement.* Report prepared for the Carnegie Corporation of New York. Denver, CO: RMC Research Corporation.

Carnegie Corporation of New York and the Center for Information and Research on Civic Learning and Engagement. (2003). *The civic mission of schools.* New York: Carnegie Corporation of New York and CIRCLE.

Flanagan, C., Bowes, J., Johnsson, B., Csapo, B., & Sheblanova, E. (1998). Ties that bind: Correlates on adolescents' civic commitments in seven countries. *Journal of Social Issues, 54*(3), 457-475.

Flanagan, C., & Faison, N. (2001). Youth civic development: Implications of research for social policy and programs. *Social Policy Report, XV*(1), 3-14.

Flanagan, C. A., Johnsson, B., Botcheva, L., Csapo, B., Bowes, J. J., Macek, P., Averina, I., & Sheblanova, E. (1999). Adolescents and the social contract: Developmental roots of citizenship in seven countries. In M. Yates & J. Youniss (Eds.), *Roots of civic identity: International perspectives on community service and activism in youth* (pp. 135–155). New York: Cambridge University Press.

Galston, W. A. (2003, September). Civic education and political participation. *Phi Delta Kappan, 85*(1), 29-33.

Kahne, J., & Westheimer, J. (2003). Teaching democracy: What schools need to do. *Phi Delta Kappan, 85*(1), 34-40, 57-67.

Keeter, S., Zukin, C., Andolina, M., & Jenkins, K. (2002). *The civic and political health of the nation: A generational portrait.* College Park: University of Maryland, The Center for Information & Research on Civic Learning & Engagement. Research funded by The Pew Charitable Trusts.

Lutkus, A. D., Weiss, A. R., Campbell, J. R., Mazzeo, J., Lazer, S., with Kulick, E., Swinton, S., & Leung, V. (1999). *NAEP 1998 civics report card for the nation* (NCES 2000-457). Washington, DC: U.S. Department of Education, Office of Educational Research and Improvement.

Melchior, A. (1999). *Summary report: National evaluation of Learn and Serve America*. Waltham, MA: Brandeis University, Center for Human Resources.

Metz, E., McLellan, J., & Youniss, J. (2000). *Types of voluntary service and the civic development of adolescents*. Unpublished manuscript, Catholic University, Washington, DC.

Niemi, R. (2000, June). *Trends in political sciences as they relate to pre-college curriculum and teaching*. Paper presented at the Social Science Education Consortium, Woods Hole, MA.

Niemi, R., & Junn, J. (1998). *Civic education: What makes students learn?* New Haven, CT: Yale University Press

Nolin, M. J., Chaney, B., Chapman, C., & Chandler, K. (1997, April). *Student participation in community service activity* (Statistical Analysis Report NCES 97-331). Washington, DC: U.S. Department of Education, National Center for Education Statistics, Office of Educational Research and Improvement.

Quest High School. (n.d.). *School foundations: Missioni/beliefs/philosophy*. Retrieved August 7, 2006, from http://qhs.humble.k12.tx.us/school_foundations/index .htm

Patrick, J. (2003). *Essential elements of education for democracy: What are they and why should they be at the core of the curriculum in schools?* Paper presented in Sarajevo, Bosnia & Herzegovena. Retreived June 12, 2006, from http://www.civiced.org/pdfs/EEOEforDemocracy.pdf

Rahm, W., & Transue, J. (1998). Social trust and value change: The decline of social capital in American youth, 1976–1995. *Political Psychology, 19*(3), 545–565.

Scales, P. C., Blyth, D. A., Berkas, T. H., & Kielsmeier, J. C. (2000, August). The effects of service-learning on middle school students' social responsibility and academic success. *Journal of Early Adolescence, 20*(3), 332–358.

Sherrod, L., Flanagan, C., & Youniss, J. (Eds.). (2002). Dimensions of citizenship and opportunities for youth development: The what, why, when, where and who of citizenship development. *Applied Developmental Science, 6*(4), 264-272.

Skogquist, B., & Mittlefehldt, B. (2001, November). *Anoka: Building effective citizens with school and community*. Presentation at National Council for the Social Studies Conference, Washington, DC.

Torney-Purta, J., & Amadeo, J. (2003). A cross-national analysis of political and civic involvement among adolescents. *Political Science and Politics, 36*, 269-274.

Walker, T (2002). Service as a pathway to political participation: What research tells us. *Applied Developmental Science, 6*(4), 183 188.

Yamauchi, L. A., Billig, S. H., Meyer, S., & Hofschire, L. (2006). Student outcomes associated with service-learning in a culturally relevant high school program. *Journal of Prevention and Intervention in the Community, 32*(1/2), 149–164.

Section II

INTERNATIONAL PERSPECTIVES ON SERVICE-LEARNING

CHAPTER 4

SERVICE-LEARNING IN ARGENTINA SCHOOLS

A Descriptive Vision Based on the Projects Presented to the "Presidential Service-Learning Award" (2000-2001)

María Nieves Tapia, Alba González, and Pablo Elicegui

ABSTRACT

Given that service-learning research in Argentina is still in an early stage, an exploratory study was necessary to establish the most significant variables, dimensions and indicators, and applicable models of analysis of the service project that had been developing in the Argentine educational system. The investigation was based on the analysis of 6,100 applications submitted to the "Premio Presidencial Escuelas Solidarias" (Solidarity Schools Presidential Award)[1] in 2000 and 2001.[2] The primary objectives of the investigation were to determine whether there was a characteristic profile of the schools that carried out community service-learning projects and to establish the general characteristics of these projects especially of those that could be

Advancing Knowledge in Service-Learning: Research to Transform the Field, 67–88
Copyright © 2006 by Information Age Publishing
All rights of reproduction in any form reserved.

considered service-learning in the strict sense. Research offered statistical data on schools engaging in service by geographical location, level, kind of administration (state or private), and social context. Service projects data include the most frequently addressed issues and the most habitual beneficiaries. Using four criteria—student participation, service goals, learning goals, and at least one formal curricular link—the research identified 57% of all projects as service-learning, and the most frequent curricular links were studied. The research also described students' mandatory/voluntary participation, the projects' financial resources, and the alliance between schools and nongovernmental organizations (NGOs) or government agencies to develop their service projects.

INITIAL DEFINITIONS: COMMUNITY SERVICE-LEARNING AND SERVICE-LEARNING PROJECTS

The pedagogy known in the United States as "service-learning," "*voluntariado educativo*" in Brazil, and "*aprendizaje-servicio*" in many Spanish-speaking countries has been defined in Argentina as a "service performed by students, aimed at attending to a real need of the community, and oriented in an explicit and planned way to enhance the quality of academic learning" (Programa Nacional Educación Solidaria, 2004).

For the purposes of this study, we will use this definition as a reference point, realizing that this option sets very precise boundaries regarding the extent of service-learning in relation to other types of service or community projects that could be initiated in the educational environment.

We should also point out that in schools, real-life the boundaries between "community service," "learning," and "service-learning" are not always fixed during the life of a project, nor are they always easily identified on first analysis. This has made it necessary to create comprehensive expressions that embrace the corpus of educational projects involving community outreach or service initiatives.

Furco and Billig (2002) proposed "a neutral" expression—community service-learning—as:

> a generic term to refer to both community service and service-learning activities as currently practiced. The use of the term is not meant to be restricted to the enhancement of academic achievement as an educational objective. While the term is somewhat awkward, community service-learning offers the advantages of apparent familiarity: neutrality between the two contested terms and a suitably balanced emphasis on both community benefit and community objectives. (p. 14)

Likewise, the expression "*proyectos educativos solidarios*," used in the *Premio Presidencial Escuelas Solidarias* (Solidarity Schools Presidential Award)

(PPES/SSPA), refers to the broadest field of service projects developed in educational settings, including nonsystematic community initiatives, institutional community service, and service-learning (Tapia, 2000). In this chapter, the term service-learning will be used in the strict sense, referring to those activities that aim simultaneously at community outreach and learning, and community service-learning as a comprehensive term representing all service motivated activities or activities oriented towards community outreach developed in the school environment (Billig, 2004; Cairn & Kielsmeier, 1995; Kendall, 1990; Tapia, 2000).

SOURCE OF INFORMATION

The main source of information of the research was the archive of applications for the PPES/SSPA, which was convened in 2000 and 2001 by the National Ministry of Education through the *Programa Nacional Escuela y Comunidad* (National School and Community Program).

Created in 2000 by the newly elected president of Argentina, who personally delivered the first awards in August 2000, the Presidential Award is a way to recognize and to gather information about schools engaging in service-learning in Argentina. In 2000-2001, the award distributed grants from $1,500 to $10,000 to service-learning projects already taking place[3] (Tapia & Mallea, 2003).

The invitation to apply for the Presidential Award was addressed to all educational institutions already developing community service projects. In 2000-2001, roughly 6,160 applications were received from teacher training colleges and schools of all levels (K-12) and all types (common, special, adults, professional formation centers, informal education, etc.), from all types of administrations (public, private), and from all environments (urban and rural) possible in the Argentine system.[4] For purposes of this study, the higher education applications were excluded to focus on the 4,391 K-12 schools that submitted applications.

In order to present their project for the award, schools were required to complete an official form, with a detailed questionnaire requiring information about the institution and the service project that was being carried out.[5] The forms had to be signed by the principal as a legal statement. Many schools attached to the form pictures, testimonies, press clips, and videotapes about their projects.

During 2002-2003, Centro Latinoamericano de Aprendizaje y Servicio Solidario (CLAYSS, Latin American Center for Service-Learning) had access to all of the forms submitted to the PPES/SSPA in 2000 and 2001, the main source of information for the research[6] in this chapter.

These forms offered several advantages and some limitations as a source of knowledge. The main advantage was definitely the comprehensiveness of the projects available. Forms constituted a rich source both in quantity and in variety, offering the possibility to infer conclusions with certain reliability. At the same time, it must be said that the forms had all the restrictions and limitations of a document with a predetermined format, submitted to a government body, and in view of being awarded a prize. The fact of reporting to a government body with the aim of winning a prize biases the information presented, as reference is made almost exclusively to achievements, while difficulties and failures are minimized or omitted. However, given that this is an exploratory and quantitative investigation, this last limitation does not affect the data central to the study.[7]

Although the sources defined the field of investigation, this does not pretend to describe all the Argentine institutions that carry out service projects, but only those institutions with service projects that received information about the award and made the decision to apply.

THE RESEARCH DESIGN[8]

Construction of Analysis Constructs

The rich and somewhat overwhelming data provided by the 6,100 Presidential Award files needed to be organized in order to establish some generalizations regarding community service-learning projects, and specifically service-learning projects, in an attempt to establish a systematic description of the situation at a national level.

Two different analysis constructs were designed to analyze the available sources including all the units of analysis.

The first analysis construct (C1) included 4,391 K-12 educational institutions that presented their service projects to the Presidential Award in 2000 and 2001. The units of analysis of this construct included those schools that made applications for only one of the Presidential Award editions and those that made submissions on both occasions. The goal was to investigate the scope and diffusion of community service-learning projects carried out by schools throughout the country, and advance towards an "external" description profiling the various types of educational institutions that were developing service projects in Argentina.

In C1, the unit of analysis was the school, and the data to be analyzed were:

- Province location;[9]
- Administration (state/private);

- Educational level (kindergarten, primary, secondary);
- Age of students; and
- Location (urban; urban-marginal; rural).

The second construct (C2) was made up of the 2,898 community service-learning projects presented to the 2001 edition[10] of the Presidential Award for service-learning and that were available for analysis. In this case, the units of analyses were the projects, not the schools as in Construct 1. The data to be analyzed included:

- Type of student participation (voluntary/mandatory);
- Alliances with social organizations; and
- Financial resources.

Regarding the service-learning profile, data to be analyzed were: learning goals, curricular links, evaluation and reflection, and student participation. Regarding the service profile, data allowed analysis of service goals, beneficiaries, diagnosis prior to the service, service evaluation, and types of activities carried out by the students

Design of Data Collection Tools

As a first step, we built the research matrices system. In the process, we also defined the combination of variables necessary to complete these matrices and thus test the hypothesis. Among the various sets of matrices built, some were aimed at analyzing specifically service-learning projects; that is, those projects meeting the following conditions:

a. The students must be involved in their realization;
b. The projects must have service as an objective;
c. They must have learning as an objective; and
d. They must be linked with at least one subject's curriculum (Furco & Billig, 2002; Tapia, 2000).

In agreement with the matrices constructed, taking into account the methodological decisions taken, and after lengthy examination of the information contained in the award applications and the Ministry of Education (EyC) database,[11] tools were developed, which led to the design and implementation of a detailed, workable database.

Methodological Questions Related to the Design of Data Collection Tools

One of the first problems encountered in compiling the CLAYSS database was the multitude of thematic descriptors: 461 different descriptors were identified in the practitioners' descriptions and duplicated in the original EyC databases.

For example, a project aimed at spreading the practice of vermiculture among rural producers could be classified, depending on the author, as "worm farming," "worm producer," or "vermiculture"; the original database would consider them as three different projects.[12]

The excessive number of descriptors and the weak foundation upon which they were determined made it necessary to single out three different concepts, which were found mixed into the descriptors offered by sources:

1. The theme, as the main subject, the central point that approached the project by defining its main issues.
2. The activity, as the action carried out by the students while performing the service.
3. The recipient, as the direct beneficiary of the service projects.

Themes and Subthemes

The Thematic Category was defined as a function of the relationship established within the project between the service objectives and issues.

The formula "objectives + issues" was used, for example, to establish the project theme of an information campaign on a health issue (e.g., a prevention campaign against *Mal de Chagas* disease.[13] If the application form included in the box "issues to address" and "project goals," statements regarding the local need for information, the theme would be C. Information and Communication. If instead, the form mentioned as the project goal "prevention of disease through house fumigation," the theme would be E. Health.

Using these criteria, nine thematic categories were identified, each of which included a group of sub-themes. The subtheme is a subset of the central theme built in order to describe the theme itself or to describe the activity (e.g., computer science or technology as a subset of education) or of a specific activity (e.g., tutoring, also as a subset of education). In general, the subtheme is considered a function of the "objective + activity" relationship, as seen in the Figure 4.1 (see the complete set of themes and subthemes in Exhibit 4.1).[14]

Students Participating in the Projects

The form requested the specification, by course, of the number of students participating in each service project. Because of the fragmentation of the Argentine educational system during the period under study,[15] age was a more accurate variable of analysis than grades to categorize these students in order to establish a unified record for all jurisdictions. Categories were established as follows:

- Children (5 to 11 years old);
- Adolescents (12 to 17 years old);
- Young adults (18 to 29 years old); and
- Adults (30 years old and over).

It was necessary to include these two last categories to consider primary and secondary adult schools working on service projects.

Community Service and Service-Learning

One of the main questions to consider was the distinction between non-systematic service projects or community service and the service-learning projects as defined in this investigation (see Exhibit 4.1).

In the forms submitted to the Presidential Award, teachers were not asked to define their own practice as community service or service-learning,[16] but they were asked other information that could be used to distinguish between service-learning initiatives and types of service projects.

Using that information, it was possible to identify the project features that are accepted characteristics of service-learning in most definitions (Conrad & Hedin, 1991; Corporation for National Service, 1994; Furco & Billig, 2002; Tapia, 2000): service activities must be carried out by students, and the project must have learning goals and service goals and must be linked to curriculum.

A progressively exclusive formula was designed to identify the field of projects of service-learning in the strict sense. First of all, the formula excluded the projects in which students were not performing the service actions (i.e., service was performed by teachers or parents). From the remaining projects, those with no service activities performed by students (applications including only learning activities) were excluded.

Projects with student participation and service activities including at least one curricular connection were considered "service-learning." The results showed that 1,663 projects were considered to be service-learning, making up 57% of Construct 2.

Exhibit 4.1. Themes and Subthemes

A. Education	B. Civic and Community Participation	C. Information and Communication	D. Environment	E. Health	F. Sociocultural Animation–Historical and Cultural Heritage–Tourism	G. Productive Service Projects	H. Attention to Socioeconomic Issues (Poverty)	Others
A.1. Alphabetization	B.1. Public commitment and civic participation	C.1. Public interest information campaigns	D.1. Environmental education	E.1. Health education prevention and the treatment of illnesses and addictions	F.1 Promotion and preservation of the historical and cultural heritage	G.1. Community orchards and farming	H.1. Nutrition	
A.2. Tutoring	B.2. Ethic and civic formation/development and education in values	C.2. Communication in remote areas	D.2. Urban environment	E.2. Organ and blood donation	F.2 Community support for sports activities, recreation and the positive use of free time	G.2. Technological production	H.2. Clothing	
A.3. Promoting reading	B.3. Promoting cooperativism	C.3 Communication at the service of NGOs/social marketing	D.3. Prevention and rational use of natural resources	E.3. Eating disorders	F.3 Artistic and cultural activities at the service of the community	G.3. Craft production	H.3. Housing	
A.4. Education in computer science and technology	B.4. Bartering clubs				F.4 Field trips and postgraduation excursions with service aims		H.4. Integrating diversity	
A.5. Training					F.5 Designing of regional tours		H.5. Campaigns	

RESULTS OF THE INVESTIGATION

Following is a summary of the main findings.

Construct 1: Solidarity Schools

Construct 1 included 4,391 educational institutions, which accounted for almost 11% of all schools in the country. This segment of the system included schools from all jurisdictions, both state and privately run, urban and rural, with thousands of students or with very few, and of all levels and orientations.

Geographic Distribution

All provinces and the capital district participated in the Presidential Award with no less than 20 institutions each. As population and the number of schools greatly differ from one province to another, it was important to establish the percentage of Solidarity Schools over the total number of schools in each jurisdiction. Based on the total number of educational institutions in each province,[17] the percentage of Solidarity Schools in relation to the total of educational institutions in each province (see Figure 4.1) was established.

Development indexes[18] did not seem to have any bearing on the number of Solidarity Schools per jurisdiction: Provinces with very different poverty levels presented similar levels of Solidarity Schools participation. In a first analysis, political reasons and communication systems inside the local educational level seemed to be the most influential variables, but the question is still open to further investigation.

Solidarity Schools by Education Level
Schools from all educational levels made applications for the Presidential Award, submitting no less than 1,600 projects each. The level with the highest representation in absolute terms was secondary (13 to18 years old). Considering the percentage of Solidarity Schools of the total for the same level, participation was around the national average of 10%, except for the secondary level, in which 13% of schools participated as shown in Figure 4.2.

Solidarity Schools by Area
About 68% of all Solidarity Schools were located in urban areas and almost 25% were in rural areas. If we consider that rural schools represent 32% of all schools in the country,[19] the percentage of rural Solidarity

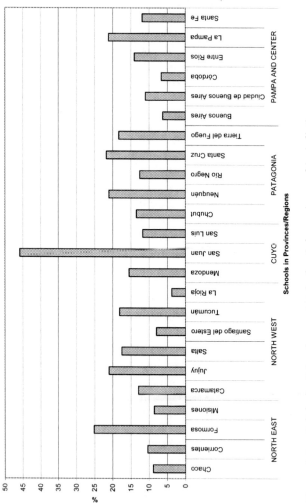

Figure 4.1.   Solidarity Schools over total schools by region and jurisdiction.

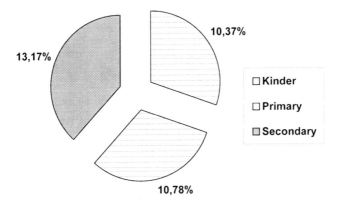

Figure 4.2. Solidarity Schools by educational level.

Schools compared to urban ones is slightly below the proportion between urban and rural schools in the whole system.

Student Enrollment in Solidarity Schools

Almost half the Solidarity Schools had between 100 and 400 students enrolled; slightly more than one fourth of the schools had a student population of about 401 and 1,000. Nineteen percent of the schools with 100 or less students and about 8% of the very large ones (with more than 1,000 students) represent slightly less than one fourth of Solidarity Schools.

Solidarity Schools by Type of Administration

Of the schools under study, almost 81% were public schools run by the provinces, and almost 20% were public schools with private administration. Considering that 78% of the schools in the whole educational system are state run (Ministerio de Educación data, 2001), the percentage of state and privately run Solidarity Schools seem to reproduce almost exactly the national distribution between both sectors. The proportion of Solidarity Schools under private or state management is very similar with the Solidarity Schools under study representing a little more than 10% of all state run schools and 9% of all privately run schools as shown in Figure 4.3.

Construct 2: "Community Service-Learning" Projects

Recipients of the Projects

As shown in Figure 4.4, more than half of the projects had as recipient the general community. The percentages for other recipients—children, adolescents, elderly, youth, and adults—are shown as well.

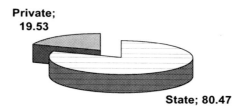

Figure 4.3.   Solidarity Schools by type of administration (in percentage total).

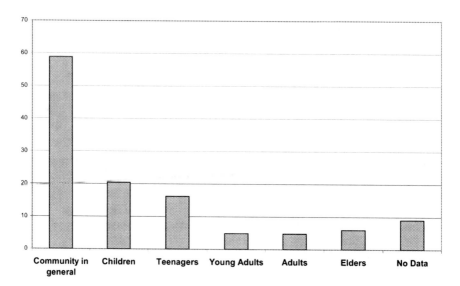

Figure 4.4.   Community service-learning projects by recipients: Percentage of national total.

The majority of the projects serve in the same area as the school. This held true in state schools as well as private ones. However, the latter have a higher percentage of service in areas outside their own region or district: more than a quarter of the projects in private schools serve an area outside the school's location. This could be due to affluent private schools preferring to work in other communities of a less favorable social standing, frequently in very remote places. Projects by recipient localization are shown in Figure 4.5.

Themes of the Community Service-Learning Projects

Projects themes most often chosen (17.8%) were productive service, such as community orchards, micro business, technical and craft productions organized for the benefit of an NGO or a needed population, and

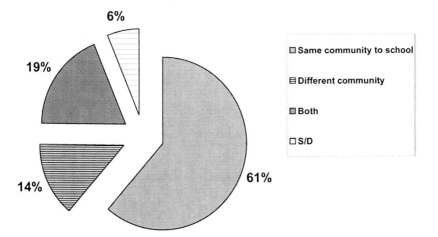

Figure 4.5.   Projects by recipient localization.

others; attention to socioeconomic problems, such as projects dealing with hunger, homelessness, and others (17%); education (14.8%); and civic and community participation projects (11%), including advocacy projects and other forms of civic participation.

Fields and Curricular Disciplines Involved

Language and humanities were the most chosen disciplines in community service-learning projects (60%). The contents of natural sciences (55.3%) and social sciences (52%) seemed to also be among the most frequently linked with the service-learning projects, while exact sciences and technology were linked to projects in about 40% of cases.

Type of Student Participation

Student participation was voluntary in 60% of all projects studied. A little more than 11% of student participation was mandatory, and almost 17% of them combined some mandatory activities with voluntary participation;12% of the projects did not include information on this subject.

Resources Used in Community Service-Learning Projects

The resource used in about 90% (2,631) of community service-learning projects was the voluntary participation of teachers and students, as seen in Exhibit 4.2. These results are consistent with the high percentage of voluntary type of student participation, as mentioned above. They also show the degree of dedication of thousands of Argentine teachers, who not only donate their time freely to accompany the students in activities that are mostly done in extracurricular time, but also contribute fre-

**Exhibit 4.2.   Funding and Resources Most Frequently Used
(in percentage over total projects)**

Funding and Resources	Percentage Over Total Projects
Volunteer work by teachers and students	90.79%
Institutional hours	62.42%
Parents' Associations	45.34%
Businesses or private companies	42.37%
Communitarian organizations	42.82%
Government organizations	39.61%
Other sources	16.22%

Note: Multiple responses possible.

quently out of their meager salaries to finance costs involved in service projects.

Date of Commencement of the Projects

According to the available data, the oldest community service-learning initiative applying to the Presidential Award dated back to 1933, which was rather surprising. What was not surprising is that only 10 of the 457 projects providing data began before democracy was regained in December 1983.[20] Of all the projects providing data, 98% began during the democratic period, and 76% began after the beginning of the Federal service-learning program "Escuela y Comunidad" in 1997, during the period of national socioeconomic crisis.

Duration of the Community Service-Learning Projects

Of all the forms analyzed in Construct 2 (2,898), we found data referring to the initiative's duration in 2,609 forms. Of this total, more than half indicated that they lasted between 1 month and 1 year. Project duration ranged from 1 month to 366 months. The latter corresponded to a school developing service-learning initiatives for more than 30 years. However, to interpret this information correctly it was necessary to keep in mind that the duration indicated might refer to one continuous project or a succession of different community service-learning projects with the same or different recipients.

According to the data analyzed, the average duration of community service-learning projects is approximately 1 year and 4 months. Data suggest that service projects were not planned as small projects lasting only a few weeks, but as a long-term activity. In almost 18% of all projects analyzed, the schools maintained their commitment to the community for more than 2 years; in 34 cases, they sustained it for 8 or more years.

Projects' average duration also suggests that a high proportion of the students involved are capable of maintaining their community service efforts for at least one academic year.

In order to express the duration of projects in terms that are more comparable to other studies carried out internationally, a very conservative estimation was calculated.[21] If students dedicate a minimum of 4 hours a month to work for the community service-learning project, then the average duration of the community service-learning projects analyzed would be approximately 63 hours, more than three times the 20 hours average duration of service-learning projects in the United States (Furco, 2004).

Links With Community Organizations

Among the most relevant information to come from the investigation is the finding that almost 70% of registered projects took place with some kind of connection or alliance with one or more civic organizations or social institutions (see Figure 4.6). About 18% of analyzed projects were carried out in association with four or more organizations. These figures are consistent with the high percentage of projects taking place with material support from civic organizations.

Service-Learning Projects: Proportion Over Total and Main Features

Following the methodology already described above, it was possible to differentiate service-learning projects (student participation + service + curriculum links) from community service (student participation + service). According to these criteria, slightly more than 57% of total

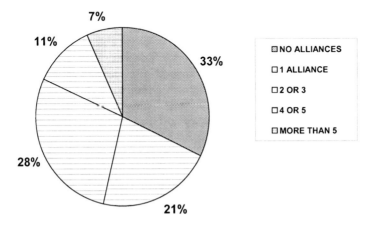

Figure 4.6.   Community service-learning projects by links with organizations (percentage of total projects).

projects presented to the Presidential Award in 2001 may be defined as service-learning projects.

Service-learning is being practiced throughout the country, with percentages in most of the provinces between 40% and 70%. It also cuts across all themes with more than half the projects in each theme engaging in service-learning projects. No significant differences were noticed between service-learning projects and community service projects concerning the most frequent themes, the main recipients (the general community), and the main curricular link with language and humanities.

Regarding the number of links established with organizations and institutions, it is important to underline that the proportion of service-learning projects linked with one or no more than four organizations (87.4%) is 20% higher than the average for community service-learning projects that have links with the same number of organizations and institutions (68%). This could indicate that service-learning projects give rise to projects with more complex planning, not only from the pedagogical point of view but also concerning links with the community.

There was a significant degree of participation of secondary school students in service-learning projects, as seen in Figure 4.7. Of the projects studied, more than 72% corresponded to this level, almost 10% more than the degree of participation of this same level in the overall number of community service-learning projects (66%).

Analyzed sources also offered important information about student participation in different stages of service-learning projects. In about 84% of analyzed service-learning projects, mention is made of diagnosis activities carried out. In a little more than 91% of these cases, there was student involvement; in 53% of cases, there was involvement of the organizations or institutions connected with the project. These high percentages reveal a value added to service-learning projects. On the one hand, the students are offered the opportunity to learn how to go about making diagnosis and applying their knowledge to develop the tools needed; on the other hand, there is a clear intention to attend to demands that are real and effectively felt by the community to be served, listening to the beneficiaries and potential partners from the initial stages of the project.

Students participated in planning service-learning projects in a little more than 77% of the cases. If considered in the total participation of students throughout the project, this shows a high degree of child and youth involvement. The educational value of this participation can also be applied in this field, as it helps develop planning skills.

The same is not true for the evaluation stage, where student participation percentage dropped sharply—only in 33% of service-learning projects is there explicit reference to student participation in the evaluation of the project. This is probably due to a deeply-rooted evaluative cul-

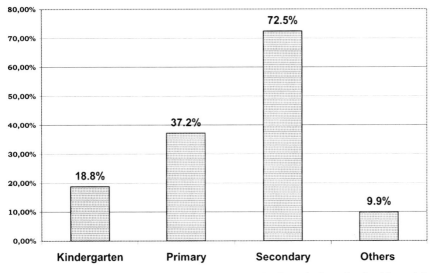

Note: "Others" includes adult schools, work training schools, and other schools with special regimes, such as special education schools and workshops.

Figure 4.7.   Service-learning projects by educational level.

ture among teachers and administrators, which excludes self-evaluation almost absolutely.

CONCLUSIONS AND PERSPECTIVES FOR INVESTIGATION

This research tried to give a first picture—surely incomplete, but already defined and based on quantitative and documented data—of Argentina Solidarity Schools and of their community service-learning projects.

As we have pointed out in this chapter, Solidarity Schools encompass such a wide range of schools of any type that it is not possible to identify a unique, specific profile for Solidarity Schools, as was the original purpose of the research. Conclusion seems to be that in Argentina every kind of school is doing community service-learning: public and private, urban and rural, with thousands of students or with a few, in provinces with high levels of poverty and in the richest districts.

Data show that previous hypotheses,[22] such as "service-learning is something religious schools do" or "Solidarity Schools are mostly rural," are hard to sustain based on quantitative data. A deeper exploration of qualitative aspects, such as the profile of directors and teachers, institutional openness to innovations, or the simultaneous presence of other teaching innovations and the like, could perhaps contribute to identifying common profiles among Solidarity Schools.

Eloquent about the solidarity school profile is the fact that almost 70% of service projects under study developed alliances with community organizations or local public institutions. The image that emerges from the research is that Solidarity Schools are capable of establishing alliances and are part of complex communitarian networks. These findings reveal a sharp change of paradigm in regard to the traditional model of the Argentina school, usually isolated from reality, and also differs from the model of school community-center that proliferated during the years of the socio-economic crisis.[23]

Regarding community service-learning projects, research offered the more detailed picture available at that point in Argentina. According to analyzed data, projects are carried out by children and adolescents, with a slight majority of children, and the most attended groups are children and adolescents. The overwhelming majority of the projects take place in the same community where the school belongs. In other words, and considering that 60% of Argentine children and adolescents were in a situation of poverty during the period under study, it may be stated that most of the projects studied were performed by poor students who contributed from their own poverty to serve other poor children and adolescents, and their own community.

The fact that 60% of projects are carried out with the voluntary participation of the students and are financed by teachers and students themselves, with help from school funds and/or resources provided by community organizations, shows the kind of solidarity commitment present in Argentina culture and also indicates projects' local sustainability without government funding.[24]

More than half of the projects presented to the Presidential Award can be considered as service-learning projects. The fact that secondary schools were doing more service-learning projects than primary schools during the period under study may have to do with the fact that during 1997-2000, most service-learning teacher training was offered to secondary teachers.

Analyzed data present several indications about the degree of institutionalization of community service-learning projects: duration of the projects, number of alliances built with organizations, and number of curricular links, suggesting a large number of projects have gone beyond the stage of individual initiative of a teacher or particular group of students to reach an institutional level.

This study may contribute to the development of future investigations on service-learning and community service-learning projects, especially in Argentina and Latin American countries where research on service-learning is still at the exploratory level. Some of the contributions could be linked to the methodological decisions used during the design of this study, which can easily be replicated. In fact, this study was replicated in 2005 by the Federal Service-Learning Program, "*Educación Solidaria,*" to categorize all projects presented to the Presidential Award in the 2003, 2004 and 2005 editions.

During the Argentine shocking financial crisis of 2001-2002, the *Wall Street Journal* published an article under the headline "People's ingenuity sustains Argentina" (Moffett, 2002), which started by talking about the activities of a solidarity school in Greater Buenos Aires. In effect, during some of the hardest years we have lived through as a country, the Solidarity Schools contributed to keep Argentina going. We hope that this investigation may help to acknowledge, disseminate, and appreciate that contribution, as well as the daily effort that children, youth, and educators continue to make in thousands of Solidarity Schools throughout Argentina.

NOTES

1. For lack of a more accurate term in English, "*Escuelas solidarias*" will be translated hereafter as "Solidarity Schools." The term *solidaridad (adj. solidario/a)* in Spanish means "working together for a common cause, helping others in an organized and effective way, rising up as a group or nation to defend one's rights, facing natural disasters or economic crisis, and doing it hand-in-hand with others" (Tapia, 2003).

2. Research was possible thanks to Global Service Institute, Center for Social Development, George Warren Brown School of Social Work, Washington University, St. Louis, Missouri, Small Grants Research Program. For a full version of the research report, see http://gwbweb.wustl.edu/csd/service/SRGP_CLAYSS.htm

3. The political decision was not to fund just good ideas, but ongoing, sustainable, quality service-learning projects.

4. Since 2003, there are two different awards, one for schools and the other for higher education, in alternate years.

5. The presentation form was modified in 2001 according to the experience acquired by the program's technical team the previous year. The 2003-2005 forms took into account CLAYSS research to include new corrections.

6. Once evaluated for the award, files went to EyC archive, now part of the general archive of the new Federal Service-Learning Program (*Educación Solidaria*).

7. It is also true that even if the Ministry of Education did not have the operational capacity to verify reliability in 100% of the cases, observations gathered from local supervision, provincial officials, and Federal officers, seem to indicate that the information submitted by the schools tends to be fairly accurate.

8. More on the research methodology is available at http://gwbweb.wustl.edu/csd/service/SRGP_CLAYSS.htm

9. Argentina is a Federal country with 24 provinces and a capital district, Buenos Aires City.

10. Research focused in the projects presented in 2001, because the 2001 form presented richer and more reliable data about the projects than the 2000 one.

11. *Programa Nacional Escuela y Comunidad* (EyC) designed two different databases to compile some of the data from the applications. Much of the information in the forms was not entered, and in some cases information entered into the EyC database was not accurate. In an attempt to overcome these limitations, researchers analyzed and revised the original files and databases, and compiled a new database.

12. The multiplication of descriptors referencing the same types of projects was particularly serious in the case of those projects that could be classified from different points of view. For example, projects involving students and their parents learning how to make sweets and homemade preserves from produce grown in the school or home garden to enhance the family income and nutrition, could be classified using 24 different descriptors, including "nutrition," "vocational training," and "workshop for parents."

13. Chronic illness, epidemic in Argentina rural areas, transmitted by a poisonous insect called "*vinchuca.*"

14. In order to classify the projects in agreement with the methodological decisions, a grid was designed. One grid was filled out for each one of the 2,898 forms of the 2001 edition, by a team of 10 research assistants selected by their experience in service-learning projects assessment. A training seminar was organized to examine and clarify the categories selected, in order to establish common criteria among assistants, but still it is necessary to acknowledge the possibility of different interpretation of entries given the number of individuals involved.

15. After the educational reform in the 1990s, some provinces implemented the new structure of 9 years of mandatory "EGB" (general basic education) and 3 of nonmandatory "Polimodal" (high school). Other provinces chose to remain with the traditional structure of 7 years of primary and 5 of secondary school, and others established their own special structure. In 2000-2001, a 15-year-old student could be in ninth grade of EGB in Buenos Aires province, in the third year of secondary school in Neuquén, and in the fourth year of CBU in Córdoba.

16. In some surveys (Skinner & Chapman, 1999), principals and teachers were asked to define if they were engaging in "community service" or "service-learning." As Billig (2004) pointed out, the results were often contradictory and confusing, given that the same terminology used in different schools could describe opposite kinds of projects.

17. According to year 2000 statistics, Argentina Ministry of Education (www.me.gov.ar/diniece).

18. Data 2000 in: *Aportes para el desarrollo humano de la Argentina /2002. Desigualdad y Pobreza.* [Contributions to Human Development in Argentina/ 2002] in www.desarrollohumano.org.ar

19. Statistics 2002, Ministerio de Educación, República Argentina.

20. Since 1930, Argentina suffered a chronic political instability between military regimes and fragile civilian governments. In 1983, after the Malvinas War defeat, military called to free elections. President Alfonsín took office in December 1983, beginning a still uninterrupted succession of democratic governments.

21. Estimation is based on direct observation of community service-learning projects in different Provinces during 2000-2001.

22. In the late 1990s, when service-learning theory was just starting to be known in Argentina, it was frequently heard the hypothesis that Solidarity Schools were basically private, religious schools, and that service-learning activities could thrive more easily in schools with few students, in rural settlements or small urban centers.

23. Schools trying to solve by themselves the numerous and complex problems affecting students and their families (Tapia, 2000, pp. 141-150)

24. Around 10% of the projects submitted to the Presidential Award 2000-2001 received Federal funding.

REFERENCES

Billig, S. (2004). *Heads, hearts, and hands: The research on K-12 service-learning*. In J. Kielsmeier, M. Neal, & M. McKinnon (Eds.), *Growing to greatness (G2G): The state of service-learning project* (pp. 12–25). St. Paul, MN: National Youth Leadership Council.

Cairn, R. W., & Kielsmeier, J. (1995). *Growing hope: A sourcebook on integrating youth service into the school curriculum* (3rd ed.). St. Paul, MN: National Youth Leadership Council.

Conrad, D., & Hedin, D. (1991, June). School-based community service: What we know from research and theory. *Phi Delta Kappan, 72*(10), 743–749.

Corporation for National Service. (1994). *Principles for high quality national service programs*. Washington DC: Author.

Furco, A. (2004, October 8). Impacto del aprendizaje-servicio: Hacia una agenda de investigación [Service-learning impact: State of the art: Meeting the challenges of service-learning research]. *Jornada de Investigadores*.

Furco, A., & Billig, S. H. (Eds.). (2002). *Advances in service-learning research: Vol. 1. Service-learning: The essence of the pedagogy*. Greenwich, CT: Information Age.

Kendall, J. (Ed.). (1990). *Combining service and learning A resource book for community and public service* (Vols. I-II). Raleigh, NC: National Society for Internships and Experiential Education.

Moffett, M. (2002, December 19). People's ingenuity sustains Argentina. *Wall Street Journal*.

Programa Nacional Educación Solidaria. (2004). *Unidad de Programas Especiales. Ministerio de Educación, Ciencia y Tecnología. Aprendizaje y servicio solidario. Actas del 5to. y 6to.* Seminario Internacional "Aprendizaje y servicio solidario," República Argentina.

Skinner, R., & Chapman, C. (1999, September). *Service-learning and community service in K-12 public schools*. (NCES Statistical Brief 1999–043). Washington, DC:

U.S. Department of Education, Office of Educational Research and Improvement.

Tapia, M. N. (2000). *La Solidaridad como Pedagogía* [Solidarity as pedagogy]. Buenos Aires, Argentina: Ciudad Nueva.

Tapia, M. N. (2003). "Service" and "solidarity" in South American Spanish: In H. Perold, S. Stroud, & M. Sherraden (Eds.), *Service enquiry: Service in the 21st century* (1st ed., pp. 139–148). Johannesburg: Global Service Institute and Volunteer and Service Enquiry Southern Africa. Retrieved May 9, 2006, from http://www.service-enquiry.org.za/downloads/service_enquiry1 .pdf

Tapia M. N., & Mallea, M. M. (2003). *Service-learning in Argentina*. In H. Perold, S. Stroud, & M. Sherraden (Eds.), *Service enquiry: Service in the 21st century* (1st ed., pp. 203–215.). Johannesburg: Global Service Institute and Volunteer and Service Enquiry Southern Africa. Retrieved May 9, 2006, from http://www .service-enquiry.org.za/ downloads/service_enquiry1.pdf

CHAPTER 5

CRITICAL THINKING IN A HIGHER EDUCATION SERVICE-LEARNING PROGRAM

Diana Pacheco Pinzón and Frida Díaz Barriga Arceo

ABSTRACT

The presence of the critical thinking process in a service-learning program was researched with a qualitative study. Service-learning in higher education is presented as an experiential learning program that promotes socially responsible education committed to improving quality of life for everybody, everywhere. Four students were monitored during a 1-semester service-learning experience and the Critical Thinking Case (Pacheco, 2005) was applied to the entire student population of the School of Psychology running the service-learning program. Results indicate the presence of the critical thinking process in the reflection stage of the service-learning experience (i.e., reflection journals and group reflection) and via the Critical Thinking Case. Overall student performances on the Critical Thinking Case differed by the semester the students were in, with more advanced students having higher critical thinking levels on the case. The results may impact service-learning programs, their reflective processes and also impact

Advancing Knowledge in Service-Learning: Research to Transform the Field, 89–110

higher education institutions by highlighting the importance of service and critical thinking as primary objectives in higher education. Being able to prove the presence of critical thinking in the reflection processes of the service-learning program facilitates experience and instrument design (e.g., Critical Thinking Case) that will allow firm advances in the research and in design of the overall education experience.

LITERATURE REVIEW

The UNESCO (1998) report stated that higher education has the mission of contributing to sustainable development and the improvement of society as a whole. Higher education should play a significant role in social progress and in promoting change and progress in quality of life (Berry & Chisholm, 1999; Díaz Barriga & Saad, 1996; Marín, 1993; Schön, 1983; UNESCO, 1998); what Dewey calls "humane conditions" (Hatcher, 1997). In México, where this investigation took place, the higher education system tries to provide students with opportunities to develop a strong sense of commitment to others, and become more experienced at facing the complex social scenarios where real problems occur, with the aim at building a better society with a sense of quality, pertinence, equity, and the values of peace, freedom, democracy, justice, human rights, and so on (Asociación Nacional de Universidades e Instituciones de Educación Superior, 2000).

Service-learning is an educational approach to relevant community service experiences where social issues are integrated with academic course learning (Eyler & Giles, 1999; Howard, 1993), and for some "the ultimate goal for service-learning is social change, or at the very least educating students who will be agents of social change" (Eyler & Giles, 1999, p. 131).

Different authors have defined service-learning in different ways, but all agree that service-learning programs are a powerful tool to address important social issues that communities in general face today (Berry & Chisholm, 1999; Howard, 1993; Jacoby & Associates, 1996; Kendall, 1990; Sigmon, 1990; Silcox, 1993; Stanton, 1990).

Bringle and Hatcher (1995) defined service-learning as a course-based educational experience in which students "(a) participate in an organized service activity that meets identified community needs and (b) reflect on the service activity in such a way as to gain further understanding of course content, a broader appreciation of the discipline and an enhanced sense of civic responsibility" (p. 112).

To promote learning, service-learning programs must meet certain conditions:

- A high-level of integration of service experience and classroom activities;
- Quality of reflection (kind, frequency, and time);
- Relevance (students and community have a sense of service relevance for everyone);
- Direct relations with community members; and
- A manageable challenge to integrate service and academia through reflection (Eyler & Giles, 1997, 1999; Pacheco, 2003).

Reflection is a substantial element of service-learning pedagogy. Even educative experiences by themselves do not lead to the meaning-making process; it is reflection that leads to it (Bringle, 2003; Eyler, Giles & Schmiede, 1996). Reflection is a useful tool to transform raw experiences into "meaning-filled theory that is grounded in experience, informed by existing theory, and serves the larger purpose of the moral growth of the individual and society" (Rodgers, 2002, p. 863). After reading Dewey's work, Rodgers (2002) presented four criteria he felt characterized Dewey's concept of reflection: "reflection is a meaning-making process ... reflection is a systematic, rigorous, disciplined way of thinking ... reflection needs to happen in community ... reflection requires attitudes that value the personal and intellectual growth of oneself and of others" (p. 845).

Service-learning experiences require engagement and a commitment to all kinds of learning and abilities, including critical thinking (Duffy & Bringle, 1998; Eyler & Giles, 1999; Eyler, Giles, & Braxton, 1997; Silcox, 1993). "The ability to function in the face of uncertainty requires critical thinking abilities...and there is a reason to think that the challenges and support provided in some service-learning programs may facilitate this development" (Eyler, 2000, pp. 12-13). A number of authors (Brandenberger, 1998; Eyler et al., 1996; Hatcher & Bringle, 1997; Silcox, 1993) mentioned that service-learning experiences can enhance critical thinking skills.

It is necessary to develop new ways to look at processes, such as critical thinking within the service-learning experiences. In this research, the case study was used to research critical thinking. The case was developed based on Paul's (1994), and Paul and Elder's (2002) critical thinking proposal. Critical thinking is the ability to review thinking systems (one's own, and those of others) through the critical thinking elements (problems, information, assumptions, points of view, consequences, concepts, interpretations), to question their sociocentric and egocentric characteristics, and open them to different frames of reference with a fair-minded intellectual approach (Paul, 1994; Paul & Elder, 2002).

Students' belief systems are highly developed, "buttressed by deep-seated uncritical, egocentric, and sociocentric habits of thought by which they interpret and process their experience, whether academic or not, and place them into some larger perspective" (Paul, 1994, p. 184). Belief systems have a tendency to be egocentric because people generally possess little insight with which to discover and become conscious of the nature of their emotions and thinking. This leads them to see everything in relationship to themselves and includes the difficulty to critically see and think about their own desires, values, and beliefs, making them self-deceptive. This prevents people from realizing that they can be wrong not only in what they think but also in the way they think. Sociocentrism refers to the group a person belongs to. People think sociocentrically when they accept as correct whatever ways of acting and believing are promoted by the social groups they belong to. When this happens within a group, it can do great harm to other groups that do not think alike (Paul & Elder, 2002). In Morin's (1999) words, "egocentrism, ethnocentrism, sociocentrism—different levels of a common propensity to place oneself at the center of the world and consider everything that is distant or foreign as secondary, insignificant, or hostile" (p. 50).

Within the service-learning tradition, Eyler et al. (1996) defined critical reflection as a "process specifically structured to help examine the frameworks that we use to interpret experience ... pushes us to step outside of the old and familiar and to reframe our questions and our conclusions in innovative and more effective terms" (p. 13). Their definition of critical reflection has some commonalities with the critical thinking definition of Paul and Elder. One important shared characteristic is their emphasis on the idea of examining our own frames of reference, which allows us to open ourselves up to other frames of reference.

Research originating in service-learning traditions indicates that "service-learning participation has an impact on ... complexity of understanding ... [and] critical thinking" (Eyler, Giles, Stenson, & Gray, 2001, p. 4). On the other hand, in their review of service-learning research over the past decade, Steinke and Buresh (2002) found that general critical thinking measures have not produced significant gains when compared with nonservice situations, although they also reported that a good quality service-learning experience produced better critical thinking skills when the research used course-related measures. It is not known of other research done in México in the context of service-learning programs, save for the work of Isla (2003) and Pacheco (2003), both done at the Marist University where the present study was done.

The primary intent in the study illustrated in this chapter is to describe the critical thinking process itself within the service-learning experience. Describing whether the process occurs in this case and how it is displayed will help to better understand the process itself and how it fits into the service-learning program.

RESEARCH QUESTIONS

1. Do students get involved in the critical thinking process of the reflection-on-action portion of a service-learning experience in an undergraduate psychology degree program? If so, how is students' critical thinking displayed during this portion of the experience?

2. How is students' critical thinking, as a specific domain process, displayed within the service-learning program of an undergraduate psychology degree program?

METHODS

Type of Study

This study is a descriptive qualitative case study (Merriam, 1988; Yin, 1994) that focuses on knowing *how* the phenomenon is displayed in natural setting. It studies the phenomenon as complex processes, not simply as outcomes, and it gives an in-depth look (Denman & Haro, 2000; Denzin & Lincoln, 2000). The case limits are the students enrolled in the School of Psychology of the Mérida Marist University, in Yucatán, México.

For question one, this research, which used a case study approach, is focused on in-depth, intensive study of the critical thinking process as part of the reflective stage in the service-learning experience context. Four students were included: two each from the fourth and sixth semesters involving service-learning program fieldwork. Selection of the four students was purposive: only those enrolled in the program of psychology, with participation in the service-learning program, working in the same setting and team, and interested in participating in the research were included (Stake, 1998; Yin, 1994).

For question two, this research gathered information in two scopes: from four students (cases) of the psychology program and from the total population of the School of Psychology. Some descriptive statistics are used to generate a general characterization of the results in the population.

Service-Learning Program in Context

The research was conducted at the Mérida Marist University, in Yucatán, México, a private university founded in 1996. The Marist University philosophy is to work for and with needy sectors of society as part of its social responsibility as an educational institution. Its motto is "Being for service."

The service-learning program is a curricular experience for all psychology undergraduate students. During the first three semesters, students visit institutions, such as schools, day care facilities, hospitals, and so on, to develop observational skills and be exposed to the different scenarios where they may work later as part of the service-learning program. At the end of the third semester, they take a workshop aimed at using service-learning principles to evaluate the fieldwork they have done in the previous three semesters. In the fourth semester, they start a four-semester experience within the service-learning program in which they are assigned to a particular scenario for the entire four-semester period.

Participants

The sixth semester students worked as part of a team and gave a six-session workshop on "sexuality, love, and loving relationships," in a government-run shelter for abused and neglected children. The fourth semester students worked as part of a team and gave an eight-session workshop about "self-diagnosis of basic human needs," in a suburban, low-income junior high school.

Instruments

For question one, there was one data source: the reflection process (journals and groups reflections).

To assist students in writing their journals and in developing the group reflections, they received a set of items based on the following schema as shown in Exhibit 5.1.

Some of the questions given to the students are found in Exhibit 5.2.

For question two, there was one data source: the Critical Thinking Case (Pacheco, 2005). developed specifically for this research. It is based on Paul's (1994), and Paul and Elder's (2002) critical thinking proposal and Morin's (1999) complex thinking concept. It consists of a two-page writ-

Exhibit 5.1.   Reflection Schemata

Smyth's (1992) Reflection Schema	Schema Used in the Study Illustrated in This Chapter
Describe	Description
Inform	Elaboration and focus (Suberck, Park, & Moyer, 1991)
Confront*	
Reconstruct	Reconstruction

*Confront is a stage that by its nature it is done within a group, it may be part of dialogue.

Exhibit 5.2.   Reflection Guidelines

What do I do? Describe some aspect or event from the session that you have participated in and using it how would you explain it in depth to understand its meaning and sense.

My answer? Describe your thoughts, actions, and feelings about this event.

How can I explain it? Clarify how you would explain the situation. Give an in-depth explanation. Try to include as much of your personal viewpoint (opinions, beliefs, and so on) as well as your viewpoint as a student (the possible theoretical explanation).

Remember that the most important thing is that you explain what happened, from your personal point of view. All answers are correct.

---

ten prompt in which students analyze a child abuse case. The case was developed thinking about "problems for which there is no single solution—only judgments and choices of alternatives. What to consider in arriving at those judgments, how to identify the alternatives and make the choices, is what the process of critical thinking is all about" (Budem, 1967, p. 3). The child abuse case was developed to include several elements that could be used to carry out the analysis. The educational, social, economical, and family frames of references were used based on the idea of looking through different frames of references, what Giroux calls the problematic nature of knowledge. Giroux (1994) stressed that when students learn to look at information through different frames of reference they "can *begin* to treat knowledge as problematic, and thus, as an object of inquiry" (italics in original, p. 201).

The Critical Thinking Case has eight open-ended questions that look for the following critical thinking elements:

- Problem;
- Information;
- Consequences;
- Contesting points of view;
- Assumptions; and
- Students' personal way of thinking about the case (Paul & Elder, 2002).

It was applied to College of Psychology student population; 125 completed cases were received. Exhibit 5.3 contains the critical thinking elements in the case and number of items. Exhibit 5.4 contains the Critical Thinking Case questionnaire.

Two experts answered the case and gave feedback. Based on critical thinking elements and the experts' answers and feedback, a rubric was

Exhibit 5.3.   Critical Thinking Elements in the Critical Thinking Case

Critical Thinking Element	Description Critical Thinking …	Question Number
Problem(s) or issue(s)	• Is defined by the *problems* it defines and solves.	1
Information	• Presupposes the collection and use of *information* in professional performance and problem solving.	2
Assumptions	• Proceeds from *assumptions* from which it logically proceeds (providing "boundaries" for the field).	3
View points	• Defines a frame of reference or *points of view* that provide practitioners with a logical map of use in considering the professional "moves" they will make.	4, 6, 7
Implications or consequences	• Generates *implications and consequences* that enable professionals to make predictions and test theories, lines of reasoning, and hypotheses.	5, 8

Exhibit 5.4.   Critical Thinking Case Questionnaire

1. What is the problem in the case-reading?
2. What evidence can you cite to demonstrate this is the problem?
3. What are the assumptions of the professionals in charge when they decide to separate the child from her family, place her in a shelter, and give her individual psychological therapy? Include any critique you may have about these assumptions.
4. The problem contained in the case-reading is seen differently by her mother and the authorities/professionals managing the case. The authorities removed the child from her family to protect her, but her mother thinks this will not solve the problem and wants her daughter back.
    Contrast the two positions by listing their respective successes and failures in handling the case, from your point of view.
5. What are the consequences of the child's separation from her family?
6. Are there complexities to the issue that are being left out given the way it is being managed? If so, please explain them.
7. Is there an alternative way to analyze the case and propose different actions?
    Yes ( ) No ( )
    Explain and support your argument
8. Comment on the possible consequences of the alternative actions you mentioned.

developed. "Rubrics are guides or scales where the progressive levels of domain are defined for the specific performance a person may attain" (Díaz Barriga, 2004, p. 54). They are ordinal scales that emphasize qualitative aspects of performance while allowing numeric scores.

The rubric used in the present study is a four-by-eight matrix with four qualitative performance levels in its columns in progressive order (exceptional, notable, acceptable, and insufficient) for each of the case items.

Exhibit 5.5.   Critical Thinking Case Rubric

Criterion	Levels			
	Exceptional	*Notable*	*Acceptable*	*Insufficient*
Problem (Item 1)	• Economic, social, gender and political factors are mentioned to give context and form to child's violence problem. • Violence in the system mentioned as are alternatives for solution (separate child and/or child is abused in shelter) • Problems contextualized within system of social injustice	• Social, economic factors mentioned, plus abuse and negligence. • Interrelationship established between the problems.	• Social and economic factors mentioned, as is abuse, though no relationship established between them. Poverty not recognized.	• Only abuse problem referred to or • Various problems mentioned, but not abuse.

The rows contain the anticipated critical thinking elements, and the cells are for the criteria developed for each item and each performance level. The exceptional level was based on the experts' answers. The rubric was discussed with the experts in terms of the case's child abuse elements. The expected answer progression in the rubric was based on the empowerment position for psychological work (Rapapport & Seidman, 2000). Exhibit 5.5 shows the Critical Thinking Case Rubric for Item 1 as an example.

To score the answers, each one is compared with the rubric. Each answer falls in one of the four critical thinking levels in each item, and depending on which level it falls, receives a numeric score (exceptional, 4; notable, 3; acceptable, 2; and insufficient, 1). A global score by subject is calculated.

RESULTS

Reflective Process

In the critical thinking analysis the emphasis is on how one thinks. The analysis is led by questions:

- Can one identify topics or issues?
- What to ask about them? How many angles, points of view, frames of reference can be considered in looking at the issue?

- Can one see that different angles respond to different egocentric and sociocentric beliefs?
- Can one see that one's own sociocentric and egocentric beliefs have ethical implications and consequences?
- Can one see that the language used comes from sociocentric and egocentric postures?
- Is one conscious of some different egocentric and sociocentric beliefs?

In considering these questions and others a critical thinker is able to realize that he or she, like everybody else, is able to think erroneously and narrowly, to think with strong biases (Morin, 1999; Paul, 1994; Paul & Elder, 2002).

In the following quote there is a set of reflections of student A (fourth semester) that exemplify how she dealt with alternative points of view and frames of reference while questioning her own point of view, and thus realized the limits of her own position. She was also able to discover some of her sociocentric beliefs about the deterministic influence of the context on people living in low-income communities and its consequences: that they prevent people from changing and having a better quality of life:

> Something that I have learned from the lives of people living in marginal zones is that they do not let children be children; they give them responsibilities early on and when they are in adolescence their personality is practically formed. (Reflective journal, 3rd session)

In the reflection process, student A was questioned, confronted, and her conception was *problematized* (Moral, 1995). In her 3rd session reflective journal, she wrote:

> this is an evaluation for me. How much do I think positively and not fall into what cannot be done?

> but now, how to change the personality of an adolescent who is already more or less like an adult?... How to change her?... parents already gave ... values. So, this is my question, yes we can, but how, because it is very difficult. (Group reflection, 5th session)

In the final session, student A mentioned that her ideas (assumptions and preconceptualizations about a deterministic and pessimist view of development and conceptualization of psychology) had been challenged and changed because of the confrontation of the service-learning experience. She also said she had been made aware that her conception of psychology had been incorrect. As Elder and Paul (2002) said, "an important part of critical thinking is the art of bringing what is subconscious in our thought to the level of conscious realization" (p. 34):

> If I repeat it you will know it is significant. I said it yesterday in Humanistics [course], I am a psychology student and the psychologist being a person that helps to bring change for better quality of life, it was ironic to say that it is difficult to change a person. At the moment they [the junior high students] began to open my eyes, this was my best learning and I cannot get stuck saying ... it is difficult, I have to be open to changes. (Group reflection, 8th session)

In the following quote, student B (sixth semester) reflected on his own conceptualizations and their implications. The consciousness and management of one's own conceptualizations so as to be open to different ways of seeing and living in the world can help people to recognize that those conceptualizations are powerful tools that affect decision making (Freire, 2001; Morin, 1999; Paul, 1994; Paul & Elder, 2002). If this does not occur, one's worldview (based on conceptualizations) is perceived as the only valid one. Elder and Paul (2001) said, "[o]ur lack of insight into the basic meanings in our native language is compounded by our lack of insight into the social indoctrination we have undergone.... We can use concepts from our native language to critique social indoctrination. Command of language makes social critique possible" (pp. 42-43):

> The boys and girls stay in this reality ... produced by each of our perceptions ... made from the concept of "abandonment," "intrafamily violence," "rape," "abuses" I could see the impact we have as a society and that we have had towards these "types of reality" that in one way or another are "uncomfortable" and call for deeper conscientization ... [sic]. (Sixth semester, reflective journal, 5th session)

Making one's conceptualizations explicit is the start of making one's belief system conscious. One step forward is to question the beliefs dictated by membership in a particular social group. When a critical thinker (Díaz Barriga, 2001) questions him or herself about concepts and ideologies, he/she is challenging his/her sociocentric beliefs, and is able to realize that particular conceptualizations have helped "societies to justify differential treatment and injustices within a society, nation, or culture" (Paul & Elder, 2002, p. 190). In the following quote, there is a reflection of student B (sixth semester) where he expressed how society treats people in different ways based on particular conceptualizations:

> sometimes it seems that socially we act like societies from past centuries that "grouped" all those who were "very different" and sent them to an institu-

tion far from the city ... or at least from the "good part". (Reflective journal, 2nd session)

The critical thinking process enables people to differentiate the ideological use of the words. This allows questioning previously held beliefs and assumptions and identified "contradictions and inconsistencies in personal and social life" (Paul, 1994, p. 185). The following quote exemplifies how student B identifies his own contradictions:

> Also, it is clear that sometimes it is a little difficult for me to separate the vision of "shelter children/adolescents" this makes me feel very badly [sic], ... I see myself as incongruent with myself, as if really this social prejudice weighs so much in me ... and in reality on many other occasions, in which I have worked or dealt with people in different types of scenarios, realities, and "pasts," I have been able to talk and interrelate, dialogue more freely than these preconceptions. (Reflective journal, 2nd session)

A critical thinker also understands that by protecting his/her belief system, keeping it untouched, he/she is being unfair to others, can actually harm them, and can lead to ethically wrong behavior. The critical thinking approach pays attention to belief claims, not just for their truth content but because they form part of a belief and action system that affects society's power structure. Its creed is that society's members will not be free if their belief system remains unanalyzed and untouched. To act without knowing the reasons behind the action, means a society's members have no control over their lives and destinies (Burbules & Berk, 1999). Elder and Paul (2001) commented that "[t]o become a proficient critical thinker ... they must develop the ability to mentally 'remove' this or that concept from the things named by a concept and try out alternative ideas, alternative 'names,'" (p. 42) as shown by the following student reflections:

> I think I have a good and interesting personal challenge. I no longer want to limit my thinking [by] what I feel could be an offense or something very direct for someone ... I just need to trust a little or a lot more in myself and know how to understand other people, but not labeling them.... That is why I want to finish cleaning my mind of this and many other prejudices that I may have as far as my culture, society, and person. (Student B, reflective journal, 2nd session)

> for me (working in the shelter) was an impressive paradigm change. When they [professors at the university] told us where we were going to do these practices, the scenario where we were going to be ... I expected something horrible. I expected that the children would be ... terrible. Allowing us ... to

go out in real life and dare to get near people ... not leave us with false images ... arrive and say, how cute they are, in the end they are children. (Student C, 6th semester, group reflection, 6th session)

To be a critical thinker implies that one is willing to fairly treat all other postures and frames of reference in a way that develops more equitable human relationships. As critical thinker, one must display reciprocity, and consider alternative viewpoints ant treat them alike. Morin (1999) mentioned that one should "understand the ideas or arguments of another worldview" (p. 50). Paul and Elder (2002) commented: "[c]ritical thinkers strive to adopt a point of view that is fair to others, even to opposing points of view.... Good thinkers, then, consider alternative points of view as they reason through an issue" (p. 113). This is exemplified by the following student reflection:

I think some of my teammates are not that interested and don't give importance (and even meaning) to the service-learning we have been doing in the shelter since fourth semester ... however, I need to acknowledge ... that without them [teammates] I don't think I would have been able to do what we have done up to today. We are a team, and in them I have been able to find a creative resource for materials and drawings. (Student B, reflective journal, 1st session)

Questioning as part of the critical thinking process can lead students to reevaluate themselves. Bolivar (1995) said that in the deepest level of reflection, judgment of practice is aided by contents, values, and critical ideas about the kind of citizens and society one wants to belong to, bringing "the moral and ethical aspects of social compassion and justice ... along with the means and the ends" (Mohlman & Berstein, 1991, p. 39). The following quotes, from student B, exemplify this questioning as part of the critical thinking process:

but I also invariably see myself as a member of this pseudoreality producing society. The truth is the idea scares me, maybe not for belonging physically to this society, but ideologically. This is when I wonder again, what have we done and are we doing for these kids? (Reflective journal, 5th session)

In the same session, student B continued:

Unfortunately, our sociocultural reality ... is terribly unjust and pitiless; it is even incongruent and at times very tough on those who try to break types and get ahead in all senses of the word. Is all this work really worth it? I have asked myself this question and what I can ... say is that *YES*, it is worth it and it deserves all our work and dedication, at least *my* work and *my* dedication.

As part of the critical thinking process, it is important to discover possible implications of one's own actions. As noted in the following paragraph, student B also reflected on psychology and empowerment as part of the ethical-social view. He mentioned that one of the desirable implications of the work being done at the shelter is the teenagers' empowerment, which is congruent with his posture in the Critical Thinking Case:

> In the psychological aspect our general objective ... is to give them ... the sense that [even though] there are a lot of stressful problems ... they are able to search for and see how this situation is affecting them ... to not feel just affected and to search for the way to know why, to see what alternative I am looking for ... lots of this is self-help, the ability to take control of problems and power ... understand them and not feel so overwhelmed and so hopeless. (Group reflection, 1st session)

This service-learning experience forced the students to face ill-defined situations that cannot be handled well purely through technical rationality (Schön, 1983, 1987). Student C had many doubts about how to handle some situations, in particular the issues of how to behave with the teenagers and how to handle the affective relationship with them. Facing an unstructured and ill-defined situation, full of conflict, she wrote:

> from the experience of past workshops in which I got too involved with the kids ... [administrators] had already told us: "When you get really involved you cannot avoid them becoming involved with you" and then, how do you break this off? It is very difficult for me. But ... then what do you do with them?... When we worked with small children I cuddled them.... For example, [a shelter teenager] just came in and sat on my classmate's legs and then with me. Suddenly with the older ones, I stroke one on the back, and I think that they are already older and that they can think wrongly, or the caregivers.... Suddenly I want to hug them, but I cannot ... it is a doubt. (Group reflection, 3rd session)

The suggested reflection structure proved very effective for students to comment on as is shown in the following quote:

> but one of the most gratifying and useful experiences that I have had are these "reflection from action and practice" ... I think it is vitally important if we want to keep automatism, lack of feeling and inefficiency from taking us over as future professionals (of me as a future professional) ... but I want to

and must develop my critical and problem-solving capacity and my creativity more in each act and thought. (Student B, reflective journal, 5th session)

Critical Thinking Case

Performance of the student A on the Critical Thinking Case falls within the Acceptable level (1.76 – 2.50) with a critical thinking score of 1.88.

The critical thinking process of the student B is clear in his Critical Thinking Case answers and in his reflective process. He had one of the three best Critical Thinking Case performances (2.75), and was qualified at the Notable performance level (2.51–3.25). Exhibit 5.6 shows a summary of performance in the Critical Thinking Case for student B. Shaded areas represent the performance level the student obtained for each of the items.

The critical thinking process of the student C is clearer in her answers to the Critical Thinking Case than in her reflective process. Her overall Critical Thinking Case performance was the highest possible (2.50) within the Acceptable critical thinking level.

Regarding the School of Psychology student population that solved the Critical Thinking Case, the percentage of the Acceptable and Notable critical thinking levels increased from the second to the eighth semester, meaning that as students advanced through the program their critical thinking level as shown on the Critical Thinking Case increased. The inverse occurred in the Insufficient level, with fewer students at this level in the more advanced semesters as shown in Figure 5.1. No folios attained an overall Exceptional level, though some students did achieve this level on individual items. The illustrative examples of students' performance in Item 1 at different critical thinking levels are shown in Exhibit 5.7.

Exhibit 5.6. Summary of Performance of Student B in the Critical Thinking Case for Student Folio # 97

	Levels			
Item	*Exceptional (4)*	*Notable (3)*	*Acceptable (2)*	*Insufficient (1)*
Problems or issues		■		
Evidence				■
Assumptions		■		
Contrasting points of view			■	
Overlooked complexity		■		
Consequences (case management)		■		
Alternatives of subject	■			
Implication of alternatives		■		

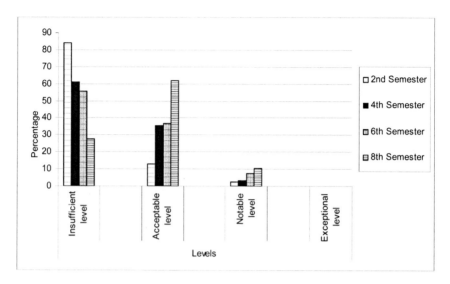

Figure 5.1.   Critical thinking level by semester.

Exhibit 5.7.   Example of Student Answers to Item 1: Problems and Issues by Performance Level

Answer by Level	Comment
Notable "From my point of view there are a number of problems and I do not think it could be said to be just one. There is the problem of public education, which does not have teachers trained to identify the causes of the problem and try to help them; they just leave "problem" children in the line of those that do not move up a year. I also see the lack of employment, the poverty that millions of people in México and the world live in. I see the exploitation of many companies, especially of women, which prevents nearness to children. I see many rooted macho behaviors; I see a government agency desensitized to this kind of event. I also see alcohol and intrafamilial abuse problems." (Folio # 110)	The student mentions family violence and stresses the problems that contextualize the violence problem. She also mentions educational problems. She points out several socioeconomic problems: unemployment, poverty, exploitation and discrimination against women at work, and their consequences as barriers for family quality of life. These elements indicate an unjust social system and allow a vision of the problem that goes beyond the child's immediate family problems. She also stresses cultural problems like machismo. The only element she does not catch is the violence of the authorities' solution.
Acceptable "Child abuse, poverty, family deterioration, addiction, machismo, unemployment, work exploitation, discrimination." (Folio # 1)	Several problems are mentioned but the student does not interrelate them, missing the complexity of the situation.
Insufficient "The child's scholastic failure and her problems with interacting with others." (Folio # 113)	The student mentions some of the child's problems that are important, but are not those that led to her being in the shelter.

DISCUSSION

The reflective process was studied in a search of evidence that might clarify the critical thinking process in the reflection stage of service-learning experience.

In response to research question one, results showed that, in general, the different levels of the critical thinking process were "experienced" by the students, whether in their reflective journal or as part of a group reflection in the service-learning program. Indeed, according to the suggested reflection schema, it can be said that in the reflection process the students were able to identify issues, frame and reframe them, confront and restructure themselves as a result (Bringle, 2003; Eyler & Giles, 1999; Paul & Elder, 2002).

The reflective process in this service-learning program was an ongoing process, and promoted the connection between the service and academic work and pushed students to broaden their points of view of the topics about which they were reflecting. The actual experience the students had in the field was also used as a material for the reflection process itself. It was continuous, connected, challenging and contextualized (Eyler et al., 1996). In the present study the reflection processes allowed the students, and pushed them, to make sense of the service-learning experience by promoting interaction between the students themselves, between theory and practice, between their experience "and other experiences, between that experience and the knowledge that one carries, and between that knowledge and the knowledge produced by thinkers other than oneself" (Rodgers, 2002, p. 848).

In response to research question two, the present study was focused on display of critical thinking process as specific domain skills (McPeck, 1994). For this reason there was no point in using content-free measures for data collection. Instead, the idea in this study was to research critical thinking by going beyond content-free or self-report measures, meaning a competency measure of the critical thinking process itself was needed. In response, the Critical Thinking Case was developed. Most research on critical thinking has employed student self-report measures on a number of factors (Tsui, 1998). General ability critical thinking tests have also been used, though it is now recognized that many intellectual skills are context-specific (McMillan, 1987). Critical thinking research in the service-learning tradition has also largely involved self-report measures (Steinke & Buresh, 2002).

Overall student performance on the Critical Thinking Case differed by the semester the students were in, with more advanced students having higher critical thinking levels on the case. This is similar to Tsui's (1998) report on meta-research using 62 critical thinking studies in which students experience critical thinking.

CONCLUSIONS

One reason to implement service-learning programs within the curriculum is to change education profoundly. This forms part of an overall ambition to move from traditional, classroom-oriented higher education to socially responsible education. The former provides knowledge that is disconnected from reality and shapes professionals with little or no ability to socially transform their immediate surroundings due to their minimal training in reading and responding to society's needs. Through the definition and implementation of service-learning programs, the latter generates socially responsible knowledge and shapes professionals that deliberately develop the ability to critically read reality and commit themselves to it; professionals who perceive themselves as transformers of their social surroundings.

It is urgent to consider models such as service-learning, which, when applied within a curriculum, have an enormous potential to involve students (at least while they are at a university) in the reading and addressing of social problems. This implies that the different disciplines should be critically analyzing these problems and proposing visions of possible change and concrete, transformative actions (Prilleltensky, 2000).

It is necessary to amplify knowledge of the reflection processes. This would lead to deeper levels of reflection that allow a critical reconstruction of experience and practice in which the goal is to rebuild practice, collaboratively and cooperatively, as something problematic that can attain an ethical-social level (Dewey, 1938; Freire, 2001; Mohlman & Berstein, 1991; Paul, 1994; Paul & Elder, 2002; Rodgers, 2002; Schön, 1983, 1987).

Critical thinking is a complex process involving higher-order thinking skills. In the present research, the critical thinking process was displayed in a service-learning program as part of the experience's reflective stage. The reflection process of the service-learning experience allowed students to bring some elements of their own belief system to a conscious level and thus made them the subject of inquiry (Giroux, 1994; Moral, 1995; Paul, 1994; Paul & Elder, 2002), leading to later transformations. The students exhibited many of the elements that define a critical thinker (Díaz Barriga, 1998; Elder & Paul, 2002; Paul, 1994). This is particularly relevant given the lack of research in this area. Eyler (2000) and Steinke and Buresh (2002) stated the need to go beyond self-report measurements and find new ways of collecting data on the service-learning experience.

Being able to prove the presence of critical thinking in the reflection processes of the service-learning program facilitates experience and instrument design (e.g., Critical Thinking Case) that will allow firm advances in the research and in design of the overall education experience.

REFERENCES

Asociación Nacional de Universidades e Instituciones de Educación Superior. (2000). *La educación superior en el siglo XXI. Una propuesta de la ANUIES* [Higher education in the 21st century]. Distrito Federal, México: ANUIES.

Berry, H., & Chisholm, L. (1999). *Service-learning on higher education around the world: An initial look.* New York: The International Partnership for Service-Learning.

Bolívar, A. (1995). Reconstrucción. In L. M. Villar (Ed.), *Un ciclo de enseñanza reflexiva. Estrategias para el diseño curricular* [Reflective teaching cycle: Curriculum design strategies] (pp. 237–265). Bilbao, España: Ediciones Mensajero.

Brandenberger, J. (1998). Developmental psychology and service-learning: A theoretical framework. In R. Bringle & D. Duffy (Eds.), *With service in mind: Concepts and models for service-learning in psychology* (pp. 68–84). Washington, DC: American Association for Higher Education.

Bringle, R. (2003). Reflexión: Hacia el éxito de los programas aprender-sirviendo. In D. Pacheco, M. Thullen, & J. C. Seijo (Eds.), *Aprender sirviendo. Un paradigma de formación integral universitaria* [Service-learning: A university educational approach for community and solidarity values] (pp. 33–45). Distrito Federal, México: Editorial Progreso.

Bringle, R., & Hatcher, J. (1995, Fall). A service-learning curriculum for faculty. *Michigan Journal of Community Service Learning, 2,* 112–122.

Budem, K. (1967, July). What do *you* think, teacher? *Peabody Journal of Education, 45,* 2–5.

Burbules, N., & Berk, R. (1999). Critical thinking and critical pedagogy: Relations, differences and limits. In T. Popkewitz & L. Fendler (Eds.), *Critical theories in education: Changing terrains of knowledge and politics* (pp. 45–67). London: Routledge.

Denman, C., & Haro, J. (2000). Introducción: Trayectoria y desvaríos de los métodos cualitativos en la investigación social. In C. Denman & J. Haro (Eds.), *Por los rincones. Antología de métodos cualitativos en la investigación social* [At the corners: Qualitative methods in social research—An anthology] (pp. 9–55). Coahuila, Sonora: El Colegio de Sonora.

Denzin, N., & Lincoln, Y. (2000). The discipline and practice of qualitative research. In N. Denzin & Y. Lincoln (Eds.), *Handbook of qualitative research* (2nd ed., pp.1–28). Los Angeles: Sage.

Dewey, J. (1938). *Experience and education.* New York: Macmillan.

Díaz Barriga, F. (1998). *El aprendizaje de la historia en el bachillerato: Procesos de pensamiento y construcción del conocimiento en profesores y estudiantes del CCH/UNAM*

[History learning in high school: Thinking processes and knowledge construction in professors and students of the CCH/UNAM]. Unpublished doctoral thesis, Universidad Nacional Autónoma de México, Distrito Federal, México.

Díaz Barriga, F. (2001). Habilidades de pensamiento crítico sobre contenidos históricos en alumnos de bachillerato [Critical thinking abilities on historical content matter in high school students]. *Revista Mexicana de Investigación Educativa, 6*(13), 525–554.

Díaz Barriga, F. (2004). Las rúbricas: Su potencial como estrategias para una enseñanza situada y una evaluación auténtica del aprendizaje [Rubrics: Their potential as strategies for situated teaching and authentic assessment of learning]. *Perspectiva Educacional 43*, 51–62.

Díaz Barriga, F., & Saad, E. (1996). Un modelo de formación en la práctica del psicólogo educativo a través de la integración docencia-servicio-investigación [An educational model in the practice of educational psychologist through the integration of teaching-service research]. *Revista CNEIP, 1*(2), 95–126.

Duffy, D., & Bringle, R. (1998). Professor McKenna teaches introductory psychology. In R. Bringle & D. Duffy (Eds.), *With service in mind: Concepts and models for service-learning in psychology* (pp. 111–118). Washington, DC: American Association for Higher Education.

Elder, L., & Paul, R. (2001). Thinking with concepts. *Journal of Developmental Education, 24*(3), 42–43.

Elder, L., & Paul, R. (2002). Critical thinking: Distinguishing between inferences and assumptions. *Journal of Developmental Education, 25*(3), 34–35.

Eyler, J. (2000, Fall). What do we most need to know about the impact of service-learning on student learning? [Special issue]. *Michigan Journal of Community Service Learning,* 11–17.

Eyler, J., & Giles, D., Jr. (1997). The importance of program quality in service learning. In A. Waterman (Ed.), *Service-learning: Applications from the research* (pp. 57–77). Mahwah, NJ: Erlbaum.

Eyler, J., & Giles, D. (1999). *Where's the learning in service-learning?* San Francisco: Jossey-Bass.

Eyler, J., Giles, D. E., Jr., & Braxton, J. (1997, Fall). The impact of service-learning on college students. *Michigan Journal of Community Service Learning, 4*, 5–15.

Eyler, J., Giles, D. E., Jr., & Schmiede, A. (1996). *A practitioner's guide to reflection in service-learning: Student voices and reflections.* Nashville, TN: Vanderbilt University.

Eyler, J., Giles, D. E., Jr., Stenson, C., & Gray. C. (2001). *At a glance: What we know about the effects of service-learning on college students, faculty, institutions, and communities, 1993-2000* (3rd ed.). Nashville, TN: Vanderbilt University.

Freire, P. (2001). *Pedagogía de la indignación* [Pedagogy of indignation]. Madrid, Spain: Morata.

Giroux, H. (1994). Toward a pedagogy of critical thinking. In K. Walters (Ed.), *Rethinking reason: New perspectives in critical thinking* (pp. 199–204). Albany: State University of New York Press.

Hatcher, J. (1997, Fall). The moral dimensions of John Dewey's philosophy: Implications for undergraduate education. *Michigan Journal of Community Service Learning, 4,* 22–29.

Hatcher, J., & Bringle, R. (1997). Reflection: Bridging the gap between service and learning. *Journal of College Teaching, 45,* 153–158.

Howard, J. (1993). Advocating for community service learning at the University of Michigan. In J. Galura, R. Meiland, R. Ross, M. J. Callan, & R. Smith (Eds.), *Praxis II. Service-learning resources for university students, staff, and faculty* (pp. 39–55). Ann Arbor: University of Michigan.

Isla, M. L. (2003). Percepción que los estudiantes de psicología tienen sobre la supervisión de las prácticas-servicio en la Universidad Marista. In D. Pacheco, M. Thullen & J.C. Seijo (Eds.), *Aprender sirviendo. Un paradigma de formación integral universitaria* [Service-learning: A university educational approach for community and solidarity values] (pp. 111–117). Distrito Federal, México: Editorial Progreso.

Jacoby, B., & Associates. (1996). *Service-learning in higher education.* San Francisco: Jossey-Bass.

Kendall, J. (1990). Combining service and learning: an introduction. In J. C. Kendall & Associates (Eds.), *Combining service and learning: A resource book for community and public service* (Vol. 1, pp.1–55). Raleigh, NC: National Society for Internships and Experiential Education.

Marín, D. (1993). *La formación profesional y el curriculum universitario* [Professional education and higher education curriculum]. Distrito Federal, México: Diana.

McMillan, J. (1987). Enhancing college students' critical thinking: A review of studies. *Research in Higher Education, 26*(1), 3–29.

McPeck, J. (1994). Critical thinking in the "trivial pursuit" theory of knowledge. In K. Walters (Ed.), *Re-thinking reason: New perspectives in critical thinking* (pp. 101–118). Albany: State University of New York Press.

Merriam, S. (1988). *Case study research in education: A qualitative approach.* San Francisco: Jossey-Bass.

Mohlman, G., & Berstein, A. (1991). Synthesis of research on teachers' reflective thinking. *Educational Leadership, 48*(6), 37–44.

Moral, C. (1995). Información. In L. M. Villar (Ed.), *Un ciclo de enseñanza reflexiva. Estrategias para el diseño curricular* [Reflective teaching cycle: Curriculum design strategies] (pp.173–204). Bilbao, Spain: Ediciones Mensajero.

Morin, E. (1999). *Seven complex lessons in education for the future.* Paris. UNESCO

Pacheco, D. (2003). Percepción de los estudiantes acerca de los procesos aprender-sirviendo en la escuela de psicología. In D. Pacheco, M. Thullen, & J. C. Seijo (Eds.), *Aprender sirviendo. Un paradigma de formación integral universitaria* [Service-learning: A university educational approach for community and solidarity values] (pp. 33–45). Distrito Federal, México: Editorial Progreso.

Pacheco, D. (2005). *Critical thinking and social and personal responsibility in a higher education service-learning program.* Unpublished doctoral dissertation, College of Education, Autonomous University of Yucatán, México.

Paul, R. (1994). Teaching critical thinking in the strong sense: A focus on self-deception, world views, and a dialectic mode of analysis. In K. Walters (Ed.),

Re-thinking reason: New perspectives in critical thinking (pp.181–198). Albany: State University of New York Press.

Paul, R., & Elder, L. (2002). *Critical thinking: Tools for taking charge of your professional and personal life.* New York: Prentice Hall.

Prilleltensky, I. (2000). Bridging agency, theory, and action: Critical links in critical psychology. In T. Sloan (Ed.), *Critical psychology: Voices for change* (pp. 67–81). London: Macmillan Press.

Rapapport, J., & Seidman, E. (2000). *Handbook of community psychology.* New York: Kluwer.

Rodgers, C. (2002). Defining reflection: Another look at John Dewey and reflective thinking. *Teachers College Record, 104*(4), 842–866.

Schön, D. (1983). *El profesional reflexivo. Cómo piensan los profesionales cuando actúan* [The reflective practitioner: How professionals think in action]. Barcelona, Spain: Paidós.

Schön, D. (1987). *Educating the reflective practitioner: Toward a new design for teaching and learning in the professions.* San Francisco: Jossey-Bass.

Sigmon, R. (1990). Service-learning: Three principles. In J. C. Kendall & Associates (Eds.), *Combining service and learning: A resource book for community and public service* (Vol. 1, pp.56–64). Raleigh, NC: National Society for Internships and Experiential Education.

Silcox, H. (1993). *A how to guide to reflection: Adding cognitive learning to community service programs.* Philadelphia: Brighton Press.

Smyth, J. (1992). Teachers' work and the politics of reflection. *American Educational Research Journal, 29*(2), 267–300.

Stake, R. (1998). *Investigación con estudio de casos* [The art of case study research]. Madrid, Spain: Morata.

Stanton, T. (1990). Liberal arts, experiential learning, and public service: Necessary ingredients for socially responsible undergraduate education. In J. C. Kendall & Associates (Eds.), *Combining service and learning: A resource book for community and public service* (Vol. 1, pp.175–189). Raleigh, NC: National Society for Internships and Experiential Education.

Steinke, P., & Buresh, S. (2002). Cognitive outcomes of service-learning: Reviewing the past and glimpsing the future. *Michigan Journal of Community Service Learning, 8*(2), 5–14.

Surbeck, E., Park, H., & Moyer, J. (1991). Assessing reflective responses in journals. *Educational Leadership, 48*(6), 25–27.

Tsui, L. (1998, November). *A review of research on critical thinking.* Paper presented at Association for the Study of Higher Education Annual Meeting, Miami, FL.

UNESCO. (1998). *Declaración mundial sobre la educación superior en el siglo XXI. Marco de acción prioritaria para el cambio y el desarrollo de la educación superior* [World declaration of higher education for the 21st century: Vision and action and framework for priority action for change and development in higher education]. Paris: Conferencia Mundial sobre la Educación Superior.

Yin, R. (1994). *Case study research: Design and methods.* Beverly Hills, CA: Sage.

Section III

IMPACTS OF SERVICE-LEARNING

CHAPTER 6

AN EVALUATION OF ACADEMIC SERVICE-LEARNING

Student and Community Perspectives on Lessons Learned

Lori Simons and Beverly Cleary

ABSTRACT

A triangulation mixed-methods design was used to measure differences in service-learning outcomes for 260 service-learning participants enrolled in educational psychology courses during the academic years 2002-2003 ($n = 77$), 2003-2004 ($n = 101$) and 2004-2005 ($n = 82$). The results indicated that service-learning students improved their political awareness, diversity attitudes, and preference for engaging in long-term service commitments from the beginning to the end of the semester. The results further indicated that service-learning influences student personal, interpersonal, and social development through social, emotional, and cognitive learning, and it empowers teachers working in an urban environment to use different pedagogical methods because of the "extra-hands" in class.

Advancing Knowledge in Service-Learning: Research to Transform the Field, 113–135
Copyright © 2006 by Information Age Publishing

INTRODUCTION

Much research has been written about the benefits of service-learning (Eyler, 2000; Harkavy, Puckett, & Romer, 2000; Moore, 2000). The number of quantitative studies evaluating the impact of service-learning on students' academic learning (Eyler, 2000; Vogelgesang & Astin, 2000), personal and interpersonal development (Eyler & Giles, 1999; Eyler, Giles, Stenson, & Gray, 2003; Moely, McFarland, Miron, Mercer, & Ilustre, 2002), and civic engagement (Eyler et al., 2003; Gallini & Moely, 2003; Moely, McFarland, et al., 2002) have increased dramatically in the last decade. Simultaneously, qualitative studies examining the influence of service-learning on students' stereotypical attitudes (Eyler & Giles, 1999; Rockquemore & Schaffer, 2000) and multicultural competencies (Boyle-Baise & Kilbane, 2000; Howard-Hamilton, 2000; Root, Callahan, & Sepanski, 2001) have multiplied and strengthened the argument for multicultural service-learning as a culturally responsive pedagogical method in higher education (Boyle-Baise, 2002; O'Grady, 2000; Root et al., 2002). Roldan, Strage, and David (2004) found that the trend in investigations substantiating the benefits of service-learning has linked service-learning to enhanced student learning. For example, service-learning is associated with student improvement in comprehension and application ability (Eyler & Giles, 1999; Litke, 2002; Strage, 2000). Investigators have also documented impacts of service-learning on student personal and interpersonal development (Eyler & Giles, 1999), such as:

- Leadership skills (Moely, McFarland, et al., 2002; Vogelgesang & Astin, 2000);
- Diversity attitudes (Boyle-Baise & Kilbane, 2000; Rockquemore & Schaffer, 2000; Root et al., 2002); and
- Personal efficacy (Green, 2001; Quezada & Christopherson, 2005).

Finally, service-learning is associated with students' social development, such as their ability to develop relationships with community recipients (Brody & Wright, 2004) and to increase levels of social responsibility and community or civic engagement (Delli Carpini & Keeter; Gallini & Moely, 2003; C. A. Payne, 2000; Reinke, 2003).

Two problems have caused controversy over the benefits of service-learning in the research. The first is associated with methodological limitations. The majority of studies have measured changes in students' attitudes before and after the service experience with qualitative methods using single, convenient samples. With this method, it is not possible to detect whether the reported changes are attributed to the service experience because the studies assess attitudes instead of behaviors with either:

- Single-item surveys (Rockquemore & Schaffer, 2000);
- Reflective essays (Green, 2001); or
- Ethnographic techniques (Boyle-Base & Kilbane, 2000).

The second problem in this area of research is the paucity of studies focusing on the impact of service-learning on the community noted by Cruz and Giles (2000), Ferrari and Worrall (2000), Jacoby (1996), and Schmidt and Robby (2002). The few studies that have assessed community outcomes conduct case-study accounts or collect evaluations by program supervisors rather than measure the effects on actual service recipients (Ferrari & Worrall, 2000; Schmidt & Robby, 2002).

A primary objective of the study discussed in this chapter is to address some of these gaps in the research on service-learning and student development. The study was a 3-year investigation of an academic service-learning program in an educational psychology course. It adds to previous investigations by offering a more rigorous design. We have incorporated a triangulation mixed-methods design, which includes quantitative and qualitative analyses (Creswell, 2005) and multiple measures of attitudes and behaviors. Four sources were used to gather information on student development, with each source including multiple formats: pre/post surveys, journals, teacher surveys, and open-ended questions. Two surveys were administered, one at the beginning and one at the end of the course for service-learning participants. Each survey included six self-report measures assessing student grade point averages (GPAs) and personal and social development. Service-learning students were also required to write one journal entry for each day of service. Journals encouraged students to generate three types of data:

1. A descriptive account of actual events that occurred during the participants' service-learning experience;
2. An ongoing report of their emotional and cognitive reactions to the events they encountered; and
3. An overall integration of the course content and service experiences.

This study utilized qualitative and quantitative methodologies to enhance the reliability of the findings for student development.

In addition to addressing some of the limitations in the service-learning research, a second objective of the study was to extend the research on service-learning and community recipients. Researchers sought to evaluate with quantitative or qualitative methodologies the effects of service-learning for community recipients and to determine the relationship between teacher satisfaction with service-learning students and the service-learning program. Two surveys were administered to teachers at the course end, a questionnaire designed for teachers' appraisals of students' performance and open-ended questions designed to identify the teachers' level of satisfaction with the service project. Specifically, this study sought to answer the following four questions:

1. Are there differences in academic learning and personal and social development from the beginning to the end of the semester for service-learning students?
2. Are there differences in satisfaction levels of student performance for teachers at an elementary school, after-school program, alternative school, and community organization?
3. What and how did the students "learn" from engaging in an academic service-learning program?
4. What effects does service-learning have on teachers? Moreover, how do teachers benefit from the service-learning program, how do the children in their classrooms/programs benefit from service learning, and does service-learning influence their pedagogical techniques?

METHOD

Participants

College students from a private teaching university in a northern metropolitan area completed a survey about their educational psychology course. Data were gathered from 260 students at the beginning and at the end of the semester during three academic years (2002-2003, 2003-2004, 2004-2005), the retention rate from pretest to posttest was 97%. As indicated in Exhibit 6.1, most students identified themselves as white and female. GPAs reported by high school (freshmen) or college (sophomores and above) students were in the "B" range. Majors were grouped into categories of arts and sciences, preprofessional programs, and education. Education was treated as a separate category due to the large number of students in that field. Service-learning students from Sample 1 (2002-2003) did not significantly differ from those in Samples 2 (2003-2004) and 3 (2004-2005). An analysis of variance and chi-square tests were used to compare demographic characteristics of service-learners in Samples 1, 2, and 3.

Exhibit 6.1.   Descriptive Data for Service-Learning Students During Academic Years 2002-2003, 2003-2004, and 2004-2005

	Respondents		
	Sample 1	*Sample 2*	*Sample 3*
	%	*%*	*%*
Variables	*(n = 77)*	*(n = 101)*	*(n = 82)*
Age			
Mean years	20.36	19.44	19.60
SD^a	7.14	2.25	2.11
Gender			
Male	13	29	20
Female	87	71	80
Ethnicity			
African American	13	14	1
Asian American	1	1	6
Hispanic	4	0	1
White	78	81	90
Other	1	1	2
Do not wish to answer	3	3	2
Year in College			
First	47	32	29
Second	25	49	38
Third	18	9	24
Fourth	10	10	9
Mean GPA	3.14	2.89	3.25
SD	.53	.56	.48
Major			
Arts and sciences	45	45	42
Preprofessional programs	3	3	10
Education	52	51	46
Undeclared	0	1	2
Volunteer Experience	39	27	24
Mean hours	1.32	1.06	.86
SD	2.47	2.60	2.54
Service-Learning Placements			
Elementary school	62	64	49
After school	36	18	20
Alternative school	0	10	28
Community organization	2	8	3
Continued service	36	44	40
Future service-learning	68	67	70

[a]Standard deviation.

Service was carried out at different community sites, including:

- A public elementary school after-school program;
- A community organization for children with behavioral problems; and
- An alternative school for adolescents with learning and behavioral problems.

More than half of the service-learning students (60%) worked as tutors while the remainder worked as mentors (30%) and social-recreational leaders (10%).

Measures

Demographic Questionnaire, developed by the researchers, was used to gather information on gender, race, age, GPA, area of study, year in school and volunteer experience.

Civic Attitudes and Skills Questionnaire (CASQ), developed by Moely, Mercer, Ilustre, Miron, and McFarland (2002), assessed civic attitudes and skills. The CASQ, an 84-item self-report questionnaire, yields scores on six scales:

1. **Civic Action.**   Respondents evaluated their intentions to become involved in the future in some community service or action;
2. **Interpersonal and Problem-Solving Skills.**   Respondents evaluated their ability to listen, work cooperatively, communicate, make friends, take the role of the other, think logically and analytically, and solve problems;
3. **Political Awareness.**   Respondents evaluated themselves on items concerning awareness of local and national events and political issues;
4. **Leadership Skills.**   Respondents evaluated their ability to lead and effectiveness as a leader);
5. **Social Justice Attitudes.**   Respondents rated their agreement with items expressing attitudes concerning the causes of poverty and misfortune and how social problems can be solved; and
6. **Diversity Attitudes.**   Respondents described their attitudes toward diversity and their interest in relating to culturally different people.

Internal consistencies for each scale ranged from .69 to .88, and test-retest reliabilities for each scale ranged from .56 to .81 (Moely, Mercer, et al., 2002).

The CASQ also measured students' views of their courses on three course satisfaction scales:

1. **Course Value.**   Respondents evaluated how important or useful material covered in the academic course had been;

2. **Learning About Academic Field**.   Respondents evaluated the content of his/her academic course, such as understanding and application of the course concepts, interest in the field, and understanding a professional's role in the field of study; and

3. **Learning About the Community**.   Respondents evaluated how much they had learned about the community, different cultures, working with others effectively and seeing social problems in a new way.

Internal consistencies for each scale ranged from .81 to .82 (Moely, Mercer, et al., 2002).

Civic Attitudes Scale (CAS), developed by Mabry (1998 as cited in Bringle, Phillips, & Hudson, 2004), assessed students' attitudes related to community service. Scores for the civic attitudes scale ranged from 5 to 25; a higher total score indicates a positive attitude toward engaging in community service. Alpha coefficient for the total civic engagement scale is strong ($\alpha = .81$).

Community Service Self-Efficacy Scale (CSSES), developed by Reeb, Katsuyama, Sammon, and Yoder (1998 as cited in Bringle et al., 2004), measured students' confidence in making a clinically significant contribution to the community through service. Ten items were added together to produce a full-scale score. Test-retest reliability for this scale is modest ($r = .62$).

Community Service Involvement Preference Inventory (CSIPI), developed by C. A. Payne (2000), assessed how students become involved in community service. The CSIPI is a 48-item paper and pencil inventory designed to assess four preferences:

1. **Exploration Involvement Preference.**   This score reflects the affective nature of apprehension common in new experiences, and it demonstrates the behavioral perspective that commitment is short term and is usually at the convenience of the helper.

2. **Affiliation Involvement Preference.**   This score reflects behavior motivation for recognition and commitments tend to be infrequent and shorter in duration.

3. **Experimentation Involvement Preference.**   This score reflects the desire to make a difference in the lives of others and to learn more about the community).

4.   **Assimilation Involvement Preference.**   This score reflects cognitive processes with career and lifestyle decisions based on the service experience as a way to understand what it means to be a responsible citizen.

Scores for each preference ranged from 12 to 60, and the total score served as an indicator for how students prefer to become involved in community service. Internal consistencies are modest for the following preferences: Exploration ($r = .63$), Affiliation ($r = .70$), Experimentation ($r = .74$), and Assimilation ($r = .70$).

Service-Learning Performance Checklist, developed by D. A. Payne (2000), measured teachers' views of the students' performance during the service-learning project. Scores for each item ranged from 1 to 5; the higher score indicates greater teacher satisfaction with students' performance on a specific task. Alpha coefficient for 25 items is high ($\alpha = .81$).

Service-Learning Teacher Survey, a truncated version of this scale developed by D.A. Payne (2000), gathered teachers' satisfaction with the service-learning project. Researchers added four open-ended questions to Payne's original three questions to identify the major advantages and disadvantages of service-learning. Questions were:

- What did you like the most about having this student come to your class/program?
- What did you like the least about having this student come to your class/program?
- What would you change about this service-learning project if you had another student come to your class next semester?
- What could the university do to make the students' visits more important to you?
- What were the major benefits for your students and the Widener student(s)?
- What were the major benefits for you?
- Have you changed your teaching methods as a result of your involvement in this project?

Texas Social Behavior Inventory-Short Form (TSBI), developed by Helmreich and Strapp (1974 as cited in Bringle et al., 2004), measured self-esteem and social competence. The TSBI is composed of 32 items, and items are added together to produce a full-scale score with a higher score indicating greater social competence. Reliability coefficients are high ($r = .85$).

Volunteer Functions Inventory, developed by Clary and colleagues (1998 as cited in Bringle et al., 2004), assessed six functions that are served through volunteer activities including values, understanding, social, career, protective factors, and enhancement. Each subscale consisted of five items that assesses the students' degree of motivation in making decisions to volunteer. Each subscale score was obtained by calculating the mean score; a higher score indicates a greater sense of importance associated with motivation. Internal consistency for each subscale is greater than .80.

Design and Procedure

A triangulation mixed-methods design was used to evaluate differences in service-learning outcomes for 260 students during the academic years 2002-2003 ($n = 77$), 2003-2004 ($n = 101$) and 2004-2005 ($n = 82$). Creswell (2005) wrote that a triangulation mixed-methods design refers to simultaneously collecting quantitative and qualitative data and merging the data and the results to understand the problem under investigation. The rationale for this design is to use quantitative data to enhance the reliability of qualitative results, and to use qualitative techniques to refine quantitative outcomes by providing information about the setting.

All of the respondents completed an informed consent form and a survey measuring academic learning and personal and social development. Students completed the survey; placed it in a coded, confidential envelope; and gave it directly to the researcher. Surveys took about 45 minutes to complete. Students were required to complete the survey again postservice (i.e., after completing 16 hours of service) and to write one journal entry for each day of service. Teachers also completed a posttest survey that measured their overall level of satisfaction with this service project and evaluated each student's performance. The surveys, which were administered to teachers at the site, surveys took approximately 20 minutes to complete. The teacher response rate was 40%, which is congruent with survey research (Rosenthal & Rosnow, 1991).

Analysis

Quantitative analyses were conducted to generate two types of outcomes: (1) evaluate changes in attitudes, skills, and behaviors before and after service for service-learning students; and (2) assess teacher satisfaction with service-learning students at four placement sites.

Qualitative analyses were used to construct a common framework of student learning and teacher empowerment. The constant comparative method was used to identify common themes that described "what" and "how" the students learned through their service experiences (Creswell, 1994, 1998, 2005). Two independent coders read the journals and identified each student's isolated thought as a unit of analysis. These 1,623 units underwent an item-level analysis so that similar thoughts were combined with each other to construct a common framework. Open coding of the individual thought units consisted of naming and categorizing the data according to the service-learning framework of Eyler and Giles (1999) and the course content of educational psychology.

An axial coding procedure was also conducted to explore the learning process associated with service-learning. Axial coding consisted of connecting the individual thoughts to central concepts of one of the following learning theories:

- Social (Gardner, 1993, 1999),
- Emotional (Salovey, Brackett, & Mayer, 2004),
- Cognitive (Salovey et al., 2004), and
- Multicultural (Boyle-Baise, 2002; Howard-Hamilton, 2000).

Individual thought units were coded as social learning (i.e., intrapersonal, interpersonal) when they indicated students' abilities to identify, monitor, and discriminate feelings as means of guiding behavior or understanding the behavior of others (Gardner, 1993, 1999; Salovey et al., 2004). The units were coded as emotional learning when they reflected students' expression of feelings and were coded as cognitive learning when they reflected students' thoughts, judgments, or reasoning abilities (Salovey et al., 2004; Slavin, 2003). The units were also coded as multicultural learning when they reflected knowledge of cultural identity for self and others, understanding of cultural differences, and appreciation of different cultural groups (Howard-Hamilton, 2000). After the individual thoughts units were coded as a major learning process, they were compared across time over the semester. Changes in student learning were observed as they went through the service experience; and following this coding procedure, learning processes and themes were compared to students' self-reports on pretest and posttest surveys. This method served as a reliability check for qualitative findings. The discussion section addresses the discrepancies between qualitative and quantitative results.

Another content analysis was conducted to construct a framework of service-learning as a method for empowering teachers. Each teacher's response underwent an item-level analysis that resulted in 10 broad cate

gories (Creswell, 1994, 1998, 2005). Finally, these categories were organized into four domains.

RESULTS

Pretest and Posttest Differences for Service-Learning Students

Using preservice and postservice surveys, students' attitudes, skills and
behaviors were observed at two points in time. A paired-sample t test was
used to assess differences in GPAs, CASQ, Civic Attitudes, CSSES, CISPI,
TSBI, and VFI scores for service-learning students ($N = 260$). Students
made significant changes in political awareness, leadership skills, diversity attitudes, and exploration and affiliation preferences for community
involvement. Service-learning students also showed unexpected changes
in GPAs, learning about the academic field and community, social competence, and volunteering for self-understanding as shown in Exhibit 2.
These positive and negative changes indicate that personal and social
development took place among our sample of participants.

Teachers' Appraisal of Service-Learning Participants

Using a posttest survey with teachers ($N = 75$), levels of satisfaction
were observed for service-learning participants. The four teacher
variables were recoded into two variables—elementary teachers and
nonelementary teachers—because less than half of the teachers were
employed at an after-school program, alternative school, or a community
organization. An independent t test was conducted to identify differences
in student performances between elementary and nonelementary
schoolteachers. Elementary schoolteachers ($M = 4.73$) reported greater
levels of satisfaction with students' concern and compassion for the
children than non-elementary schoolteachers ($x = 4.50$), although this
finding was significant at $p < .06$.

What and How Did the Students "Learn" From Participating in Service-Learning?

The content analysis that was conducted on 260 journal reflections replicated and extended the framework of Eyler and Giles (1999) by suggesting students develop a deeper understanding of course concepts, acquire
self-knowledge, and learn to value relationships with culturally diverse

Exhibit 6.2.   Means and Standard Deviations on GPAs and Personal and Social Development Measures for Service-Learning Students

Measures	Pretest		Posttest		df	t
	M	SD	M	SD		
GPA	3.17	.53	3.06	.55	225	2.50*
CASQ						
Civic action	26.54	4.28	26.28	4.51	232	1.07
Problem solving	41.16	4.54	36.55	5.18	212	13.34***
Political awareness	14.18	2.78	17.66	4.31	243	−13.28***
Leadership	13.27	1.80	13.70	1.61	232	−2.92**
Social justice	28.90	3.45	29.17	4.07	231	−1.01
Diversity	12.68	2.09	14.00	2.85	244	−8.10***
Course value	39.34	5.49	38.59	6.03	234	1.86
Learning about academic	20.69	3.12	19.66	3.16	226	5.36***
Learning about field	23.69	3.94	23.11	3.59	224	1.98*
CSIPI						
Exploration	34.62	4.06	32.34	4.01	223	6.41***
Experimentation	41.30	5.45	41.37	5.68	235	−.18
Affiliation	26.53	5.76	29.34	6.35	226	−7.32***
Civic attitudes	20.09	3.26	20.28	3.19	132	−.79
Self-efficacy	39.57	5.57	39.41	5.76	130	.33
Social competence	61.89	11.07	58.56	7.92	116	4.03***
VFI						
Values	20.21	2.92	20.60	3.91	125	−1.21
Understanding	20.41	2.67	16.10	2.36	130	18.56***
Social	16.21	4.81	16.04	3.95	128	.43
Career	15.77	2.29	15.73	2.80	129	.16
Esteem	19.06	2.76	19.06	3.25	126	-.52
Protective	12.99	2.87	12.96	3.06	131	.12

$*p = < .05. **p = < .01. ***p = < .001.$

community recipients. The first learning outcome articulated in student journals was described as academic learning. Almost all (99%) of the data coded identified content knowledge; 86% of the coded data identified application of concepts. For example, one student wrote:

> I felt like this course was similar to learning to play baseball. If you want to hit a ball, you have to get out there with a bat. There is no way that I could have understood how risk factors such as low socioeconomic status, race, and family characteristics could influence the learning process unless I worked with the children in an urban environment. The context humanized the theories of Piaget, Tantum, Bronfenbrenner, Vygotsky and Bruner.

Eyler and Giles (1999) suggested that service-learning contributes to students' self-esteem, career decisions, and reward in helping others. One-hundred percent of the coded data detected that students acquire self-knowledge and career information, and 94% of the coded data also revealed that they gain self-confidence and find reward in helping others. Students valued their chances to experience "real world" interactions, to learn about them, and to make sure teaching or counseling was a career that they wanted to pursue. One student's comment illustrated personal growth through finding reward in helping others:

> The kids have taught me just as much, if not more than I have taught them, and I look forward to teaching these students more and more each day, because of the great sense of satisfaction that comes with experience.

Eyler and Giles (1999) addressed the impact of service-learning courses relative to reducing stereotyping and community connections. Sixty-four percent of the data coded identified reduced stereotyping, 77% of the data coded described community connections, and 66% of the data coded illustrated social responsibility as a third and final learning outcome. Two students' notations illustrate reduced stereotyping and community connections.

> After walking down the hall with some of the children, a little girl stated that she wanted to be a janitor. Another student informed her that she could not be a janitor because she is a girl and she is White (as he pointed to the poster of people and careers). This experience has made me more sensitive to working with diverse children.

> I think the most important lesson that I learned through service-learning is not to stereotype based upon first appearances. My experience at Main Street taught me a good lesson of how easily stereotypes are proven wrong. I also felt that I belonged at this school and my race and gender were not factors in my relationships with the children and teachers.

Although not all students acquired the same learning outcomes, there was a striking similarity in the learning processes that took place in their service experiences.

Exhibit 6.3 outlines those learning patterns, grouped into preservice, during service, and postservice themes. In the preservice stage, many students began their service experience with either excitement or apprehension about working in an urban environment. Learning was viewed in terms of emotional, cognitive, or multicultural processes. For example, students who engaged in emotional learning had idealistic views of helping. One student stated, "I knew it would make me feel great to participate in this project." Students who engaged in cognitive learning

**Exhibit 6.3.   Major Learning Processes and
Time Patterns Associated With Student Learning**

Time Patterns	%	Learning Process	Units of Analysis
Preservice	52	Emotional	• Nervous and excited; first day and I got those first day of school jitters all over again.
	23	Cognitive	• Apprehensive; preconceived notions about the school; stereotypes about the school.
	23	Multicultural	• Concerned if the children would reject me when they see this "White guy" coming into their classroom.
During service	81	Social/interpersonal	• Enhanced my beliefs in the good of others; developed partnerships/relationships; opened my eyes to a reality that I did not know existed.
	78	Social/intrapersonal	• Learned not to stereotype. The children would smile every time I was there and it made me feel good; the children would get excited to me; reflected on who I am and who I will strive to be as a teacher.
Postservice	77	Emotional	• Felt upset that I had to leave; empathy and compassion; concern; gratitude; shocked by the hugs; overwhelmed; felt good to give back; loved working with this group.
	71	Cognitive	• Saw changes in the students' abilities or behavior; made a difference; helped confirm or disconfirm my career choices; contributed to my confidence; it was a surreal experience; learned I must think outside of the "box."
	58	Multicultural	• I expected all of the children to be bad; learned I can work in an diverse atmosphere/individuals; expectations and attitudes changed; learned about a different culture; my views changed, less judgmental and reframe from stereotyping; shocked over educational injustices.

had preconceived notions about working in a specific or their selected school district, and those who engaged in multicultural-learning expressed concerns that the children would reject them because of their ethnicity.

Most of the students in during service changed their thoughts and attitudes about the community. It was clear that interpersonal and intrapersonal learning occurred through the students' relationships with teachers and children. Interpersonal learning was viewed when the students were more concerned about the meaning of the service experience for others. As one student stated, "This experience opened my eyes to a reality that I did not know even exists and I am concerned for the children when I leave; who is going to help them?" In contrast, intrapersonal learning was noted when the students were attentive to the influence of service on one's feelings, thoughts, and behaviors; for instance, one student noted, "This experience taught me not to undervalue myself." Students' intrapersonal and interpersonal learning led to their emotional, cognitive, and multicultural reflections postservice.

In the postservice stage, most students experienced emotional and cognitive learning. Emotional learning was observed when students associated empathy and compassion with the service experience. One student commented, "It felt good to help the children read and I am upset that the project is over." Cognitive learning was viewed when a student associated the service experience with critical thinking skills and observed, "This was a surreal experience that helped me think outside of the box."

In conclusion, high frequencies were found for academic learning, and personal and social development as learning outcomes, that explain "what" the students learned, while moderate frequencies were found for social (i.e., interpersonal, intrapersonal), emotional, and cognitive learning as processes that explain "how" the students learned from participating in service. Multicultural learning was also identified as a learning process but was cited less often.

What Did the Teachers Gain From Service-Learning?

As shown in Exhibit 6.4, few teachers made comments regarding student improvement; however, they did request that the same student could assist them throughout the year instead of for one semester. Four major themes emerged from the coded data about the benefits of service-learning from the teachers' point of view including:

1.   Children and classroom;
2.   Pedagogical and/or instructional methods;
3.   Teacher education and/or student development; and
4.   Community-university partnership.

One teacher's remarks addressed all four themes:

> It takes a village to teach students, and your students have become a part of our village. This project has restored my faith in the goodness of others and in the university. The students gained real-life experience while they

**Exhibit 6.4.   Thematic Analysis of Service-Learning
as a Teacher Empowerment Method**

%	Domains	Categories	Units
96	Children and classroom	Rapport	• Worked well with students. • Children responded positively to the students, natural characteristics of a teacher
		Made children feel special	• One-one attention. • Made the children feel as though someone cared about them. • Influenced the children's self-esteem. • Provided mentoring and support.
		Fulfilled a community need	• Willingness to jump in. • Provided individual instruction. • Assisted with the students who were developmentally delayed and academically behind. • Children's PSSA score increased.
81	Teacher education–student development	Real-life experience	• Application of course concepts. • Reaffirmed career decisions. • Students learn what grade level they wanted to teach. • Gained first-hand experience. • Learned how to deal with disruptive children.
		Urban education	• Students had an opportunity to adapt to another social climate. • Gained knowledge of working with students who are from lower SES and academically behind. • Got a picture of urban education.
66	Community-university partnership	Renewed my faith in a caring community	• Connected to the university. • I depend on the students for individual instruction with the children. • Students had an impact on the children and the class. • Student became part of the class/school/community. • Gained a sense of who I will be working with in the future.
		Students helped me	• Assisted with teaching; taught me to be flexible. • Reduced my level of stress. • Students supported me.
65	Pedagogical methods	Changed instructional methods	• Used individual instruction methods. • Relied on the students for one-on-one instruction. • Extra hands in the classroom allowed for activities that would have been impossible with 30 plus 6-year-olds.
		Learned new skills	• Learned to be flexible. • Learned from the students to be more student-centered and hands-on with children. • Increased my awareness of my teaching skills.

(Exhibit continues on next page)

Exhibit 6.4. Continued

%	Domains	Categories	Units
31	Requests	Time	• Limited time. • Would like students to come longer than 15 hours. • Longer time. • Have student continue throughout the year. • Continue program in the future.
		Students	• Send more students. • Have the same student throughout the years. • Had to share students. • Have more than one student in a classroom.

assisted in overcrowded classrooms and worked with students who may have fallen behind or through the cracks of the institution. The students have made a difference in the lives of the children and me. I have reshaped my own techniques and have learned from them to be more student-centered in my approach to teaching.

DISCUSSION

The current study contributes to new information about preservice differences between service-learning and nonservice-learning students. This is one of the first studies to use a triangulation, mixed-methods design to demonstrate that participation in service-learning affects students' academic learning and personal, and social development. Incorporating multiple methods and assessing community recipients allowed the authors to test for preservice and postservice differences and assured the reliability of findings beyond considering only a single method. The quantitative and qualitative data suggest that all participants and recipients involved in this service-learning study benefited from their participation.

Service-learning participants showed expected changes in their knowledge of local politics, leadership skills, diversity attitudes and exploration and assimilation preferences for community involvement. However, they also showed unexpected changes in GPAs, learning about the academic field and community, problem-solving ability, social competence, and self-understanding motives. Findings that students are less apprehensive about engaging in community service and are more likely to make lifestyle decisions that involve service experiences are somewhat consistent with previous research of C. A. Payne (2000), who found that service-learning students increase their apprehension about making long-term commitments to service from the beginning to the end of the semester. Likewise, findings that students increased their diversity attitudes and multicultural competencies are incongruent with previous research on diversity attitudes (Moely, McFarland, et al., 2002). There are two possible explanations for the inconsistent results in previous and current research. First, the lack of a control group prohibits measuring service-learners' motives for participating in service-learning; therefore, "sample-selection" and "good-subject" biases (Rosenthal & Rosnow, 1991) may have been retained in the results of this study. Second, homogeneity effects are probably associated with the large proportion of education majors within the sample. Education majors are exposed to the field during their first year; therefore, they are likely to have a deeper understanding of the social injustices in an impoverished community. Increases in diversity attitudes and assimilation preferences for engagement indicate an increase in awareness of power distributions in educational institutions that contribute to inequities in our societies. Most of the students worked as tutors with ethnically and economically diverse children who were academically behind in the public education system. Service-learning gave the students an opportunity to see how the children are affected by limited resources and overcrowded classrooms, thus increasing their political awareness, leadership skills, and openness to cultural differences, and decreasing their self-interest motives for participation in service.

Another objective of this study was to determine if differences existed between qualitative and quantitative findings of personal and social development for service-learning students. The qualitative data presented in the study suggest that students gain self-knowledge, become more aware of different cultures and the community, and learn to take responsibility for social issues through their participation in service-learning (Eyler & Giles, 1999; Green, 2001; Strage, 2000). Similarities between the qualitative and quantitative findings were observed in students' personal and social learning outcomes; and the consistency of data on students' surveys and in journals contribute to the confidence in the authors' claims that students benefit from engaging in this pedagogy.

Three discrepancies were also observed between qualitative and quantitative data concerning students' academic learning, social competence, and community self-efficacy. In their journal entries, most of the students described content knowledge and application. However, students' GPAs and problem-solving skills did not improve from the beginning to the end of the semester as expected. Inconsistent findings in qualitative and quantitative data may be attributed to the different assessment methods that were used to measure academic learning. Similarly, in their journals, almost all of the students described skills to work effectively with community recipients and to acquire a sense of personal efficacy, although students' social competence and self-efficacy scores did not improve at the course end. There are two plausible reasons for the mixed results: (1) students rated their competence and efficacy levels extremely high at preservice; and (2) questionnaires measuring competence and efficacy may not be sensitive enough to detect changes in these scores over the course of the semester. Findings about academic learning, self-efficacy, and social competence should be examined further in future studies so that results are more reliable and valid.

The qualitative data also provided an opportunity to observe the learning processes that took place during the service-learning experience. Previous research has illustrated that service-learning is effective in facilitating student learning (Eyler & Giles, 1999; Rockquemore & Schaffer, 2000), yet little is known about how students actually learn. By detecting social, emotional, cognitive, and multicultural learning through the content analysis, learning processes were observed as students moved through a semester of service-learning. This allowed the authors to identify common trends in students' learning development because they expressed common reactions during the semester. Almost all of the students spoke about learning through interactions with community recipients, reflecting on the impact that the program had on their thoughts and feelings and considering the impact that they had on the program. Many students also described emotional and cognitive reactions to their service experience. Service-learning gave students opportunities to use social, emotional, and cognitive learning, which in turn promoted their academic learning, personal growth, and social competencies. The qualitative data provide a procedural framework of how learning occurs through service-learning, and the integration of both qualitative and quantitative data enhances the evaluation of this model.

A final objective of this study was to explore service-learning as a method for promoting teacher satisfaction and empowering teachers in an urban setting. Although differences were not observed between elementary and non-elementary schoolteachers, the teachers were satisfied overall with the students and the service-learning program. In fact, the major limitation to the service-learning project was time. The majority of teachers stated that they wished the students could work with them for more than 15 hours and more than one semester. Similarly, almost all of the teachers noted that the students provided individual attention to the children, which, in turn, made the children feel special and helped them improve academic ability. More than half of all teachers also felt that this service assisted them with their classroom management because they were able to work with children in groups and to utilize pedagogical techniques that would be inappropriate for large classrooms. Likewise, the majority of teachers felt that the service project benefited the university students by providing real-life experience and exposing them to urban education.

More than half of the teachers felt that the benefits for university students were equally valuable for them and thus restored their faith in the university. All of the teachers requested that the program be continued so as to further build upon this partnership. The qualitative findings on the benefits from service-learning for teachers are not only encouraging, but also critical to the university, whose mission is predicated on service-learning and citizenship. Researchers observed how service-learning allows a university to establish a partnership with a community that was previously disconnected from the institution while also fulfilling a community need that is advantageous for teachers and children. The qualitative data provide a framework that describes how service-learning directly and indirectly empowers teachers in an urban context.

While the study adds to the service-learning research, the results should be viewed in light of a few key limitations. First, the Widener student population and the community recipient population are demographically homogenous. Student participants were predominantly white, came from middle-class backgrounds, and usually were the first-generation to attend a 4-year college. The teachers were predominantly white, and the children were predominantly African American. Second, the students worked in public schools and community organizations in an urban area where the majority of children were from low-income families, scored below the basic proficiency level on the Stanford Achievement Test, and received either Title I or special education programs (Pennsylvania Department of Education, 2001-2002). Third, since quantitative and qualitative data were collected at two different points in time from surveys and journals, there are likely testing-effects, social-desirability effects, and self-report biases associated with the results. Finally, the lack of control group and randomization methods preclude inferring causality between academic service-learning and student and community outcomes. Future research should replicate this study and use randomization and control group methods to make conclusions that are more definitive about service-learning student and community outcomes. This would make an interesting future study.

REFERENCES

Boyle-Baise. M. (2002). *Multicultural service learning*. New York: Teachers College Press.

Boyle-Baise, M., & Kilbane, J. (2000). What really happens? A look inside service-learning for multicultural teacher education. *Michigan Journal of Community Service Learning, 7*, 54–64.

Bringle, R. G., Phillips, M. A., & Hudson, M. (2004). *The measure of service-learning*. Washington, DC: American Psychological Press.

Brody, S. M., & Wright, S. C. (2004, Fall). Expanding the self through service-learning. *Michigan Journal of Community Service Learning, 11(1)*, 14–24.

Creswell, J. W. (1994). *Research design: Qualitative and quantitative approaches.* Thousand Oaks, CA: Sage.

Creswell, J. W. (1998). *Qualitative inquiry and research design: Choosing among five traditions.* Thousand Oaks, CA. Sage.

Creswell, J. W. (2005). *Educational research* (2nd ed.). Upper Saddle River, NJ: Pearson Prentice Hall.

Cruz, N. I., & Giles, D. E. (2000, Fall). Where's the community in service-learning research? [Special issue]. *Michigan Journal of Community Service Learning,* 28–34.

Delli Carpini, M. X., & Keeter, S. (2000). What should be learned through service learning? *PS: Political Science and Politics, 33(3),* 635–639.

Eyler, J. S. (2000, Fall). What do we most need to know about the impact of service-learning on student learning? [Special issue]. *Michigan Journal of Community Service Learning,* 11–17.

Eyler, J. S., & Giles, D. E. (1999). *Where's the learning in service-learning?* San Francisco: Jossey-Bass.

Eyler, J. S., Giles, D. E., Stenson, C. M., & Gray, C. J. (2003). What we know about the effects of service-learning on college students, faculty, institutions, and communities, 1993-2000 (3rd ed.). In *Introduction to service-learning toolkit* (2nd ed., pp. 15–22). Providence, RI: Campus Compact.

Ferrari, J. R., & Worrall, L. (2000). Assessments by community agencies: How "the other side" sees service-learning. *Michigan Journal of Community Service Learning, 7,* 35–40.

Gallini, S. M., & Moely, B. E. (2003). Service-learning and engagement, academic challenge, and retention. *Michigan Journal of Community Service Learning, 10(1),* 1–14.

Gardner, H. (1993). *Multiple intelligences: The theory in practice.* New York: Basic Books.

Gardner, H. (1999). *Intelligence reframed.* New York: Basic Books.

Green, A. E. (2001). "But you aren't white:" Racial perspectives and service learning. *Michigan Journal of Community Service Learning, 8(1),* 18–26.

Harkavy, I., Puckett, J., & Romer, D. (2000, Fall). Action research: Bridging service and research [Special issue]. *Michigan Journal of Community Service Learning,* 113–119.

Howard-Hamilton, M. (2000, July). Programming for multicultural competencies. *New Directions for Student Services, 90,* 67–78.

Jacoby, B. (1996). *Service-learning in higher education.* San Francisco: Jossey-Bass.

Litke, R. A. (2002). Do all students "get it?" Comparing students' reflections to course performance. *Michigan Journal of Community Service Learning, 8(2),* 27–34.

Moely, B. E., McFarland, M. Miron, D., Mercer, S., & Ilustre, V. (2002). Changes in college students' attitudes and intentions for civic involvement as a function of service-learning experiences. *Michigan Journal of Community Service Learning, 9(1),* 18–26.

Moely, B. E., Mercer, S. H., Ilustre, V., Miron, D., & McFarland, M. (2002). Psychometric properties and correlates of the civic attitudes and skills questionnaire (CASQ): A measure of student's attitudes related to service-learning. *Michigan Journal of Community Service Learning, 8*(2), 15–26.

Moore, D. T. (2000, Fall). The relationship between experimental learning research and service-learning research [Special issue]. *Michigan Journal of Community Service Learning,* 124–128.

O'Grady, C. R. (Ed.). (2000). Integrating service learning and multicultural education: An overview. In *Integrating service learning and multicultural education in colleges and universities* (pp. 1–20). Mahwah, NJ: Erlbaum.

Pennsylvania Department of Education. (2001-2002). *State, district, and school report cards.* Harrisburg, PA: Bureau of Assessment and Accountability.

Payne, C. A. (2000). Changes in involvement preferences as measured by the community service involvement preference inventory. *Michigan Journal of Community Service Learning, 7,* 41–53.

Payne, D. A. (2000). *Evaluating service-learning activities and programs.* Lanham, MD: The Scarecrow Press.

Quezada, R. L., & Christopherson, R. W., (2005). Adventure-based service learning: University students' self-reflection accounts of service with children. *Journal of Experiential Education, 28*(1), 1–16.

Reinke, S. J. (2003). Making a difference: Does service-learning promote civic engagement in MPA students? *Journal of Public Affairs Education, 9*(2), 129–137.

Rockquemore, K. A., & Schaffer, R. H. (2000). Toward a theory of engagement: A cognitive mapping of service learning. *Michigan Journal of Community Service Learning, 7,* 14–23.

Roldan, M., Strage, A., & David, D. (2004). A framework for assessing academic service-learning across disciplines. In M. Welch & S. H. Billig, (Eds.), *Advances in service-learning research: Vol. 5. New perspectives in service-learning: Research to advance the field* (pp. 39–59). Greenwich, CT: Information Age.

Root, S., Callahan, J., & Sepanski, J. (2001). Service-learning in teacher education: A consideration of qualitative and quantitative outcomes. In A. Furco & S. H. Billig (Eds.), *Advances in service-learning research: Vol. 1. Service-learning: The essence of pedagogy* (pp. 223–243). Greenwich, CT: Information Age.

Root, S., Callahan, J., & Sepanski, J. (2002). Building teaching dispositions and service-learning practice: A multi-site study. *Michigan Journal of Community Service Learning, 8*(2), 50–59.

Rosenthal, R., & Rosnow, R. L., (1991). *Essential of behavioral research: Methods and data analysis* (2nd ed.). New York: McGraw-Hill.

Salovey, P., Brackett, M. A., & Mayer, J. D. (2004). *Emotional intelligence.* Port Chester, NY: Dude.

Schmidt, A., & Robby, M. A. (2002). What's the value of service-learning to the community? *Michigan Journal of Community Service Learning, 9*(1), 27–33.

Slavin, R. E. (2003). *Educational psychology* (7th ed.). Boston: Allyn & Bacon.

Strage, A. A. (2000). Service-learning: Enhancing learning outcomes in a college-level lecture course. *Michigan Journal of Community Service Learning, 7,* 5–13.

Vogelgesang, L. J., & Astin, A. W. (2000). Comparing the effects of community service and service learning. *Michigan Journal of Community Service Learning, 7,* 25–34.

CHAPTER 7

IMPACTS OF A SERVICE-LEARNING SEMINAR AND PRACTICUM ON PRESERVICE TEACHERS' UNDERSTANDING OF PEDAGOGY, COMMUNITY, AND THEMSELVES

Angela M. Harwood, Devon Fliss, and Erin Gaulding

ABSTRACT

In this chapter, the authors add to the existing knowledge base of effective practices in teacher education by addressing the central question: "What are the outcomes of a service-learning seminar and middle-school service-learning practicum experience for preservice teachers?" This study is designed to augment existing research through an analytic induction analysis of the reflective writings of preservice teachers. The authors found that preservice teachers who concurrently participated in a seminar on service-learning pedagogy and a middle-school service-learning project gained

Advancing Knowledge in Service-Learning: Research to Transform the Field, 137–158
Copyright © 2006 by Information Age Publishing
All rights of reproduction in any form reserved.

increased understanding of students, service-learning and general pedagogy, the community, and themselves.

INTRODUCTION

Enabling future teachers to use service-learning pedagogy is a central
goal for many teacher educators who work in the service-learning field,
yet relatively little is known about the most effective ways to accomplish
this goal. In this chapter, we add to the existing knowledge base of effective practices in teacher education by addressing the following central
question: What are the outcomes of a service-learning seminar and middle-school service-learning practicum experience for preservice teachers?
This study is designed to augment existing research through an analysis
of the reflective writings of preservice teachers. In this chapter, we review
the literature about preservice teachers and then present the results of our
study.

LITERATURE REVIEW

As the research on K-12 impacts of service-learning grows, the topic is
also gaining the attention of teacher educators nationwide (Council of
Chief State School Officers, 1995; Donahue, 1999; Erickson & Anderson,
1997). Teacher educators assert that involvement in service-learning
allows preservice teachers to question existing policies and assumptions
about classroom practice, to experience learning strategies consistent with
educational reforms, and to develop sensitivity to multicultural populations and societal needs (Wade, 1997). In addition, service-learning is
seen as a technique that offers preservice teachers an extended opportunity to work with youth (National Middle School Association, 1991).
Researchers who have addressed service-learning in teacher education
have given focus to the factors that influence preservice teachers' intent to
employ the pedagogy in the future and the types of experiences that
shape those intentions.

Participation in service-learning during teacher education courses,
particularly when those experiences are of high quality and when the
experiences are supported by course instructors, increase preservice
teachers' intent to incorporate service-learning in their future classrooms
(Root, Callahan, & Sepanski, 2002a). In general, experiences that involve
preservice teachers in using service-learning as pedagogy with K-12
students (e.g., completing a service-learning project during student
teaching) are more likely to lead to the implementation of service-

learning in one's future teaching (Ball, 2003; Wade & Yarbrough, 1997). Ball (2003) further argued that for service-learning to be effective,

- Service-learning pedagogy must be embedded program-wide;
- Students should be introduced to the pedagogy in the first quarter of their teacher-education program; and
- Their education in service-learning should then continue through a capstone project of designing, implementing, and reflecting upon service-learning during student teaching.

The type and structure of preservice teachers' service-learning experience makes a difference in their attitude toward the pedagogy (Donahue, 2000; Wade, Anderson, Yarbrough, Pickeral, Erickson, & Kromer, 1999). Working with informed and involved mentor teachers, help with planning and implementing projects (Ball, 2003; Flottemesch, Heide, Pedras, & Karp, 2001) and participating in a well-structured service-learning program (Allen-Campbell & Brannon, 2001) are identified by preservice teachers as important contributions to their success.

Overall, while research studies (e.g., Anderson & Guest, 1993; Boyle-Baise, 1997; Brown & Howard, 2005; Donahue, Bowyer, & Rosenberg, 2003; Freeman & Swick, 2001; Middleton, 2003; Root, Callahan, & Sepanski, 2002b; Root & Furco, 2001; Tellez, Hlebowitsh, Cohen, & Norwood, 1995; Wade & Yarbrough, 1997) have shown that service-learning can be a worthwhile and powerful experience for preservice teachers that enhances self-esteem, self-efficacy, positive views of diverse others, an ethic of caring, and additional important competencies, researchers still have much to learn about *what* aspects of service or the service-learning experience contribute to their understanding of the components of service-learning pedagogy. Ball (2003) suggested that if the goal of teacher education service-learning is to create future teachers disposed to using service-learning, then assessment of outcomes must directly address that issue, rather than vaguely looking for evidence of "teacher change" (p. 72).

Many types of field experiences have been a part of the tradition of teacher education programs. In addition to exploring service-learning field placements, teacher educators have more broadly focused on how work in schools enable preservice teachers to develop professional skills. Early field experiences are considered important in helping preservice teachers develop the ability to link theory and practice, influence teaching decisions through hands-on experience, and broaden their conception of teaching beyond time spent in front of a class of young people (LaMaster, 2001). Perry and Power (2004) argued that while college classroom learning is important for preservice teachers, the most important knowledge teachers gain is through local, systematic inquiry.

Dana and Silva (2001) and Watson and Reiman (2001) studied the role of reflection and inquiry in field experiences and the link between reflection/inquiry in successfully transitioning preservice teachers from college settings to professional positions. Bullough, Young, Erickson, and Birrell (2002) suggested that more experimentation is needed in terms of various kinds of field experience models and strategies; in particular, experiences that go beyond the traditional student teacher-cooperating teacher-faculty advisor format. Specifically, they noted the potential of field experiences that pair preservice teachers so they can collectively reflect and build upon one another's' experiences. Pryor and Kuhn (2004) and Moore (2003) also argued that a combination of experience and reflection bridges theory and practice—a common concern of teacher education programs. This type of reflective practice is considered to be critical to the development of successful educators (Perry & Power, 2004; Pryor & Kuhn, 2004; Watson & Reiman, 2001). Freudenthal (as cited in Moore, 2003) indicated that transfer between learning in teacher education programs and classroom practice is facilitated by reflection on realistic classroom situations. Brouwer (cited in Moore, 2003) asserted that "transfer of what is presumably learning in teacher education programs to actual classroom practice has been strongly linked to whether there was provision for student teachers to develop knowledge about teaching by reflecting on realistic classroom situations" (p. 32).

This current study was framed by consideration of these studies previously published in the service-learning and general teacher education literature. While prior research suggests that service-learning is a worthwhile and powerful exercise for preservice teachers, the aspects of service that contribute to their understanding of service-learning have not been fully explored. This chapter will provide information that will help to fill this acknowledged gap in the research.

METHOD

Program Description

The data reported here were collected during "Project Connect" a university-middle school collaborative service-learning experience. The collaborative is designed to allow eighth-grade students and preservice teachers the opportunity to engage in community service-learning projects together. Through this approach, between 25 and 50 preservice teachers work with 200 to 300 middle school students and provide service for 35 to 50 community-based agencies annually. They work in community-based agencies with the elderly, young children, pets and animals, the environment, or social services. The program was intentionally designed to feature strong academic components, for both university and eighth-grade students, enabling them to meet state and national standards while providing sustained, needs-centered service to community organizations. The middle school component is deeply embedded in a language arts/social studies core curriculum. (For a more complete description of this collaborative approach, see Harwood & Hart, 2000.)

The university elements of the program are designed to enable preservice teachers to gain a deeper understanding of service-learning by being exposed to a model middle school approach and by engaging as partners in implementing the program.

Preservice teachers serve as learning facilitators for groups of four to eight 8th-grade students. They are responsible for:

- Meeting the students at the school;
- Transporting them to the community site;
- Engaging in service with them; and
- Responding to eighth graders' written reflections.

Some preservice teachers opt to participate in Project Connect as a portion of their required middle school practicum (a 20-hour requirement prior to student teaching); others opt to participate as an elective.

In addition to the field experience, a specialized two-credit course, "Seminar in Service-Learning," is offered. The optional seminar is designed to complement the field experience and to give preservice teachers a full understanding of service-learning pedagogy. The major goals of the combined seminar and field experience for preservice teachers are:

- Developing an understanding of service-learning;
- Exploring their roles as teachers;
- Increasing their knowledge of community issues and agencies; and
- Learning more about themselves.

In seminar meetings, students share information about their field experience and study critical pedagogical components of service-learning. They explore the definition and underlying rationales behind service-learning; critical components of building a service-learning curriculum, such as developing projects around standards and choosing community partners;

assessment; the role of reflection; and methods of celebrating service-learning. Course requirements include submitting a final service-learning curriculum plan and writing reflections for each week of service in the field. In reflections, students are specifically asked to provide brief descriptions of what happened on site and then to comment on what they learned about middle school students, teaching, the community service site, and themselves.

Participants

Data reported in the chapter consist of preservice teachers' reflections collected during the 2003, 2004, and 2005 sessions of the combined service-learning seminar and field practicum. Data were obtained from a total of 21 participants from the 3 years, and a total of 50 reflections were analyzed. For each of the 3 years, all available reflections were used. For the nine participants in 2003, only the final, culminating reflections were included; for 2004, there were between two and six reflections from each of seven students; and for the 2005 group, there were four to six reflections from each of five students. The data sample is somewhat weighted toward the 2005 participants because access to every reflection from each student across the 3 years was unavailable. It was felt, however, that the additional depth that could be provided by as many reflections as possible justified their inclusion. In the analysis, which confirmed our decision, consistency was found in the themes across the three groups of students.

The students, preservice teachers enrolled in the secondary certificate program, were all registered for the seminar course described above and each worked with one group of eighth-grade students on site once a week for 6 weeks. Two of the students were in a master's in teaching program; the remainder were undergraduates.

Procedure

The data in this chapter consist of qualitative analysis from the reflections written by preservice teachers as they engaged in the seminar and practicum. In analyzing each set of data, we employed the analytic induction method of analysis (Bogden & Bicklen, 1992; Glasser & Strauss, 1999; Patton, 1990). In this approach, themes emerged from the data and were constantly tested and retested as additional data were analyzed. The lead author first marked each reflection with slashes to indicate data points to be coded. Then, working with the big categories implied by the focus of the reflection prompts (middle school students, teaching, the community, and self), and a category of "other" to capture items that might not fit within the stated categories, the two authors independently coded each data point. As we read and analyzed the data, we looked for emergent subcategories and made notes about them.

A total of 434 data points were coded, with an interrater reliability of 85.7%. Those data points that were primarily descriptive of what occurred on site were then removed from the data set, which left 356 data points that we continued to analyze. The data points were then disaggregated from each reflection and combined under major the category headings of students, teaching, the community, and self. After sorting data into these main categories, we created subcategories within them as themes emerged. As this was done, we decided to separate the large "teaching" category into general pedagogy and service-learning pedagogy. Finally, after subcategories were developed, some were combined with others, or shifted between large category headings (for instance, one element initially under "community" was moved to the subcategory of "working with community partners" under the larger category of understanding service-learning pedagogy).

RESULTS

We discovered six major categories of outcomes in our analysis of the preservice teachers' reflection data:

1. Understanding of students;
2. Understanding of service-learning pedagogy;
3. General pedagogical understandings;
4. Understanding of community;
5. Knowledge about self; and
6. General commentary on the impact of the practicum experience.

The findings are summarized in Exhibit 7.1 and in the following sections.

Increased Understanding of Students

There were 90 total data points in which preservice teachers expressed understanding of the middle school students with whom they were working. There were several subcategories of understanding that emerged, many of which focused on preservice teachers' identification of students'

**Exhibit 7.1.   Outcomes of Participating in a
Service-Learning Seminar and Field Practicum (N = 356)**

Outcome	Number of Responses
Increased Understanding of Students (n = 90)	
Identifying student needs	28
Recognizing student abilities	17
Social or behavioral development	14
General development	9
Student interests	9
Emotional understanding	9
Establishing bonds with students	4
Understanding Service-Learning Pedagogy (n = 91)	
Service-learning impact on students	27
Working with community partners	22
Reflection	20
Structuring service-learning approaches	15
Value of service-learning	7
General Pedagogy Knowledge (n = 64)	
Behavior/discipline	25
Structuring instruction	18
Capturing teachable moments	11
Role and impact of teachers	10
Understanding of Community (n = 62)	
Impact of service on community	26
Community-based issues	21
Operation of community agencies	15
Knowledge About Self (n = 40)	
Self as teacher	19
Attitudes/emotional awareness	12
Skill self-assessment	9
Practicum-Specific Impacts (n = 9)	

developmental levels. These ranged from understanding middle school students' needs to recognizing their abilities, social or emotional characteristics, and physical attributes. In addition, preservice teachers wrote about gaining knowledge of students' interests and establishing bonds with middle schoolers.

The data in this category most often included indications of understanding students' needs ($n = 28$), including needs for motivation ($n = 11$), structure ($n = 10$), or emotional support ($n = 7$). An example recognizing motivation needs follows:

I believe that the project we did, clearing blackberries, was perfectly timed as far as motivating the students was concerned. If we had done another week of mulching, I think the kids would have mutinied, but instead they had an activity that for once they really enjoyed and also that they were able to witness serious progress.

Preservice teachers also recognized the need to adjust the structure of activities to meet the needs of the students with whom they worked. Two preservice teachers remarked:

[Student name] is more experienced in dealing with people I think, because of his involvement in church mission trips, and what we've been doing so far has come really easy to him. Because it's a little more challenging for [name] and [name], it was good for them to get more chances to speak to people and also to get some direct pointers from me.

I learned from [the teacher] that two out of the three students are in special education. I asked [her] if it would be beneficial to provide the girls with some time to work on their reflections on site, and she thought that would be great.

Other examples from the broad category of understanding students show that preservice teachers gained new insights about the abilities of middle schoolers ($n = 17$). They often expressed a sense of excitement, or surprise. As one preservice teacher wrote:

I found that I learned a lot of interesting things about middle school students through this experience. I think we are all too often inundated with negative views on the middle school student of today. This experience showed me that these students are very independent and self sufficient.

"The students have continued to impress me," and "this showed me how well they were able to adapt to a new situation" are other representative examples coded in this subcategory.

In addition to learning about student needs and abilities, preservice teachers gained new understandings of the general developmental level and interests of middle schoolers. These outcomes included fairly sophisticated observations of group dynamics and how these dynamics shifted when certain students were absent or a parent was present, as well as observations about how the physical characteristics of middle schoolers impacted their work. Preservice teachers reported that they learned about students' interest in careers in addition to gaining insights into the world of adolescents. Across the range of responses in this category, it became apparent that participation in the service-learning project deepened preservice teachers' understanding about the students with whom they worked.

Understanding Service-Learning Pedagogy

In their reflections, preservice teachers reported 91 instances of increased understanding of service-learning pedagogy. These included recognizing the impact of service-learning on students ($n = 27$), working with community partners ($n = 22$), reflection ($n = 20$), structuring service-learning ($n = 15$) and statements expressing personal value for service-learning ($n = 7$).

The largest subcategory of service-learning understanding was a recognition of the impact the program had on eighth-grade students. Participants most often wrote about the affective outcomes for students, as exhibited in the following example: "What I saw were kids joyful to be making a difference in peoples' lives. You could see they had never been trusted with the chance to do so and they were proud of their efforts." Preservice teachers also noted 8th graders' feelings of self-efficacy, pride, or frustration. Interestingly, relatively few cognitive outcomes were mentioned, and in three of the seven items coded in this category, preservice teachers seemed to question whether those outcomes were happening and noted: "As I gleaned from the reflections, most students did not understand the permanent impact of the careless act of introducing an invasive species," and "Although I did come to the realization that the service portion of the project was definitely present, I still struggle a bit with the learning aspect."

The second largest outcome in the service-learning pedagogy category was a heightened understanding of community partners. Data points coded in this subcategory ranged from commentary about the appropriateness of sites and how partners responded to students to an exploration of the role of partners. Preservice teachers recognized that the location of sites with respect to the school had an impact, and that how the community partners interacted with students made a big difference. One preservice teacher expressed this as follows:

> I also wondered how the project would have gone if our community partner was not prepared or held low expectations of the students. There are so many confounding variables that make for a successful project, the students' excitement, our leadership, and the community partner played a role in making the project successful.

Others also commented on the importance of the connection with partners and when it worked well or when it did not:

> Maintaining dialogue between the students and the site coordinator is something that I have learned is critical to a positive service-learning experience.

Just a note for next time—the community partner will most likely need more notice so they can prepare for discussion and questions on such a topic.

Our community partner interacts with students, but she doesn't seem to take an invested interest into their lives and making connections between our work site and who they are.

The third subcategory was reflection. Preservice teachers demonstrated an ability to analyze the reflection process, indicated by their ideas for how to improve the quality of their eighth-grade students' reflections by changing the structure or mode. One preservice teacher wrote, "In the form of reflections, I witnessed how important good scaffolding is in order to help students reach learning goals and objectives." Many preservice teachers wrote about strategies they would use to help improve their students' reflections. The following is a representative example of the responses:

I had a decent talk with the kids concerning their reflections and what I expect, especially the fact that they need to think about their answers and try to relate the questions not only to the specific projects but also related issues.

Another stated, "I am going to try returning their (reflection) folders to them personally next week. I expect that this face-to-face acknowledgment will make them feel a bit more accountable for their work."

Other preservice teachers wrote about how to heighten student engagement in the reflection process. Representative quotes included: "Gleaning reflection questions from students may be more genuine since they are the ones experiencing the service and have an understanding of what is relevant and important to their projects and themselves," and "The kids were more connected to the reflection when they were allowed to present their thoughts through their own medium and questions." All of these examples and numerous others in the data indicate that preservice teachers developed a sophisticated understanding about how to facilitate reflection in service-learning.

In addition to learning about the specific elements of reflection and working with community partners, preservice teachers also demonstrated knowledge of the overall structure of service-learning. Some of their comments included: "This makes me wonder if this project could work as a culminating project," and "Overall this week made me think a lot about how I would organize a service-learning project differently." These remarks and others in this category demonstrate that the preservice teachers were thinking through issues they would need to address to successfully adopt service-learning in their future classrooms.

Finally, seven of the preservice teachers indicated a personal value for service-learning as a result of their experience. A few comments in this category included: "I have no doubt that service-learning will be an integral part of my curriculum and I am excited to see all the different avenues that it will take," and "I know in the future that I will advocate for programs like this in the schools I teach at." One student summarized her experience as follows:

> We hear so much about making learning authentic for kids, about making it real to enthrall them and get them invested in their learning. Service-learning accomplishes all of this and more. Service-learning rocks!!!

In summary, the data clearly indicate that preservice teachers learned a lot about the pedagogy of service-learning through their seminar and practicum experience.

General Pedagogy Knowledge

Preservice teachers' reflections indicated they also learned many things about teaching in general ($N = 64$), which included learning about behavior, discipline, or motivation ($n = 25$); structuring instruction ($n = 18$); capturing teachable moments ($n = 11$); and commentary on the role of teachers and their impact ($n = 10$).

Working directly with students in the practicum enabled the preservice teachers to observe and think about student behavior. Data indicate they were learning how to approach behavioral issues and that they were developing a sense of the types of behavior teachers needed to think about. As one student stated:

> I think this gets back to the need for attention and ways of dealing with inappropriate behavior properly. I think this is one of the biggest "management" issues that teachers have to deal with in their classrooms.

Other students, particularly those who worked at day care sites, made many connections between how they saw preschool teachers handle toddlers and how they envisioned themselves in their future classrooms working with their own students.

A second major general pedagogy outcome was that the project encouraged preservice teachers to think about how to structure instruction for success. Statements by the preservice teachers included: "I realize the importance of giving structure to small groups when working in the classroom so that everyone has the opportunity to excel in their own ways," and "By giving students clear instructions and expectations we are setting them up to succeed, rather than making them guess about what they need to do." Many of these comments were framed in the preservice teachers' field experiences, providing evidence that they used those experiences as a springboard for thinking about instruction in general.

The next subcategory of general pedagogy—capturing the teachable moment—provided an interesting contrast to the previous one on structuring instruction. The data points coded into this subcategory were those in which preservice teachers provided examples of how to work within the moment to shape learning. One shared an experience their group had while walking from a park restoration site back to the school. As they were walking, a car full of drunk teenagers roared by, with those inside "rudely cat-calling and waving open bottles of alcohol." After observing the eighth graders' reactions, the preservice teacher was able to respond to them. As she reported:

> As horrible as the situation was, it was also a blessing in disguise.... It was great to be able to engage the students in a conversation not only about drinking and driving but also how to be gentlemen (as 9 of our 10 students are boys). While I was in shock by the actions of those in the car, I had to immediately pull myself together and address the issue with the students. I think this has definitely helped to prepare me for the future "unknowns" in teaching.

This and other quotes coded in this category show that the preservice teachers were learning, as one remarked, to "stay on my toes and roll with the punches"—a skill that will serve them well as teachers.

As a result of participating in the service-learning project, preservice teachers also considered the impact they and other teachers could have on students. One preservice teacher commented on the importance of role-modeling; for example, "I did a ton of modeling for my students and it seemed to be very helpful in getting them more comfortable." Another said:

> Even though we only went out with the Fairhaven students for 6 weeks, I became aware of how much influence we can have on our students. We may never know how we have affected a student's life; that is why it is important for us to be aware of how we carry ourselves, especially in their presence.

Others noted the outcomes of their efforts in working with students. One wrote, "In this visit I saw some of the leadership skills and supportive group dynamics I had been trying to encourage." Overall, preservice teachers' reflections indicated that the experience helped them to think through many general issues related to teaching.

Understanding the Community

Data from this study indicate that the preservice teachers gained a better understanding of their surrounding community ($N = 62$), which included understanding the needs of community partners and recognizing how service-learning can fill those needs ($n = 26$), learning about community issues ($n = 21$), and learning how community agencies operate ($n = 15$).

In addition, preservice teachers learned about the needs faced by their agency partners and made observations about how the eighth graders fulfilled those needs. Four preservice teachers wrote specifically about how they were meeting "authentic needs" at their sites, while others wrote about specific impacts they saw students making. These ranged from the accomplishment of physical labor at environmental sites to providing much-needed extra help in elementary classrooms or preschool settings. The following example comes from a preservice teacher who worked with a local agency that conducts animal therapy:

> I had the opportunity to have a great middle school memory. I got to take pigmy goats to the nursing home.... Two goats, two bunnies, two dogs, three adults, and four outstanding students caravanning to the nursing home was a sight to see. It was amazing how each animal attracted different people.... I spoke with a man who grew up on a farm in South Dakota during the depression. He owned seven pygmy goats ... you could tell that he liked being around the goats and going back to those memories was a comforting place.

Attending community-based sites each week also enabled students to think about the issues facing communities and society in general. Considerations of societal issues ranged from the role of child care providers in society to the isolating environments in nursing homes, the expulsion rates in preschools, and gender stereotypes. Very specific understandings of issues related to individual sites were also coded in this category, such as knowledge of invasive species, herbicides and pesticides, and ecosystems.

Preservice teachers also learned what their community-based agencies did and how they approached their work. Data points coded in this subcategory included recognition of the philosophies of various agencies, the roles of people who worked there, and how agencies implemented systems to carry out their work. Overall, the data from preservice teachers indicate that they gained a better understanding of community issues, how agencies work, and the impact that service can have on community partners.

Knowledge About Self

Beyond learning about both general pedagogy and specific service-learning pedagogies detailed in previous sections, data from preservice teachers indicate that they also learned a lot about themselves ($N = 40$). This self-discovery fell into the major subcategories of understanding self as teacher ($n = 19$), analyzing personal attitudes or emotional responses ($n = 12$), and skill self-assessment ($n = 9$).

Many preservice teachers reflected on themselves as teachers. Some commented that the experience reinforced their decision to teach, while others reflected on their teaching style and/or their ability to work with students. Representative comments included: "I'm continually learning it is much easier for me to work with boys than girls ... I'm not sure why that is but it is an intriguing observation for me"; "but on a more pedagogical level I rediscovered my love for pre-teen age kids"; and "I also found out how difficult it really can be for me to strike up a conversation with kids this age ... it is somewhat funny but they can be very intimidating." Others wrote about their vision for their future classrooms: "I will take my experiences with service-learning into my classroom to help cultivate a positive learning environment that will better enable all students to succeed," and "In a dream world I'd like to start my school year off getting the kids outside the class and allowing them to talk freely and open up a little bit more than they might in a classroom."

Preservice teachers also wrote about how participation affected their emotional state or their attitudes. "It has given me more confidence in my skills as a teacher, and empathy for my students with special needs" wrote one. Another commented, "One thing that I realized about myself this trip was my tentativeness." Others wrote about the need to manage their attitudes or perceptions, as evidenced in the following quote:

> In the past, I would get so upset that kids weren't behaving the way I expected them to or working as much as I thought they should. I realized that my anxiety over managing everybody's behavior kept me from enjoying myself and kept the kids from learning how to manage their own behavior. Over the last month, I've learned to recognize that kids can manage their behavior and seek out learning ... with a little guidance of course!

Finally, preservice teachers engaged in some skill self-assessment in their reflections. Quotes coded in this subcategory included: "I have some issues with time management"; "I just wish I was more skilled at motivating the students"; and "I see now that I am less of a natural leader and more of an emergent leader." Hopefully, knowledge of their skills will enable the teachers to focus on building them while they student teach.

Specific Impact of the Practicum

Finally, one set of data points remained separate from the categories described above because the nature of the preservice teachers' comments related specifically to particular elements of this practicum or seminar experience ($n = 9$). These comments, provided by seven different preservice teachers in the sample, identified that this particular experience was different from others they had in the program. Comments included, "I really appreciated the contrast that this activity provided with my practicum classes"; "I think this practicum is unique in offering such observable opportunities because of the different structure"; and "Since I began the secondary education program, I have learned many things about teaching, but I have probably learned the most when I am actively engaged in different teaching strategies." The following quote provides an excellent summary of these sentiments:

> I think it was really great for both the students and me to experience service-learning first hand. Books and articles can only tell you so much, but getting out there and actually doing it gives it a whole new meaning. Reflecting back on the whole experience, I absolutely loved it.

In summary, the data from the project indicate that preservice teachers derived a wide range of learning from their involvement in the service-learning seminar and practicum. Analysis of their reflections indicates that they learned about students, service-learning and general pedagogical principles, the community, and themselves. A discussion of these findings follows.

DISCUSSION

Data from the preservice teachers in the study indicated that the greatest impacts of the combined service-learning seminar and field experience were increased understanding of students and service-learning pedagogy. Given that transporting students across town and working with them at community-based sites provides very different opportunities to engage in conversations of a widely varying nature, this finding is not surprising. It was quite interesting to see that preservice teachers evidenced an ability to provide deep analyses of students' needs and abilities and to critique students' educational processes based these analyses.

The second major finding, evidence of understanding service-learning pedagogy, would seem to follow from the combination of both practical experience and the readings and discussions during the seminar sessions. The weekly seminars provided students with the ideal elements of service-learning, which they then proved able to reflect on in their writings. The seminar further provided a context for students to analyze field work, giving them a forum to explore problems and suggest solutions, often providing "just in time" versus "just in case" learning. Participation in the field work gave preservice teachers an opportunity to compare and contrast what they read about service-learning with actual practice.

Perhaps the essential bridge between the field work and the seminar was the reflective writing wherein preservice teachers displayed an ability to interpret the readings through their work in the field. Pryor and Kuhn (2004) suggested "although reflection on practice is needed for professional growth, this reflection does not come naturally" (p. 251); the combination of the service-learning seminar plus a practicum addresses this concern. It is also an example Huling's (1998) call for the development of a coursework/field experience construct that links the theoretical content of course work to an observation component in the field experience, carefully moderated and guided by teacher education faculty. The joint reflection during class discussions is an alternate model, such as that called for by Bullough and colleagues (2002), which enables preservice teachers to interact with one another before, during, and after their time in the field. Further, preservice teachers in the service-learning seminar can develop practical knowledge as a community of learners reflecting on their teaching together, as suggested by Perry and Power (2004. The combination of practice and study enabled them to take a very complex pedagogical approach from the abstract to the concrete with use of examples. This led to instances of quite sophisticated analyses of key service-learning components such as project structure, the use of reflection, and working with community partners.

Finally, a third of the students in the sample indicated strongly that they valued service-learning and would look forward to using it in the future. This supports previous findings that assisting classroom teachers with service-learning projects (Root et al., 2002a; Wade & Yarbrough, 1997) and working on extensive service-learning planning assignments (Wade, 2003) can affect preservice teachers' intent to use service-learning in the future. It is possible that their ability to analyze both the students' reactions to service, and the impact they were having together at the sites would support these stated desires to use service-learning in the future.

The combined seminar and practicum also provided opportunities for preservice teachers to think about general pedagogical issues such as behavior management, motivation, and instruction. Because the practicum required them to take direct leadership with their student groups, they were able to practice and then analyze those experiences. It is not uncommon for the preservice teachers to come up against students who are not totally motivated for the project or those who do not always exhibit desirable behaviors. Often, these scenarios are discussed in both reflections and the seminar sessions. Taking the leadership role also puts preservice teachers in the position of practicing their thinking-on-your-feet skills, which might not otherwise happen prior to their student teaching internships.

The preservice teachers in the study exhibited an understanding of the community agencies with which they worked, in addition to making connections to the site-specific and societal issues embedded in those agencies. Wade (2003) claimed that student teachers did not often make such connections. Perhaps the focus question about community/issues in the reflection requirements encouraged preservice teachers to make this leap, which would support Swick's (2001) assertion that recognizing the need for service, and the structural issues that create that need, require that the "big picture" issues be built into reflection writing.

Asking preservice teachers to reflect about themselves seems to have provided them with impetus to make some important self-discoveries. Whether they wrote about their teaching skills, identified personal style or attitudes, or acknowledged how they operate as teachers, this self-understanding can give them something specific to build on during their student teaching.

Finally, the comments preservice teachers made about the particular nature of this practicum should be considered closely by teacher educators. Their comments, especially about learning the most when they engage in various teaching strategies and how the experience gave them perspectives beyond those provided by texts, are important elements for us to consider. It is perhaps unfair to hope that preservice teachers will employ complex pedagogies, such as service-learning, without having a solid exposure to them first as learners.

While this study provides teacher educators with some insights into how one specific structure—the combination of a service-learning seminar and concurrent field experience implementing a project—had an impact on preservice teachers, it also poses some issues for further exploration. How might this approach compare to others suggested by researchers in which preservice teachers gain experience in service-learning throughout their programs? What is the differential impact on preservice teachers who have only service-learning experience, without concurrent instruction specifically about the pedagogy, or without the opportunity to reflect on it with their peers? Another interesting topic would be to compare how outcomes differ when preservice teachers engage in this type of seminar plus practicum experience rather than the more traditional classroom-based experiences. Collecting comparative data between groups that have the service-learning practicum and seminar and those in the more traditional programs would help to illuminate this.

Overall, we feel that the nature of the reflection topics preservice teachers were asked to address had a direct impact on the learning they were able to derive from their experience. It would be interesting to see how reshaping or redirecting those reflection prompts might lead to different outcomes. Moreover, given the overall focus of developing content knowledge in preservice teacher education, it would be interesting to explore how service-learning projects might contribute to deepening preservice teachers' pedagogical content knowledge. Specifically, since students in the project learned about community issues, a central base of content for social studies educators, and because working at environmental sites provides obvious opportunities for science preservice teachers to gain content-specific knowledge, research on how service-learning may contribute to these areas is warranted. Furthermore, since preservice teachers in this project engaged in reading and responding to eighth graders' writing, the potential for helping them understand literacy skills and to practice teaching them could be important elements to explore in further research.

Finally, we would like to further explore the long-term impacts of participation in this project by gathering some longitudinal data on how many program graduates later implement service-learning in their classrooms. Although many graduates have communicated with us about their service-learning efforts, a formalized analysis has not been conducted of who is implementing service-learning, and who is not, or why. These and several other possibilities for scholarship in service-learning and teacher education will help all teacher education professionals to better understand how to prepare preservice teachers to implement service-learning in their future classrooms.

REFERENCES

Allen-Campbell, D. C., & Brannon, K. (2001). Project S.A.L.U.T.E.: Service and learning in urban teacher preparation. In J. A. Anderson, K. J. Swick, & J. Yff (Eds.), *Service-learning in teacher education: Enhancing the growth of new teachers, their students, and communities* (pp. 111–115). Washington, DC: American Association of Colleges of Teacher Education.

Anderson, J., & Guest, K. (1993, April). *Linking campus and community: Seattle University's community service internship for preservice teachers*. Paper presented at the National Service-Learning Conference, Minneapolis, MN.

Ball, D. (2003). Teacher education service-learning: Assessment. In Teacher Education Consortium in Service-Learning, *Learning to serve, serving to learn: A view from higher education* (pp. 67–90). Salisbury, MD: Salisbury University

Bogden, R., & Bicklen, S. (1992). *Qualitative research for education: An introduction to theory and* methods. Boston, MA: Allyn & Bacon

Boyle-Baise, L. (1997, November). *Community service-learning for multicultural education: An exploratory study with preservice teachers*. Paper presented at the College and University Faculty Assembly of the National Council for the Social Studies, Cincinnati, OH.

Brown, E., & Howard, B. (2005). Becoming culturally responsive teachers through service-learning: A case study of five novice classroom teachers. *Multicultural Education, 12*, 2–9. Retrieved November 1, 2005, from Proquest Research Library database.

Bullough, R. V., Jr., Young, J., Erickson, L., & Birrell, J. R. (2002). Rethinking field experience: Partnership teaching versus single-placement teaching. *Journal of Teacher Education, 53*(1), 68–80. Retrieved March 6, 2006, from ProQuest Education Journals database. (Document ID 98090128)

Council of Chief State School Officers. (1995). *Integrating service-learning into teacher education: Why and how?* Washington, DC: Author.

Dana, N., & Silva, D. (2001). Student teachers as researchers: Developing an inquiry stance towards teaching. In J. Rainer & E. Guyton (Eds.), *Research on the effects of teacher education on teacher performance* (pp. 91–104). Dubuque, IA: Kendall/Hunt.

Donahue, D. M. (1999). Service-learning for preservice teachers: Ethical dilemmas for practice. *Teaching and Teacher Education, 15*, 685–695.

Donahue, D. M. (2000). Charity basket or revolution: Beliefs, experiences and context in preservice teachers' service learning. *Curriculum Inquiry, 30*(4), 429–450.

Donahue, D. M., Bowyer, J., & Rosenberg, D. (2003). Learning with and learning from: Reciprocity in service learning teacher education. *Equity & Excellence in Education, 36*(1), 15–27.

Erickson, J., & Anderson, J. (1997). *Learning with the community: Concepts and models for service-learning in teacher education*. Washington, DC: American Association for Higher Education.

Flottemesch, K., Heide, T., Pedras, M., & Karp, G. G. (2001). Initial service-learning experience through the lenses of preservice teachers. In J. A. Anderson, K. J. Swick, & J. Yff (Eds.), *Service-learning in teacher education: Enhancing the growth of new teachers, their students, and communities* (pp. 126–133). Washington, DC: American Association of Colleges of Teacher Education.

Freeman, N. K., & Swick, K. (2001). Early childhood teacher education students strengthen their caring and competence through service-learning. In J. A. Anderson, K. J. Swick, & J. Yff (Eds.), *Service-learning in teacher education: Enhancing the growth of new teachers, their students, and communities* (pp.

134–140). Washington, DC: American Association of Colleges of Teacher Education.

Glasser, B. G., & Strauss, A. L. (1999). *The discovery of grounded theory: Strategies for qualitative research*. New York: Aldine de Gruyter.

Harwood, A. M., & Hart, C. (2000). Promising practice for K-16: Creating school-university service-learning collaborations. Denver, CO: Education Commission of the States.

Huling, L. (1998, December). *Early field experiences in teacher education*. Washington, DC: ERIC Clearinghouse on Teaching and Teacher Education. (ERIC Document Reproduction Service No. ED429054)

LaMaster, K. J. (2001). Enhancing preservice teachers field experiences through the addition of a service-learning component. *Journal of Experiential Education, 24*(1), 27–33. Retrieved March 6, 2006, from ProQuest Education Journals database. (Document ID 78372570)

Middleton, V. A. (2003). A diversity-based, service learning PDS partnership. *Equity & Excellence in Education, 36*(3), 231–237.

Moore, R. (2003). Reexamining the field experiences of preservice teachers. *Journal of Teacher Education, 54*(1), 31–42. Retrieved March 6, 2006, from ProQuest Education Journals database. (Document ID 275277621)

National Middle School Association. (1991). *NCATE-approved curriculum guidelines*. Columbus OH: Author.

Patton, M. Q. (1990). *Qualitative evaluation and research methods*. Newbury Park, CA: Sage.

Perry, C. M., & Power, B. M. (2004). Finding the truths in teacher preparation field experiences. *Teacher Education Quarterly, 31*(2), 125–136. Retrieved March 6, 2006, from ProQuest Education Journals database. (Document ID 275277621)

Pryor, C. R., & Kuhn, J. (2004). Do you see what I see? Bringing field experience observations into methods courses. *The Teacher Educator, 39*(4), 249–266. Retrieved March 6, 2006, from ProQuest Education Journals database. (Document ID 691401881)

Root, S., Callahan, J., & Sepanski, J. (2002a, Spring). Building teaching dispositions and service-learning practice: A multi-site study. *Michigan Journal of Community Service Learning, 8*(2), 50–60.

Root, S., Callahan, J., & Sepanski, J. (2002b). Service-learning in teacher education. In A. Furco & S. H. Billig (Eds.), *Advances in service-learning research: Vol.1. Service-learning: The essence of the pedagogy* (pp. 223–243). Greenwich, CT: Information Age.

Root, S., & Furco, A. (2001). A review of research on service-learning in preservice teacher education. In J. A. Anderson, K. J. Swick, & J. Yff (Eds.), *Service-learning in teacher education: Enhancing the growth of new teachers, their students, and communities* (pp. 86–101). Washington, DC: American Association of Colleges of Teacher Education.

Swick, K. (2001). Service-learning in teacher education: Building learning communities. *The Clearing House, 74,* 261–265. Retrieved March 2, 2005, from Proquest Research Library Database.

Tellez, K., Hlebowitsh, P. S., Cohen, M., & Norwood, P. (1995). Social service field experiences and teacher education. In J. M. Larkin & C. E. Sleeter (Eds.), *Developing multicultural teacher education curricula* (pp. 65–78). Albany: State University of New York Press.

Wade, R. C. (Ed.). (1997). *Community service-learning: A guide to including service in the public school curriculum.* Albany: State University of New York Press.

Wade, R. C. (2003). Teaching preservice social studies teachers to be advocates for social change. *The Social Studies, 94,* 129. Retrieved March 2, 2005, from the ProQuest Research Library Database.

Wade, R., Anderson, J., Yarbrough, D., Pickeral, T., Erickson, J., & Kromer, T. (1999). Novice teachers' experiences of community service-learning. *Teaching and Teacher Education, 15,* 668–684.

Wade, R. C., & Yarbrough, D. B. (1997). Community service-learning in student teaching: Toward the development of an active citizenry. *Michigan Journal of Community Service Learning, 4,* 42–55.

Watson, B., & Reiman, A. (2001). Promoting ethical and reflective professional judgment in preservice teachers. In J. Rainer & E. Guyton (Eds.), *Research on the effects of teacher education on teacher performance* (pp. 29–44). Dubuque, IA: Kendall/Hunt.

CHAPTER 8

ENGAGING SCHOLARS IN THE SCHOLARSHIP OF ENGAGEMENT

Advancing Research and Publication Knowledge and Creative Production

Kevin Kecskes, Peter Collier, and Martha Balshem

ABSTRACT

The practice and study of the scholarly application of pedagogies of engagement are important to the service-learning field because a significant aspect of faculty culture is the pursuit of an active scholarly agenda. This facet of faculty life often manifests as "traditional research," which may unfortunately work at cross purposes with the civic engagement and service-learning efforts in higher education nationwide. In recent years, considerable attention has been paid to redefining faculty work in ways that position scholarly pursuits to align with community needs. Portland State University has institutionally responded to these changing faculty needs by revising the

Advancing Knowledge in Service-Learning: Research to Transform the Field, 159–181
Copyright © 2006 by Information Age Publishing

promotion and tenure guidelines, creating a centralized faculty development unit, and implementing the Scholarship of Teaching and Research
Team (STRT) program. Now in its seventh year, STRT increases faculty
scholarly productivity and supports faculty research in the areas of the
scholarship of "teaching and learning" and of "engagement." This chapter
presents the programmatic tenets of the STRT model and shares the results
of our research on the impacts of this program on faculty.

INTRODUCTION

The practice and study of the scholarly application of pedagogies of
engagement are important to the service-learning field because a significant aspect of faculty culture is the pursuit of an active scholarly agenda.
This facet of faculty life often manifests as "traditional research," which
may unfortunately work at cross purposes with the civic engagement and
service-learning efforts in higher education nationwide. Ward (2002) challenged traditional notions of service and scholarship and argued that the
new American scholar integrates research and teaching and focuses on
ways in which these aspects of faculty life interact with the external community. In support of these new concepts of scholarship, national foundations (e.g., Carnegie Foundation for the Advancement of Teaching and
Learning) and national associations (e.g., American Association of Colleges and Universities and National Campus Compact, among others), as
well as innovative campuses, have begun to intentionally support various
forms of engaged scholarship.

Over the past decade and a half considerable attention has been paid
to redefining faculty work in ways that reflect the complexity of academic
work and to integrating that work much more intentionally with the persistent needs of communities (Boyer, 1990; Lynton, 1998). In his essay
"The Scholarship of Engagement," Boyer (1997) challenged institutions
of higher education to engage with the communities that comprise them.
Today, faculty at many institutions are expanding their professional hori-
zons by applying their expertise beyond university walls. Finkelstein
(2001), editor of the special issue of *Metropolitan Universities* on the scholarship of engagement, wrote "engaged scholars are expanding the perceptions of faculty roles and responsibilities and of the place of the
community in higher education" (p. 7). But, exactly what is engaged
scholarship?

Engaged scholarship has many names. O'Meara (2002) called it service
scholarship; Boyer (1990) discussed the scholarship of application;
Driscoll and Lynton (1999) referred to professional service; and Checkoway (2002) used the term public scholarship, which he defined as "schol-

arship for the common good." Finally, Ward (2002) used the term scholarship of engagement because of the clear connections to Boyer's earlier work and to the larger work of colleges and universities as engaged campuses. At Portland State University, we regularly use most of aforementioned terminology, plus the term scholarship of community outreach, which is the official designation for this work and appears in the institution's promotion and tenure guidelines. We have found that keeping the terminology open provides for different doorways through which diverse faculty can enter. Undergirding these various terms is Lynton's (1998) conception that faculty need to use discovery, teaching, application, and integration to connect to external communities in order to address salient public issues. To leverage the considerable intellectual skills and experiences of the professoriate to make a tangible difference in the world, faculty, as scholars, must take on world problems through disciplinary means (Boyer, 1990).

This raises another important question—how does a well-meaning institution support engaged scholarship? At Portland State University, these efforts initially took the form of revised promotion and tenure guidelines.

Portland State University

Portland State University (PSU), Oregon's only urban university, is the largest and most diverse in the state system. Serving more than 25,000 students, Portland State offers more than 100 undergraduate, master's and doctoral degrees, as well as graduate certificates and continuing education programs. In 1994, PSU completely changed its approach to undergraduate general education and implemented the program known as University Studies. University Studies has been recognized as a national model (Ehrlich, 2000; Tagg, 2003) because of the emphasis on best practices in regards to teaching and learning and the intentional integration of social responsibility into the general education program (Davidson, 1997, Davidson, Holland, Kaiser, & Reardon, 1996). This shift prompted campuswide discussions on the place of the scholarship of pedagogy and engagement with respect to promotion and tenure decisions.

The 1995-1996 revisions of the faculty "Promotion and Tenure guidelines" read as follows concerning the "evaluation of scholarship":

Scholarly accomplishments in the areas of research, teaching, and community outreach (see E.2.4) all enter into the evaluation of faculty performance. Scholarly profiles will vary depending on individual faculty members' areas of emphasis. The weight to be given factors relevant to the determination of promotion, tenure, and merit necessarily varies with the individual faculty member's assigned role and from one academic field to another. However, one should recognize that research, teaching, and community outreach often overlap. For example, a service-learning project may reflect both teaching and community outreach. Some research projects may involve both research and community outreach. Pedagogical research may involve both research and teaching. When a faculty member evaluates his or her individual intellectual, aesthetic, or creative accomplishments, it is more important to focus on the general criteria of the quality and significance of the work than to categorize the work. (Promotion and Tenure Scholarship, 2004)

These revisions explicitly acknowledged the validity of scholarship in the areas of research, teaching, and community outreach. However, it was up to the individual faculty member to make the case that efforts in the areas of teaching and learning and engagement constituted legitimate scholarship. While all faculty are generally clear as to what constitutes legitimate scholarship within the context of their discipline, many are not as clear when trying to make a case for efforts relating to pedagogy or community service. For PSU, this was both a problem and an opportunity.

A Problem and a Programmatic Response

Developed during the same time period as the revisions in the promotion and tenure guidelines, PSU's centralized faculty development unit, the Center for Academic Excellence (CAE), responded to this growing faculty need for a deeper understanding. CAE designed and tested a professional development initiative that intentionally supports the scholarship of teaching and learning, with the understanding that under this larger rubric falls the scholarship of engagement. Thus began PSU's (STRT) program, now in its seventh year of supporting faculty in their pursuit of engaged scholarship.

PSU's program is surely not the only one of its kind. At Michigan State University, an informal self-organized group of faculty secured modest funding, engaged in reading groups, and coauthored articles relating to the scholarly applications of disciplinary insights (Rosaen, Foster-Fishman, & Fear, 2001). PSU's program, by contrast, has been a formal response to this identified area of need and was thus developed with these two goals in mind.

1. To provide support for faculty scholarly productivity. Many new faculty members report being overwhelmed by the teaching and administrative demands of their university positions during a time when scholarly production is the coin most valued regarding to promotion and tenure decisions.

2. To increase support for faculty efforts in the areas of the scholar-
    ship of teaching and learning and of engagement.

In this chapter, we will both present the basic tenets of the innovative
STRT program model and share the results of the research on the
impacts of this program on faculty and their scholarly production.

The STRT Program

The STRT program is open to faculty of any rank, fixed term or tenure
related. A STRT request for proposals goes out to the entire campus community two weeks before the beginning of fall term.[1] Applicants must:

- State a specific project in the areas of the scholarship of teaching
  and learning or the scholarship of engagement;
- Explicitly state the project goal for the year (e.g., manuscript for
  submission for publication, conference presentation, or grant
  application);
- Commit to attending six group meetings over the course of the
  academic year; and
- Commit to writing a description of and reflection on their STRT
  project for *Our Voices,* a CAE publication that is edited over the
  summer and then distributed to all faculty in the fall of the next
  academic year.

Before the initial meeting, successful applicants are sorted into groups of
5 to 8 based on interest area (e.g., internationalization, technology, diversity, civic engagement); methodology (e.g., basic qualitative, quantitative,
mixed method division); or how far along each project is (e.g., grouping
beginning projects with other similar ones).

All groups of STRT participants meet together for the first and last
meeting of the year. In addition, participants meet four more times
over the academic year in their assigned groups to discuss progress on
each other's projects. This works out to two meetings per term based on
PSU's use of the quarter system. Each group is led by a facilitator and
consultant; these individuals typically have prior STRT experiences as
participants. These facilitators and consultants bring expertise to share
with the group (i.e., methodological or technical skills, publication
experience, and group facilitation skills). All participants, facilitators,
and consultants receive a STRT professional development stipend of
$500 for the year.

STRT Program Activities

While the organizing topics for each STRT group may vary from year to year, there are several program elements that remain consistent annually.

Identification of instrumental outcomes.   In the application process, participants are encouraged to identify the "product" that they plan on accomplishing for their STRT project. This is reinforced at the initial STRT meeting, where, after breaking into smaller groups, each participant is asked to briefly describe his or her project to the rest of the group including:

- The type of methodology being used;
- The instrumental outcome (presentation, manuscript, grant proposal, software, etc.);
- How far along this particular project is; and
- The kinds of help that person is hoping to get from the STRT group.

It should be noted that, while many times the consultants are the designated experts on research design, methodology, and even writing, many times it is the other members of the STRT group that actually provide invaluable assistance to each other. This sharing of expertise among participants is encouraged by the group facilitators.

Creation of project timeline.   By the second STRT meeting, participants are asked to share a timeline for their projects with the group, as well as to provide the facilitator with a written copy of the timeline. The timeline exercise, which happens very early in the STRT year, serves to make participants aware of deadlines as well as what needs to be done for completing the project on time. In addition, it helps each participant become clearer as to when they will need assistance from the consultant and facilitator in order to proceed in a timely manner.

Distribution of writing and publishing support materials.   Each year, STRT facilitators distribute materials on organizing writing and dealing with procrastination. In addition, "friends-of-the-STRT program" from the PSU library (i.e., current and past STRT participants and consultants) provide workshops on publishing outlets outside of particular disciplines.

Exploration of the meaning of the scholarship of engagement.   An additional resource for promoting discussions about the meaning of the scholarship of engagement, as shown in the Venn diagram in Figure 8.1, has been used in STRT groups for the past 3 years.

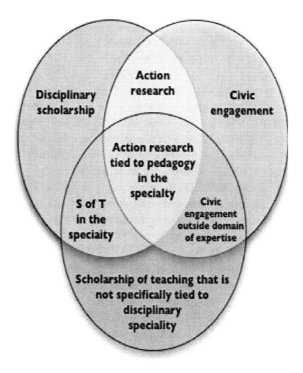

Figure 8.1.   Meaning of scholarship of engagement.

Michael Flowers, consultant for one the 2003-2004 STRT teams, developed the idea of representing the scholarship of engagement as a Venn diagram consisting of three overlapping circles—Disciplinary scholarship, Civic engagement, and Scholarship of teaching not tied to specialty (which may or may not be related to the faculty member's primary discipline). The areas where different circles overlapped yielded some "hybrid" subdomains:

- Scholarship of teaching within discipline;
- Action research;
- Civic engagement outside of domain of expertise; and
- Action research tied to pedagogy within specialty.

When this conceptual model was used in STRT team meetings, participants were surprised to find that their individual projects fit into completely different subdomains in the Venn diagram. There were projects that focused on action research, the Scholarship of Teaching within a discipline, and action research tied to pedagogy within specialty. This consistently led to active discussions about what constitutes engaged scholarship? Several facilitators noted that some group members actually shifted their projects from one subdomain of the Venn diagram to another as a result of reconceptualizing their project due to participating in the STRT team.

CAE's all-day writing retreats.   The Center for Academic Excellence sponsors four all-day writing retreats—one each during fall, winter, spring, and summer terms. While open to the entire campus community, STRT members are encouraged to take advantage of this resource, which they do in high numbers. Usually at least 80% of writing retreat participants are either current or past STRT group members.

Celebration at the final STRT meeting.   The last STRT meeting of the year is another group meeting that serves as both an opportunity to share STRT experiences across groups and to celebrate the scholarly productivity and collegiality fostered by the STRT program.

Publication of "*Our Voices*."   All STRT participants agree to write a combination description of project and reflection on the STRT experience for the, *Our Voices: The Scholarship of Teaching Resource Team*, a nonrefereed publication that participants can add to their academic vitae. Writing the piece for *Our Voices* causes participants to reflect upon the benefits they experienced as a result of being part of the STRT community of scholars.

METHODOLOGY

The initial years of the STRT program at Portland State were characterized by a very pragmatic approach that emphasized providing a viable support network for faculty trying to develop and publish research involving engaged scholarship outside of their traditional disciplinary backgrounds. Evaluation tended to focus on participants' self-reports of "what I got from participating in STRT." Participants' project summaries and reflection pieces for *Our Voices* served as the only consistent indicators of the impact of STRT participation on faculty. Qualitative content analysis of participants' reflection writings constituted the extent of program analysis of evaluation data. Early efforts at capturing an accurate tally of scholarly products were hindered by inconsistencies in regards to participant reporting of products to STRT. Therefore, for the 2004-2005 STRT program year, researchers introduced additional evaluation measures, in conjunction with continuing the content analysis of faculty members' reflections on the benefit of STRT participation on scholarly productivity.

Evaluation Measures

The 2004-2005 evaluation plan had three components.

1. **Evaluation of instrumental outcomes.** A count of the number and type of scholarly products generated by the 2001-2003 and the 2004-2005 STRT program participants
2. **An evaluation of intrinsic outcomes.** Content analysis of participants' self report data on the impact of participating in STRT.
3. **An evaluation of symbolic outcomes.** The examination of the development of shared meaning of the scholarship of engagement among program participants. This was a measure of the STRT group's shared understanding of the scholarship of engagement based on a qualitative content analysis of participants' understanding of the scholarship of engagement after participating in the STRT program.

Instrumental Outcomes

Instrumental outcomes constitute the primary coin by which faculty members establish the value of their contributions to the university, scholarly community, and larger community. They constitute a key component of making a case for promotion and the award of tenure. Engaged scholarship can be a significant element of a faculty member's promotion and tenure portfolio when institutional policies are in place that explicitly recognize its importance.

At PSU, evidence of this institutional commitment can be found in the discussion of the evaluation of scholarship that appears in the Office of Academic Affairs Guidelines for Promotion and Tenure.[2] Select points of the discussion follow.

*   Research may be evaluated on the quality and significance of publication of scholarly books, monographs, articles, presentations, and reviews in journals, and grant proposals submissions and awards. An evaluation should consider whether the individual's contributions reflect continuous engagment in research and whether these contributions demonstrate future promise. Additionally, the evaluation should consider whether publications are refereed (an important form of peer review) as

an important factor. In some fields, evidence of citation or use of the faculty member's research or creative contributions by other scholars is appropriate.

- The development and publication of software should be judged in the context of its involvement of state-of-the-art knowledge and its impact on peers and others.

- In certain fields such as writing, literature, performing arts, fine arts, architecture, graphic design, cinema, and broadcast media or related fields, distinguished creation should receive consideration equivalent to that accorded to distinction attained in scientific and technical research.

Scholarly Products Produced

For this measure, the unit of analysis was the project, not the individual participant, as many projects involved multiple faculty participants. There were originally 27 faculty projects in the 2004-2005 STRT program. Over the course of the year, two projects were abandoned before completion: one because of a faculty member's health issues and the second because the faculty participant took a position at another university. As depicted in Exhibit 8.1 the 25 remaining projects generated 41 scholarly products including conference presentations, publications, manuscripts submitted, grant proposals, and software. Exhibit 8.2 displays the national and international conferences where STRT participants were accepted as presenters, and Exhibit 8.3 lists the journals in which STRT members were published. Some STRT participants had manuscripts accepted for publication based on the current year's work, while in other cases, 2004-2005 publications actually reflected work done in the previous year's STRT program. In all instances, the only publications reported were those directly connected with STRT projects.

The level of scholarly production of the six STRT facilitators and consultants who participated in this study benefited from the supportive STRT environment. The 2004-2005 STRT facilitators and consultants published seven articles and book chapters, as well as making presentations at four conferences. It seems clear that STRT participation

Exhibit 8.1.   2004-2005 STRT Scholarly Products (n = 25)

Conference Presentations	Publications	Manuscripts Submitted	Grant Proposals	Tools Developed	Total Products
18	11	5	5 (4 funded)	2	41

Exhibit 8.2. National and International Conference Presentations

Conference	Location
Western Regional Campus Compact Consortium Meetings	Portland, OR
Sixth International Grey Literature Conference	New York, NY
National Reading Conference	San Antonio, TX
First International Conference on Enhancing Teaching and Learning Through Assessment	Hong Kong
Conference of Minority Public Administrators	Corpus Christi, TX
American Democracy Project National Meeting	Portland, OR
8th Annual Conference of Oregon Association of Teacher Educators	Portland, OR
63rd Annual Meeting of the Oregon Academy of Science	Corvallis, OR
American Society for Public Administration's National Conference	Denver, CO
International Resilience Project Conference	Halifax, Nova Scotia
Fifth International Conference on Knowledge, Culture, and Change in Organizations, at the University of the Aegean/Rhodes	Greece
International Conference on Personal Meaning.	Vancouver, B.C.
Allied Academies International Fall Conference	Maui, HI

Exhibit 8.3. Journals for 2004-2005 STRT Scholarly Products

Academic Exchange Quarterly
Academy of Management Journal
Journal of Faculty Development
Journal of Materials Education
Personnel Psychology
Publishing Research Quarterly

positively affects scholarly production, yet there is more. In addition to instrumental outcomes, faculty reported a range of intrinsic rewards they received from STRT participation.

Intrinsic Outcomes

The measure of intrinsic outcomes was based on a content analysis of project description and reflection pieces from *Our Voices*. In this analysis, two coders and an intercoder comparison were used to confirm the initial code categories. Two sets of codes were utilized. The first series of codes, based on language similarities, kept very close to the text. The second set of codes was then based on patterns we saw after this close and detailed work.

Initially, two large categories of responses were noted.

I.   **Instrumental support. The instrumental benefits of STRT participation took several forms.**   Three subthemes relating to instrumental support were identified by participants:
   A.   Money was used to fund travel and other professional activities. *STRT provides positive reinforcement by funding professional development— the university (or some part of it) supports (with money) the work I'm doing.*
   B.   STRT provided networking and contacts.
       [Through connections made by participating in STRT], we now have another group of universities that want [sic] us to work with them on our continuing research.
   C.   STRT made nondiscipline-based research legitimate as counting toward promotion and tenure.
       STRT helped to give my project greater credibility within my department where the focus is generally on pure scientific research.

II.   **Social support. Participants mentioned the value of social support to an even greater degree than instrumental support.**   Three subthemes were also identified regarding social support; the first has two parts.
   A.   Working within a community of scholars sharing similar issues helped faculty realize their goals in two areas:
       1.   **Time constraints.**   *The monthly meetings forced us to complete each step (on time) and then "led" us to move on to the next one in a timely manner.*
       2.   **The demand of departments for scholarship.**   *STRT provided an intellectual home for the nontraditional research that I do.*
   B.   The members of the STRT group provided technical skills.
       STRT was a place where people understood some of the measurement and analysis techniques I am using better than I do, and that is a good resource for me.

I was able to venture into some new methodology areas that I normally would not have utilized.

C. STRT participation re-energized faculty.
The support and community I experienced (in STRT) helped me to recharge.

Unanticipated Findings

In addition to instrumental and social support, faculty identified several unexpected benefits of STRT participation. Three additional themes emerged, the most striking of which was the positive direct effect that participants' reported STRT had upon their own teaching.

1. **Improvement of teaching.**
    My group helped me improve the way I teach and do research.
    STRT provided us with the chance to think about how effectively we are passing along our knowledge and love of knowledge to our students.
    The questioning process [from the STRT meetings] provided me with a framework I use in my daily teaching.

It should be noted that we expected to find an indirect effect of STRT participation on teaching, perhaps through the mediating effect of increasing engagement. But participants clearly articulated that there was a direct effect on classroom teaching.

Additional unexpected findings had to do with increased connections between the university and the larger community as well as among faculty members from different disciplines.

2. **Connection between the university and the community.**
    [Participating in our STRT project] helped students see the connection between what they learn and their personal responsibilities to the community. STRT helped me formulate a community project, which is not normally done in my area of physics.

3. **Enjoyment of collegiality and an increased sense of a campus community.**
    I always enjoy the interactions with faculty from other departments in the university—there are few opportunities for this at a huge school like PSU. My favorite byproduct of STRT is the cross-disciplinary relationships and how these "embed" me into PSU in a very tangible way.

Overall, what was underlying each theme was a tone of emotional enthusiasm.

> *The greatest feeling is that we have accomplished something that ordinarily we would have left on our "to do someday" list. STRT intensified my sense that I can be a better professor with the help of my colleagues.*

The themes that emerged from the qualitative analysis of the effect of STRT led us to undertake an even broader evaluation of the effects of STRT participation on faculty.

Symbolic Outcomes

In order to be able to tell how STRT program participation really affects faculty, we would really like to know if participating in STRT changes faculty *behaviors* in regards to the scholarship of engagement. The first step to realizing this goal is to begin to better understand how (or whether) being part of the STRT program impacts faculty members' ideas about the meaning of the scholarship of engagement.

Theoretical Foundation

The theoretical foundation for the intervention comes from sociology, specifically Mead (1934) and Symbolic Interactionism. He contended that meaning develops through social experience and that social experience consists of the exchange of symbols (language, gesture, ideas) as part of interaction with others. STRT activities are designed to promote interaction between group members and discourse on the scholarship of engagement within a context that is personally relevant to the participant faculty: their own research projects.

Anthropologists Romney, Weller, and Batchelder (1986) argued that, when exploring a new "cultural domain" (e.g., the scholarship of engagement), it is important for researchers to explore the degree of "cultural consensus" about that particular cultural domain that exists among those members of an "indigenous population" (i.e., faculty who are engaging in the scholarship of engagement) that have first-hand experience within that domain. Instead of imposing some a priori definition, the culturally-sensitive researchers instead rely on the information that is held in common by actual participants. That is why our first step is to examine what the scholarship of engagement means to STRT participants. Until we are clear what the "shared meaning" of the scholarship of engagement is for STRT faculty, it is impossible to identify which behaviors are valid indicators of that concept.

Measure of the Meaning of Scholarship of Engagement

While the STRT program has some normative expectations in regards to the scholarship of engagement (e.g., we see this as a viable and worthwhile form of scholarship that builds connections between the university, students, and the community and promotes valid scholarship usable for faculty promotion and tenure cases), it is essential to understand participating faculty experiences in *their own words*. This is why qualitative methodology is the appropriate approach to understanding this situation.

When researchers examined the shared meanings about the scholarship of engagement that developed among STRT participants, an initial distinction was made between meanings associated with "The Nature of Engaged Scholarship" and those related to "The Effects of Engaged Scholarship."

The Nature of Engaged Scholarship

Several themes emerged from an analysis of responses related to the nature of engaged scholarship. While several participants pointed out that engaged scholarship can take different forms, there was even more agreement that engaged scholarship focuses on topics of interest to the community, treats the community as peers, and, many times, both advances disciplinary knowledge and has practical value to community.

Scholarly engagement can take different forms. Three of 19 STRT participants mentioned this idea. As one participant noted: *Learning can take many forms so engagement will mean vastly different things to people in the various disciplines on campus.* A second participant elaborated on this idea:

> Because my research encompasses two very different spheres, the form this takes varies. My research into fans of Japanese animation involves some very complex decisions regarding academic distance and active involvement. By contrast, my work with rubrics is fairly easy to define and extend. My latest extension in this regard has been some workshops I have been doing with the School of Nursing at Oregon Health and Science University.

The involvement of the community, as equal partners with faculty, in research (engaged scholarship) was found in two related themes.

1. **Engaged scholarship focuses on topics of interest to the community.**   This concept was mentioned by five of 19 STRT

participants. This idea was enthusiastically supported by several STRT team members.

Engaged scholarship means that my research and my teaching should focus more on topics which address involvement in our social environment [our community, our city, our classes, our students]. An essential part of teaching mathematics for social justice is establishing connections between school mathematics and issues that affect students as individuals and as community members.

2. **Engaged scholarship treats community members as peers.**   This theme was also mentioned by five of 19 STRT participants. One faculty member pointed out:

   The focus of our research should not be just on a practical impact (in the community). Instead, [engaged scholarship] is research designed with the community or community members as a kind of peer group, in addition to the scholarly peer group we all have.

A second faculty member continued this theme: *The community then becomes a great resource from which to draw ideas, explore research, and involve the community as part of the data collection process.* The idea of the community as a resource fits nicely with a separate theme that emphasized the reciprocal benefits of engaged scholarship.

3. **Engaged scholarship both advances disciplinary knowledge and has practical value to community.**   Mentioned by 6 of 19 participants, this was one of the most popular themes. One faculty member pointed out: *[engaged scholarship] means linking the academic/ literature/ history of a subject with community based applications or activities.*

A second participant used an example to make a distinction between the scholarship of learning and the scholarship of engagement.

> *In a program where students collect environmental data we could study the effect of that experience on student learning. That would be the scholarship of learning. However, if we were to study how that experience has impacted not only student learning but also actual change in the environment due to student activities, that would be scholarship of engagement.*

While engaged scholarship can take many forms, what remains common is the emphasis on partnerships with the community and reciprocal benefits. Twelve of the 19 STRT participants mentioned one of the three community-related themes.

Effects of Engaged Scholarship

The second large group of shared meanings, relating to the effects of engaged scholarship, can be further divided into effects on students and effects on the scholar/researcher.

Several themes relating to the effects on students emerged. Participants agreed that participating in classes that emphasized engaged scholarship resulted in greater engagement by the students with their community, with their own learning, with each other, and with their teachers. There was also an acknowledgment that this approach did a better job of connecting classroom learning to real world problems than more traditional approaches.

- Resulted in greater engagement in community by students. Six of 19 STRT participants mentioned this theme.
  I ask my students to engage ... with their own lives and with other activities (jobs, volunteer work, hobbies, religious activities, etc.). Provides students with ... opportunities so that [the test of classroom knowledge] is realized by actual work that is aimed at a community audience.

- STRT resulted in greater engagement in learning by students. Here, again, 6 of 19 STRT participants echoed this theme in their responses.
  The scholarship of engagement means active learning for students. My students did not simply learn about the structure of the government; they chose a community problem about which they cared passionately, studied public policy alternatives, and proposed solutions to the appropriate community or government agencies.

- Resulted in greater engagement with each other and teacher. While only 2 of 19 mentioned this theme, it does represent another facet of engagement. *In my teaching, it means that I ask my students to engage not only with each other, but with me, also, of course.*

- STRT connected academic learning to real world problems. This theme was noted in responses of four of the 19 STRT participants.
  [Engaged scholarship] helps students connect academic learning to real world problems. I try to get them to integrate what is happening to them at PSU with other aspects of their lives, to integrate learning into those lives as opposed to seeing college as a means to an end.

Two final themes emerged relating to the "Effect of Engaged Scholarship on the Scholar/Researcher." STRT participants talked about how engaged scholarship affects faculty members in terms of connections to the community and to the university.

1. **STRT participation** involves spending time in and connecting with community. The greatest agreement associated with this theme, as it was mentioned by nine of 19 STRT participants.

   [The effect on me of] engaged scholarship that is put into practice is that my research and I are connected to a community broader than just that of the university. As an educator at PSU (where the motto is 'Let knowledge serves the city'), in a city with a rapidly changing demographic, community engagement is the best form of both connection and social activism.

2. **Connecting with the campus community.** Three of 19 STRT participants mentioned this theme.

   [One effect of engaged scholarship is to] enrich the knowledge and the learning experience of university ... researchers and faculty. In my research, it means doing what I ask of my students: interacting with my communities at PSU [from my immediate colleagues], to the department as a whole.

To summarize the themes that emerged relating to the effects of engaged scholarship, engagement and connection underlie all of the effect of engaged scholarship on students and faculty members. For students, effects included increased engagement with learning, their communities, each other, their teachers, and a greater connection of classroom learning to real world problems. The greatest effects of engaged scholarship on faculty had to do with increased connectivity—with the campus as well as the larger, beyond-the-university communities.

DISCUSSION

In this chapter, the innovative STRT program model at PSU has been described. In retrospect, promoting the scholarship of engagement and the scholarship of teaching and learning at Portland State was as much a community-building exercise as a question of supporting scholarly productivity. The success of the PSU STRT program provides support for the perspective that efforts to bring faculty and staff together around the theme of engaged scholarship and the scholarship of teaching and learning benefit from interdisciplinary communities of scholars that are supportive and energizing.

In the case of traditional scholarship, the local campus community can not often substitute for the national network of like-minded disciplinary scholars. However, in regards to promoting the scholarship of engagement and the scholarship of teaching and learning it can. The STRT program honors and applies what we know about learning communities and serves as a reminder that, as engaged faculty, we should always remember to apply what we know about learning to ourselves as learners.

We have also presented the results of research on the impact of this program on faculty and their scholarly production. The STRT program was developed with two goals in mind. The first was to provide support for faculty scholarly productivity. The measure of instrumental outcomes for 2004-2005 STRT participants—41 scholarly products generated from 25 projects—suggests the STRT program works with regard to meeting the first goal. Faculty are constantly faced with demands upon their time to participate in a range of university activities designed to promote campus unity, collegiality, and service in the form connections to the larger community, which, though in accord with the values of an engaged faculty, serve to take them away from the development of the publications and research necessary to advance their university careers. STRT offers faculty opportunities to stay true to their values of service while still advancing their scholarly agendas.

The second goal of the STRT program was to increase support for faculty efforts in the areas of the scholarship of teaching and learning and of engagement. Evidence of the impact of STRT on faculty in these areas can be found in the measures of both intrinsic and symbolic outcomes. In the discussion of social support, from the content analysis of the *Our Voices* reflection writings, participants noted that STRT provided *"an intellectual home for the non-traditional research"* as well as *"a place to venture into some new methodology areas that I normally would not have utilized."* This theme of STRT providing a context for interdisciplinary research or research outside-of-discipline to be viewed as legitimate scholarship was echoed by another participant, *Being part of STRT helped me formulate a community project which is not normally done in my area.*

In addition, the measure of symbolic outcomes suggests that a shared understanding of the scholarship of engagement developed among 2004-2005 STRT participants. Engaged scholarship was characterized by STRT participants in terms of "higher quality interactions." Students received increased engagement in learning, communities, and with each other. Faculty received increased engagement with other faculty. Students formed connections between classroom learning and the real world. Faculty formed connections between the university and community and between departments and faculty across disciplines.

We contend that STRT is an effective tool for promoting faculty production in relation to engaged scholarship, but it is much more than that. At PSU, STRT is a context for recognition, achievement, and acknowledgement of accomplishments in the areas of the scholarship of teaching and learning and engaged scholarship. It is also a context for the creation of a sense of scholarly community, and, as the foregoing quotations have indicated, this is as important to STRT participants as is the instrumental support provided by the program. This sense of scholarly community, moreover, is created in service to an emerging paradigm for scholarly self-definition. As STRT participants interact across disciplinary lines, they discover challenges and issues that seem characteristic of the scholarship of engagement in any field. In one STRT group, for instance, an oral historian and an environmental scientist discussed the challenges related to conducting community-based research in the context of a one-term course. Does one privilege the student's experience or the quality of the research? And if the research is not high quality enough to be useable to policymakers, does not that disappointment in itself affect the student experience and sense of self efficacy? This is an interesting interdisciplinary discussion; it also raises potential ethical implications for community-based research and associated scholarly pursuits (Kecskes, Barber, & Edwards, 2005).

It is fitting that this process takes place on our local campuses. Traditionally, our scholarly communities, the locales in which like-minded scholars gather to share their interests and make their reputations, are national. On our own campuses, we may enjoy a feeling of personal comfort and belonging, but it is often only loosely connected to our central areas of scholarship. STRT, however, brings scholarly community and local face-to-face community together. It is apt for this to happen in the context of advancing the scholarship of engagement, which speaks to both intellect and heart.

LIMITATIONS OF CURRENT EVALUATION STRATEGIES

The limitations of the evaluation measures used in this study have to do with issues of incomplete data. Regarding the instrumental measure of scholarly products, as noted earlier, several of the 2004-2005 publications actually reflected work done in the previous year's STRT program.

Reflecting a different aspect of this same issue, there is, likewise, not a mechanism in place to collect a count of scholarly products related to STRT activities that take place in the year(s) following STRT participation. For example, the conference presentation of the STRT year may become the refereed publication in 2 more years after multiple rewrites and revisions. Unless a faculty member is still active in STRT, we have no way of knowing if a faculty member's earlier STRT participation directly led to a subsequent publication.

SUGGESTIONS FOR FUTURE RESEARCH

We propose that the broadness of the Scholarship of engagement makes it an ideal theme to be explored as part of STRT team efforts in subsequent years. Because there is a real lack of consensus within academia and the civic engagement community as to what constitutes the scholarship of engagement, this seems to be a discussion where PSU faculty, reflecting upon the shared meanings of engaged scholarship that develop as consequences of STRT participation, can make important contributions.

CONCLUSION

The STRT program works at PSU; the lessons we have learned are applicable for others interested in developing similar programs at other institutions. On a practical level, the central organizing mechanism that drives the STRT program is fairly easy to replicate. For a relatively small investment, other universities can create a legitimizing organization that facilitates the development of communities of engaged scholars. What a STRT-like program does is to coordinate a range of activities, that while not directly connected to the scholarly goals of a single academic department, promote faculty productivity and collegiality. Specific activities include: bringing together faculty across academic ranks (tenure line, fixed term, and research staff); identifying potential facilitators and "consultants"—individual's with methodological and/or faculty productivity support skills (librarians, writing coaches); matching up these facilitators and consultants with groups of participating faculty; coordinating a year-long schedule of regular gatherings; and providing an outlet for scholarly products, like PSU's *Our Voices* magazine.

The STRT program's emphasis on engaged scholarship increases its applicability for faculty seeking to advance their academic careers. The program's emphasis intentionally mirrors a shift among national academic disciplinary societies; increasingly more associations include engaged scholarship as "legitimate" scholarship. In a recent review chapter, Morreale and Applegate (2006) note that as a result of a seed grant program funded by the Carnegie Foundation's Academy for the Scholarship of Teaching and Learning, the National Communication Association and 10 other associations produced a series of monographs on disciplinary styles relating to the engaged scholarship of teaching and learning. Other national disciplinary associations that promote engaged scholarship through different programs include the American Sociological Association, American Political Science Association (APSA), American

Historian Association (AHA), and the American Association of Law Schools (Morreale & Applegate, 2006).

Ultimately, the applicability of STRT and similar programs will depend on the degree to which universities value engaged scholarship when making tenure and promotion decisions. Many institutions are currently revising their promotion and tenure guidelines to accommodate the scholarship of engagement.

In conclusion, the PSU STRT program is successful. Our research demonstrates that engaging faculty in a program of activities that both encourages their research on service-learning and civic engagement, while at the same time involving them in a community of scholars with shared interests, results in increase scholarly productivity, a more connected campus community, and new insights into the meaning of the scholarship of engagement.

NOTES

1.   A description of the STRT program and the STRT application form can be found on the CAE Web site http://www.pdx.edu/cae/strt.html

2.   See Evaluation of scholarship information E.2.a, b, c: Research and Other Creative Activities (Research). Retrieved May 10, 2006, from http://oaa.pdx.edu/PromotionAndTenureScolarship5

REFERENCES

Boyer, E. L. (1990). *Scholarship reconsidered: Priorities of the professoriate*. Princeton, NJ: Carnegie Foundation for the Advancement of Teaching.

Boyer, E. L. (1997). The scholarship of engagement. *Journal of Public Service and Outreach, 1*(1), 11–20.

Checkoway, B. (2002). Renewing the civic mission of the American research university. *Journal of Public Affairs, 6*(Suppl. 1), 265–294.

Davidson, S. L. (1997). Divide and flourish: Nursing the nucleus of faculty change. *Journal of Public Service and Outreach, 2*(1), 26–32.

Davidson, S. L., Holland, B., Kaiser, M., & Reardon, M. (1996). Leading large-scale institutional change: Successes and challenges. Practical changes at a large urban public university: Portland State University. In L. R. Sandman (Ed.), *Fulfilling higher education's covenant with society: The emerging outreach agenda* ((pp. 47–50). East Lansing, MI: Michigan State University. Retrieved June 9, 2006, from http://www.msu.edu/~partners/pubs/capstone/ch3_2.html

Driscoll, A., & Lynton, E. (1999). *Making outreach visible: A guide to documenting professional service and outreach*. Washington, DC: American Association for Higher Education.

Ehrlich, T. (2000). *Civic responsibility and higher education*. Phoenix, AZ: Oryx Press.

Finkelstein, M. A. (2001). The scholarship of engagement: Enriching university and community. *Metropolitan Universities—An International Forum, 12*(4), 7–9.

Kecskes, K., Barber, K. E., & Edwards, P. (2005). Professionalizing community-based research. *Academic Exchange Quarterly, 9*(1), 263–268.

Lynton, E. A. (1998). Reversing the telescope: Fitting individual tasks to common organizational ends. *AAHE Bulletin, 50*(7), 8–10.

Mead, G. H. (1934). *Mind, self, and society* (C. W. Morris, Ed.). Chicago: University of Chicago Press.

Morreale, S., & Applegate, J. (2006). Engaged disciplines: How national disciplinary societies support the scholarship of engagement. In K. Kecskes (Ed.), *Engaging departments: Moving faculty culture from private to public, individual to collective focus for the common good* (pp. 264–277). Boston: Anker.

O'Meara, K. A. (2002). Uncovering the values in faculty evaluation of service as scholarship. *Review of Higher Education, 26*(1), 57–80.

Promotion and tenure scholarship: E. evaluation of scholarship. (2004). Retrieved Mar. 16, 2006, from Portland State University, Office of Academic Affairs Web site: http://oaa.pdx.edu/PromotionAndTenureScolarship5

Romney, A. K., Weller, S. C., & Batchelder, W. H. (1986). Culture as consensus: A theory of culture and informant accuracy. *American Anthropologist, 88*(2), 313–338.

Rosaen, C., Foster-Fishman, P., & Fear, F. (2001). The citizen scholar: Joining voices and values in the engagement interface. *Metropolitan Universities—An International Forum, 12*(4), 10–29.

Tagg, J. (2003). *The learning paradigm college*, Boston: Anker.

Ward, K. (2002). *Faculty service roles and the scholarship of engagement*, Indianapolis, IN: Jossey-Bass.

Section IV

THE INFLUENCE OF PAST SERVICE-LEARNING RESEARCH ON PRESENT THINKING

CHAPTER 9

THE WISDOM OF DELPHI

An Investigation of the Most Influential Studies in K-12 Service-Learning Research in the Past 25 Years

Robert Shumer

ABSTRACT

Did you ever wonder what the most influential studies were in K-12 service-learning research? A two-round Delphi study involving researchers and practitioners identified many sources and reached consensus on 9 research reviews and studies that had the most impact on the service-learning field. Analysis and discussion of these important studies revealed several common elements of service-learning practice. Program quality was considered to be of greatest importance. Implications of this review suggest that rather than focus on outcomes, future research on service-learning should emphasize how to create, sustain, and evaluate high quality programs.

Advancing Knowledge in Service-Learning: Research to Transform the Field, 185–204
Copyright © 2006 by Information Age Publishing

INTRODUCTION

The Growing to Greatness study (National Youth Leadership Council, 2004) produced interesting and important information about the field of K-12 service-learning. It described the prevalence of service-learning in schools and provided several articles about research evidence, the impact of healthy youth development programs, the development of service-learning in the Learn and Serve initiative, the profiles of many state implementations, and profiles of several community-based organizations that utilize service-learning. As we reflect on all the information provided, we need to ask what the report adds to the long history and tradition of service-learning, and specifically, what it contributes to the further knowledge about this phenomenon called service-learning? We need to understand what we have learned from previous research that sheds light on what we need to do and to include in future research ventures.

In order to answer this question a small group of noted researchers and practitioners (20+) from around the country were convened to describe what they thought were the most important/influential studies that shaped K-12 service-learning research. Conducting a Delphi study, using two rounds of dialogue and discussion, it was determined that there was some consensus on the most influential works. The first round produced 18 research studies/citations that were deemed important to the field because they framed the basic core of knowledge. In the second round, participants reranked the studies, identifying those that had the most significant impact on our research knowledge base. These were the studies/bodies of knowledge that most influenced the participants in the Delphi study and were the items participants felt most people referred to as seminal works in the field.

Analysis of importance was based on two criteria: frequency of listing (the number of times a study was listed by respondents) and average score (based on placement from 1 to 18). This meant that in the first round, for example, the most frequently mentioned study was listed by 9 of the 11 participants (in any rank). There were two items that were listed 9 times. The lowest average score (reflecting the highest placement on the list) in Round I was 2.5 for *The Michigan Journal of Community Service Learning*, but it was only listed two times in the frequency section.

In the second round, selections were again made on the greatest frequency and the lowest average score (based on ranking from 1-18). An additional category was added, based on the number of placements in the top 1-2 or 1-3 rankings, in order to break potential ties on the other two criteria. For a study/review to be selected as the most influential it had to have the most citations, have the lowest average score among those studies with the highest number of citations, and finally, had to have the highest frequency of placements in the 1-3 levels among those with the highest number of citations.

Based on these criteria, the results of the Delphi study suggested that the following items were deemed most important to what we know about service-learning. Recommendations were divided into four categories:

Research Reviews
- Conrad and Hedin (1989/1991)
- Billig (2000)

Research Studies
- Melchior and Bailis (1993-1998)
- Conrad and Hedin (1980)
- Eyler and Giles (1999)
- Newmann and Rutter (1985)

Standards of Good Practice
- Alliance for Service-Learning in Educational Reform (Close-Up Foundation, 1995)

Collections
- *The Michigan Journal of Community Service Learning*
- The research book series, *Advances in Service-Learning Research*

Each item is summarized to describe the knowledge contributed to the service-learning research literature. Since the ASLER standards (1995) were not specifically based on research, they are not covered in this report. The purpose of this chapter is to present these major studies and to determine how they frame our needs for future research.

RESEARCH REVIEWS

School-Based Community Service: What We Know From Research and Theory (Conrad & Hedin, 1991)

This was one of the first major research reviews published on service-learning. Long time researchers from the University of Minnesota and Hopkins High School (Minnesota), the coauthors reviewed what was known about service and experiential learning programs for the National Center on Effective Secondary Schools at the University of Wisconsin and then rewrote the review for the 1991 issue of *Phi Delta Kappan* focusing on service-learning.

In their discussion of the research, they began by suggesting that service is an idea that many people view as good, but is not of critical importance to education or the wider society. They questioned whether interest by politicians and educators would be sustained, or whether pressures for higher test scores and improved basic skills would keep youth service on the fringes of the educational agenda. These concerns seem as timely today as they were 15 years ago.

They discussed the rich history of service, from Kilpatrick's (1918) urging the adoption of the "project method," to the Progressive movement, through the Citizen Education project of the 1950s, to the calls for more active, engaged educational programs in the 1970s, to the reports on educational improvement (Boyer, 1983; Goodlad, 1984; Harrison, 1987). In both Boyer and Harrison's work, we see a call for a mandatory 120 hours of service for high school graduation and an actual labeling of credit given for student service, according to Harrison's (1987) *Student Service: The New Carnegie Unit*. Using this historical backdrop, Conrad and Hedin attempted to gather "evidence" to make the case for community service and experiential learning as a viable educational strategy. They acknowledged that very little has been proven by educational research. One can always find research evidence to support a case. They then explained the difficulties of doing research on service programs because service is not an easily definable activity, such as taking notes at a lecture. Add to this dilemma the fact that service "has a wide range of plausible outcomes," making it difficult to determine the "appropriate dependent variables" and you begin to understand the difficulty of isolating service-learning as a defined intervention in any research study.

There are two types of research evidence: quantitative and qualitative. In the quantitative arena related to intellectual development, Conrad and Hedin (1980) cited their own study, where they found that problem-solving ability increased more for students in community service (and other experience-based programs) than for comparison groups. Improvement occurred most when the problems were similar to those presented and when the programs specifically focused on problem solving.

Besides the intellectual gains derived from service, they also found social/psychological development as well. Again referring to their own 1980 study, they found students in community service, community study, career internships, and outdoor adventure all made gains in social and personal responsibility. Citing other researchers (such as Hamilton & Zeldin, 1987), they documented positive outcomes, including

- More favorable attitudes toward adults;
- More positive attitudes toward others;
- A greater sense of self-efficacy;

- Higher self-esteem;
- More active exploration of careers;
- A better sense of social competence; and
- Enhanced moral and ego development.

They also cited effects on those served. While most research has focused on impact on volunteers, two areas of study, tutoring and peer helping, have yielded strong outcomes on those receiving service. Tutoring has consistently been found to be an effective method of instruction, shown to be more effective at raising academic outcomes than computer assisted instruction. Peer programs have been shown be effective on a variety of outcomes, including reducing actual drug use of those served.

There are mixed results from quantitative studies. Studies of the impact of community service on increasing political efficacy and later civic involvement are divided. Some show positive results, others show no effect. On tests of general knowledge, service programs only rarely result in higher test scores (with the exception of youth engaged in tutoring).

While the authors indicated in their report that quantitative studies have been mixed (although in a consistently positive direction), qualitative data have demonstrated more powerful impacts. The gaps between qualitative and quantitative work suggests a practice so complex that it demands equally varied types of assessment. Including qualitative data helps to enrich the knowledge base and provides particular and peculiar impact on each individual.

Conrad and Hedin (1980) also discussed the connection between the two forms of evidence. In the quantitative analysis of their national study of 4,000 students, they found 75% reported learning more or much more than in their regular classes. Analysis of student journals in intensive service programs connected to the curriculum revealed the particular learning that came from service. In this study, 95% of the students reported learning more or much more than from their regular classes. Some of the findings included:

- There is power in being in a new role;
- Relationships with children are more compelling reasons to act responsibly than demands and sanctions of school authorities;
- Service experiences widen the range of people, places, and problems encountered by youth; and
- Service experiences can lead to new ways of knowing and understanding.

From these contexts, 'more' begins to take on new meaning. It does not refer to the actual amount, necessarily, but to the significance of the experience. Youth begin to learn what is important in life and service experiences help them to understand who they are and where they are going.

Conrad and Hedin (1991) ended their review by suggesting that the case for community service as a legitimate educational practice was supported by many forms of research. While the results are mixed, there is little question that service-learning is deserving of support from practitioners and policymakers.

Research on K-12 School-Based Service-Learning: The Evidence Builds (Billig, 2000)

Dr. Billig, one of the leading researchers in the country on service-learning and related subjects, began her review with a quote from Conrad and Hedin, suggesting that the issues raised by them remain current. This introduction provides us with a sense of historic continuity, where one author builds on the foundation of previous work. So it is with the Billig review, sponsored by the Kellogg Foundation's *Learning In Deed* initiative. In fact, this sponsorship and the focus of the review embody the change that occurred in the service-learning world from 1991 to 2000. The Kellogg Foundation, along with the Corporation for National and Community Service, raised the prominence of service-learning to new levels. Note that while the focus of the Conrad and Hedin review was on community service and other experiential learning programs, Billig's review was directed specifically toward service-learning research. Her article reviewed service-learning studies completed between 1990 and 1999.

She began the review with a series of questions about service-learning: "Is it a program or a philosophy? What are the key elements? What do best practices look like? What are the effects and impacts? Do characteristics and relationships influence outcomes?" (p. 659). The function of this article was to show that 10 years of research has addressed many of these issues.

Billig cited the tremendous growth of service-learning. She compared programs from 1984, where 27% of high schools had community service and only 9% had service-learning, to 1999, where 64% of all public schools and 83% of high schools had some form of community service (p. 659). Nearly one third of all public schools and one half of public high schools provide service-learning programs.

Service-learning is supported by public opinion. Adults thought that the focus on civic education and positive youth development were good goals. Members of the public did express concern that service-learning would "detract from basics" and were concerned about student safety and mandatory service.

Similar to the Conrad and Hedin review, Billig briefly traced the history of service-learning. While acknowledging ancient roots, she focused on more recent understandings from the National Society for Experiential Education and the Corporation for National Service. There was consensus on major components of good service-learning: active participation, thoughtfully organized experiences, focus on community needs, school-community coordination, academic curriculum integration, structured time for reflection, opportunities for application of skills and knowledge, extended learning opportunities, and development of a sense of caring for others. Referring to more recent publications by notable authors Furco, Sigmon, and Toole and Toole, she raised important questions about the various components of good programs/good practice. Service-learning is viewed as a way to focus schools on developing caring, responsible individuals who understand democracy and the meaning of civic responsibility. She mentioned the quality standards developed by ASLER (1995) as guidelines for effective practice.

Billig began the actual review by citing the limitations of the work. Most examples came from research conducted through program evaluations. Programs vary immensely across many ranges; few use control groups or tracked impacts over time. Many studies are not easily replicated and the data are not easily validated.

Despite these limitations, the body of evidence is promising. Much of the impact is supported by similar results found in higher education. The findings of the studies reviewed are not simply isolated studies, but part of a body of research that clearly points in a positive direction. For each area, Billig assembled an array of studies and specific results that support the general findings of outcomes and impact.

Outcomes and Impacts

- Service-learning has a positive effect on the personal development of public school youth.
- Students who participate in service-learning are less likely to engage in "risk" behavior.
- Service-learning has a positive effect on students' interpersonal development and the ability to relate to culturally diverse groups.
- Service-learning helps develop students' sense of civic and social responsibility and their citizenship skills.
- Service-learning provides an avenue for students to become active, positive contributors to society.

- Service-learning helps students acquire academic skills and knowledge.
- Students who participate in service-learning are more engaged in their studies and more motivated to learn.
- Service-learning is associated with increased student attendance.
- Service-learning helps students to become more knowledgeable and realistic about careers.
- Service-learning results in greater mutual respect between teachers and students.
- Service-learning improves the overall school climate.
- Engaging in service-learning lends to discussions of teaching and learning and of best ways for students to learn.
- Service-learning leads to more positive perceptions of schools and youth on the part of the community members (pp. 660-662).

Billig identified several other "mediators" that influence outcomes and affect program and learning quality:

- Intensity and duration of programs are related to project outcomes;
- Increased responsibility, autonomy, and student choice affect impact;
- Direct, sustained contact with clients is responsible for more robust outcomes; and
- Different kinds of reflection and specific teacher qualities affect the outcomes of service-learning programs (p. 662).

Billig ended the article by citing a need for more and better research. There is a need for more multi-site, experimental, and quasi-experimental longitudinal studies. Such studies help to make causal claims. Better qualitative studies are also needed to provide better understanding of how service-learning works and more detail about the uniqueness and process of programs.

She concluded that despite the growth in service-learning programs, few researchers have been drawn to the field. There is a huge need for more funding and better long-term studies. Citing the Conrad and Hedin review, she ended as they did a decade before:

> Only time will tell whether the current interest among politicians and educators in strengthening the service ethic of our nations' youth will be sustained or whether new priorities or the same old pressures for higher basic skills will keep youth service on the fringes of the political and educational agenda. (p. 663)

There is irony and history in these remarks. Two decades, two reviews, and the conclusions remain the same. While the evidence in the last decade builds a stronger and more focused argument for service-learning, the need, the will, and the political and educational drive remain at bay. The jury is still out, and researchers hope to convince others there is sufficient evidence with which to continue.

RESEARCH STUDIES

Several studies were listed as being significant and important. Space limits the discussion to three reports or series of reports: the Melchior and Bailis studies from 1992-1999, the Conrad and Hedin study in 1979-1980, and the Eyler and Giles study in higher education (1999). Each has made an enormous contribution to the field.

Melchior and Bailis (1992-1998)

The works by Melchior and Bailis, from Brandeis University, were considered by the Delphi group as exemplars of well-designed, well-implemented, and well-reported studies. Not only were the studies methodologically well planned, the more impressive contribution was the explanations for the data and the insights drawn from the results. The evaluation studies reported here include:

- The 1992-1995 study of Serve America, conducted with Abt Associates, was an examination of 13 programs in four states, including school-based and community-based programs. The study involved almost 500 students.
- The 1994-1997 study of Learn and Serve America programs, sponsored by the Corporation for National Service, consisted of 17 programs in nine states. This study included 10 high schools and 7 middle schools, all considered to be experienced in service-learning pedagogy.
- The Active Citizenship Today (ACT) initiative study ran from 1995 until 1998 and involved 580 middle and high school students.

An excellent summary of these reports is found in the chapter they wrote for *Service-Learning: The Essence of the Pedagogy* (Melchior & Bailis, 2002). This analysis is based primarily on that chapter and on a summary of their Learn and Serve study.

The focus of these studies, especially those dealing with civic measures, was on a sense of personal and social responsibility for others and for community involvement. Melchior and Bailis also dealt with constructs of leadership, diversity, and development of communication skills. Finally, they emphasized involvement in service and the total hours engaged in service during the previous half year.

The Learn and Serve and Serve America studies also looked at academic and behavioral outcomes, including

- Attitudes toward formal school and school engagement;
- School performance (grades, attendance, suspensions, and failures);
- Involvement in risk behavior (becoming a teen parent, drug and alcohol use, delinquency); and
- Violence.

The ACT study included personal knowledge of community, sense of belonging, and attitudes toward teamwork.

This series of studies, using several analytical approaches, produced important results. For high school students in Serve America, they reported positive impacts on students' attitudes toward social welfare, communications skills, involvement in volunteer service, and total hours of service. For middle schools, the only statistical results were for service hours. For Learn and Serve America, many areas were affected significantly, including:

- Service-leadership;
- Awareness of community issues;
- Capacity to address needs;
- Commitment to address needs;
- Acceptance of diversity;
- Involvement in service; and
- Service hours.

For middle schools in Learn and Serve America, only involvement in service was reported as significant. In the ACT studies, significant impact was found in communication skills, civic attitudes, and service leadership. Other outcomes involved social studies grades, reduction in arrests, reductions in teen pregnancy, and reduction in class failures. ACT also showed impact on teamwork.

Some of the relative findings involved only modest impacts of from 2% to 5% on most issues, and 5% to 8% on attitudes. Most youth have a well developed sense of civic responsibility, reflected in baseline data that were high across groups.

Discoveries indicated that impact on attitudes and behaviors was directly related to service experiences and had less impact on broad measures. Service experiences most closely tied to course curriculum produced measurable results. These results confirmed what Westheimer and Kahne (2000) and Hamilton and Zeldin (1987) found: service experiences can be designed to shape different skills and outcomes, and different program designs produce different outcomes.

Melchior and Bailis also found that program quality and intensity affect outcomes. Program design and implementation "play a major role in the degree to which theory plays out in practice." Clearly differing hours of service affected impact: high school students showed more impacts and also engaged in 40% more service hours. The ACT study showed that time-on-task was related to program impact.

These studies also shared information about quality characteristics of service experiences (similar to Conrad and Hedin). Students reported many site traits that led to good learning:

- Challenging tasks;
- Important decision making;
- Adult interest in the youth;
- Freedom to explore their own interests;
- Variety of tasks to do; and
- Real responsibilities.

There was consensus on these characteristics of quality site experiences over 2 decades worth of work.

Examination of long-term impacts produced important findings. Performing a follow-up study one year later indicated that one-time involvement in service-learning was not likely to produce long-term impacts. They concluded that short-term programs yielded short-term results. Those who continue show impacts over time. Without continued involvement, almost all program impacts disappeared.

In one unusual finding, service-learning programs had negative impact on English grades, and had a positive impact on mathematics and science grades. Researchers were not sure if this was simply a statistical aberration or if service-learning somehow had a distracting impact on student performance.

Implications of these studies were clear: service-learning can play a role in meeting the challenges of developing youth civic engagement and participation. It can also lead to higher grades and provide meaningful experiences for active and effective citizens. Service-learning clearly can build knowledge and skills. It definitely helps youth feel more confident, take action, and build a commitment to participation over longer times. It is involved in more substantial and substantive service experiences and can generate lasting results.

These research pieces make it clear that we need to examine the nature of quality experiences. Programs need to be well and fully implemented if they are to generate results. We still struggle with developing reliable measures for active and sustainable programs; and we need to invest in learning about the long-term impacts of service-learning and pay much more attention to program design and implementation processes.

Conrad and Hedin (1980) National Study of School-Sponsored Experiential Learning Programs

The study of 27 programs, which involved direct participation in community (community service, community study, career internships, and outdoor adventure), highlighted some of the early, important findings in the service-learning field. While some of the study has already been discussed, notable findings from the rest of the study include information about the length and duration of programs, academic impact, and development of social responsibility. In comparing the outcomes of the programs, the authors reported that youth improved their school grades as a result of the experiential learning programs. More importantly, Conrad and Hedin found that the existence of a reflective seminar contributed most to the self-reported grade improvement of the students, along with evidence that programs that were intense (several hours per week) and had program lives of many months proved to have the most impact on intellectual development.

They also learned that students grew in areas of social responsibility (caring for others, demonstrating social responsibility by responding favorably to questions on a social responsibility scale). Students also indicated that they were able to demonstrate more effective moral reasoning when confronted with examples of social dilemmas.

Besides the intensity and duration concerns raised by the study, Conrad and Hedin found there were favorable characteristics of good community learning sites. Having real responsibility, facing challenging tasks,, having a caring adult to interact with, being allowed to choose activities, and having a variety of tasks to perform were all associated with better community-based learning environments.

Thus, the message of the Conrad and Hedin legacy is that intensity and duration matter. Quality of reflection, nature of tasks, and student choice were all important attributes of successful community-based learning programs.

Where's the Learning in Service-Learning?
(Eyler & Giles, 1999)

This popular book, a report on two studies conducted by the authors over a period of 6 years, has proven to be the most frequently mentioned study in higher education. The Comparing Models of Service-Learning initiative, sponsored by the Fund for the Improvement of Postsecondary Education (FIPSE), was actually inspired by the Conrad and Hedin study of 1980. The authors of this initiative suggested they wanted to do for higher education what Conrad and Hedin had done for K-12: assess the impact of experiential and service-learning programs on students. No similar national study had been conducted in higher education. Eyler and Giles engaged over 1,500 students from 20 colleges and universities to examine possible changes in problem-solving and critical thinking abilities, as well as changes in the complexity of their thinking. The second study, funded by the Corporation for National Service, involved 67 students in interviews that explored student experiences with reflection (and led to the publication of *A Practitioner's Guide to Reflection in Service-Learning*, [Eyler, Giles, & Schmiede, 1996]).

The findings of Eyler and Giles' studies reveal much about what we know about the learning in service-learning. It is the learning, they suggest, that is one of the primary goals of educational institutions, whether in higher education or in the K-12 arena. While the book is replete with discussion about the learning process and service-learning, several points can be highlighted that summarize their findings. Major findings include:

- Learning begins with personal connections;
- Learning is useful;
- Learning is developmental;
- Learning is transforming; and
- Citizenship rests on learning.

In the specific areas of the study, the authors concluded that service-learning has several other effects. It reduces negative stereotypes and has an impact on personal and interpersonal development. Program quality affects student learning, and in good programs, students report learning more. Not only do they learn more, they have better understanding. The authentic situations found in service-learning also lead to the generation of more questions by students.

Service-learning influenced critical thinking and problem solving. While not affecting critical thinking directly, it did affect student ability to identify social issues and made them more open to new ideas. The quality of programs, including application, structured reflection, and community voice, were predictors of their ability to see consequences of actions. As the service and learning were integrated into classroom focus and reflection, ability to engage in problem analysis increased.

Service-learning was also shown to have an impact on student perspectives. The nature of the experience helped change their view of social problems. Sometimes the experiences created disorienting dilemmas that helped give students new perspectives on social issues. High quality placements, where students had real responsibility and challenging work, helped them see issues in new ways.

There were several forms of civic participation identified in the studies. These included political participation, participation in voluntary associations, generation of social capital, and several elements of citizenship. These components involved values, knowledge, skills, efficacy, and commitment.

Eyler and Giles found that there were many characteristics of effective programs, including:

- Application (the degree to which students link service to classroom activities);
- Reflection (how service is connected to learning); and
- Intensity of reflection on the service experiences.

Eyler and Giles also found that intensive reflection, using writing or discussion, was necessary for impact. Community voice was determined to be an important predictor of personal development.

Gender differences were noted. Females were more likely to experience positive changes from service experiences. Not surprisingly, females also participated in service-learning in higher proportions than males.

Several principles of effective service-learning were noted:

- There was a clear connection between the service and learning;
- There was continuity of experiences over time;
- The context of the service was interesting and meaningful;

- There were real challenges in the service and learning experiences; and
- There were individuals in the process who provided coaching and support, all were necessary for high quality programs.

The authors developed a series of questions that affect the quality of academic service-learning programs. In many ways these items are similar to those found in the Billig review and in the Conrad and Hedin studies.

- Do students have opportunities to do important work and take on responsible roles?
- Is the service work continued over a sustained period of time?
- Are there close connections between academic subject matter and what students are doing in the community?
- Is reflection about the service integrated into classes through frequent opportunities for discussion and written analysis or projects?
- Does reflection challenge students to go beyond description and sharing of feelings to analysis and action planning?
- Do students work with people from diverse backgrounds?
- Are community partnerships developed in partnership with the community?

Eyler and Giles (1999) ended the book with a prophetic quote from T.S. Eliot:

> We shall not cease from exploration
> And the end of all our exploring
> Will be to arrive where we started
> And Know the place for the first time. (p. 208)

This book affirmed the importance of the Conrad and Hedin study: there is a need to understand where and how learning occurs through service. Eyler and Giles demonstrated that service-learning, in higher education settings, has important characteristics and traits that make it effective. As with the Billig pronouncements, choice, connection of the reflective practice to academic constructs, challenges of the activities and of the learning, continuous involvement, and context all determine the quality of the experience. As they stated, reflective practice becomes the "hyphen" in service-learning, connecting the experiences with the intentional learning required of academic institutions.

A Profile of High School Community Service Programs (Newmann & Rutter, 1985-1986)

In this review of more than 900 high schools in 1985, Newmann and Rutter found that roughly 27% of all high schools had some form of community service and 9% had some form of community service connected to the curriculum (service-learning). This study was one of the first to document the prevalence of community service and service-learning in the field, demonstrating that a minority of schools had such programs in 1984. The study has been used as a baseline document by which to compare growth with more current studies of the dissemination of service-learning programs across the country. It helped to quantify the presence of service and service-learning programs in schools and established a working understanding of the differences between programs that were simply service efforts and those that were connected in some way to the curriculum.

COLLECTIONS OF RESEARCH

The Michigan Journal of Community Service Learning and the Advances in Service-Learning Research Series

These two items, a journal and a book series, were listed in the Delphi study as two of the most important collections of research on service-learning at the K-12 levels. They were cited as the most broad-based assemblage of research in the past decade.

Michigan Journal of Community Service Learning

The *Michigan Journal of Community Service Learning* was cited as important to research on K-12 education because it included research on teacher education. Such a topic was deemed a critical component of K-12 development. For example, in the fall 2000 volume of the journal, Boyle-Baise and Kilbane presented a qualitative study of 24 preservice K-12 teachers involved in a multicultural teacher education course. They discussed what "really happened" in helping preservice teachers learn about multicultural issues, describing the strong "self-growth" that occurs in service-learning courses, but also commenting on the more limited understandings of families and community strengths and problems.

Other prominent researchers on service-learning and teacher education who published in these volumes were Root, Callahan, Anderson, Wade, and Swick. The journal has been instrumental in including teacher education research as a regular part of its offerings, and in so doing, has served as a bridge between K-12 education and higher education.

Advances in Service-Learning Research

The *Advances in Service-Learning Research* series (Billig, 2002-2005) was considered important because it presented some of the most current research in the field. Developed as a series to highlight some of the best presentations/papers presented at the annual International Service-Learning Research Conference, the book series has showcased the most highly regarded research studies shared through a peer-review process.

A product of many people, spearheaded by Billig, Furco, and other long-time researchers from the 1980s and 1990s who participated in the National Society for Internships and Experiential Education Research Special Interest Group, the series quickly has become one of the research standards for the field. Billig, the series editor, has co-edited volumes with many notable researchers in the field, including Callahan, Furco, Eyler, Root, and Welch. Each volume in the series includes studies and reports presented at the fall conference, guaranteeing that the research is current and reviewed for both conference presentation and then reviewed again for publication. The series is not limited to K-12 research, and like the *Michigan Journal of Community Service Learning*, is one of the better sources of material that bridges the information landscape of K-12, higher education, and community-based studies.

SUMMARY

We have ended this review "where we started." The issues and findings from the first major study (Conrad & Hedin, 1980) are restated and reaffirmed through the many important research efforts of the past 25 years. That service-learning has impact is beyond doubt. How often and how significant that impact depends mainly on issues of quality of implementation: the nature of the tasks, the intensity and duration of the service experiences, and the processing of the experiences (reflecting, assessing, and performing new tasks).

From Conrad and Hedin we learned that intensity, duration, and reflection matter. Quality programs must last over time and be based on attention to student assessment of their learning. From quantitative studies we learned about general outcomes from service and experiential activities. From qualitative research we learned of the particulars of outcomes, including depth and details of what was achieved.

From Billig, we learned that there have been few controlled studies and that much of our information is from anecdotes. She claimed we need more quantitative studies that use experimental and quasi-experimental designs. She added that the factors that contribute to quality include responsibility, autonomy, and student choice. Teacher quality and the kinds of reflection affect outcomes. It is important to have direct, sustained contact between students and those they serve in order to have good impact.

Melchior and Bailis reminded us that service experiences most closely tied to curriculum had the best effects. The more challenging the activities and the more personally engaging the service, the more likely change would occur. Their findings about the importance of responsibility and the nature of the tasks reinforce the studies by Conrad and Hedin and Billig's review: the nature of tasks and how they are processed are important to achieving good outcomes.

Eyler and Giles found many of the same things in higher education that Conrad and Hedin discovered in K-12 education. High quality service-learning presented students with dilemmas that needed solutions, provided opportunities for critical thinking, and allowed transformational experiences that proved very valuable to students across the country. Connections, continuity, context, challenge, and coaching all proved to be important elements of quality service-learning programs.

Newmann and Rutter showed us that service-learning has indeed grown in size and application in K-12 schools since the 1980s. They suggested that as service-learning programs grow to scale, there are issues about expansion that may influence the quality of the experiences.

The *Michigan Journal of Community Service Learning* and the *Advances in Service-Learning Research* series demonstrate that the field of service-learning research has indeed come of age, producing a continuous supply of research studies that increase our knowledge of all the relevant topics raised over the years. Especially relevant for K-12 research is the impact of teacher education programs in preparing high quality teachers who can deliver high quality programming.

IMPLICATIONS

What does this all mean for the future direction of service-learning research? Most significantly, it suggests that researchers need to change the focus of their work. Instead of concern for the number of programs in operation and all the outcomes produced by service-learning initiatives, we need to turn our attention to the process of creating high quality service-learning models. Simply put, 25 years of research has shown that quality matters. It is the quality of programs that predicts positive outcomes. All the quality indicators mentioned in these research studies/ reviews should become the areas of focus for future research.

Questions about how one creates a high quality service-learning program become paramount. What kind of training and education is necessary for quality programs? What kind of assistance for curriculum development, community site development, and coordination practices are necessary to ensure the high quality of task processing and subsequent high quality learning and impact?

As Conrad and Hedin stated almost two decades ago, there is no doubt that service-learning is a serious educational philosophy and pedagogy. What is in doubt is how we create high quality programs. Based on the review presented in this chapter, the research effort of the next decade should be focused as much on questions of implementation strategy as on measuring the existence and outcomes of service-learning programs.

REFERENCES

Alliance for Service-Learning in Educational Reform. (1995). *Standards for school-based and community-based service-learning programs.* Alexandria, VA: Close-Up Foundation.

Billig, S. (2000, May). Research on K-12 school-based service-learning: The evidence builds. *Phi Delta Kappan, 81*(9), 658-664.

Billig, S. H. (Series Ed.). (2002-2005). *Advances in service-learning research.* Greenwich, CT: Information Age.

Boyer, E. (1983). *High school: A report on secondary education in America.* New York: Harper & Row.

Boyle-Baise, M., & Kilbane, J. (2000, Fall). What really happened? A look inside service-learning for multicultural teacher education. *Michigan Journal of Community Service Learning, 7,* 54-64.

Conrad, D., & Hedin, D. (1980). *Executive summary of the final report of the national experiential education project.* St. Paul, MN: Center for Youth Development and Research, University of Minnesota.

Conrad, D., & Hedin, D. (1991, June). School-based community service: What we know from research and theory. *Phi Delta Kappan, 72*(10), 743-749.

Eyler, J., & Giles, D. E., Jr. (1999). *Where's the learning in service-learning?* San Francisco: Jossey-Bass.

Eyler J., Giles, D. E., & Schmiede, A. A. (1996). A practitioner's guide to reflection in service-learning: Student voices and reflections. Nashville, TN: Vanderbilt University.

Goodlad, J. (1984). *A place called school.* New York: McGraw Hill.

Hamilton, S., & Zeldin, S. (1987, Winter). Learning civics in the community. *Curriculum Inquiry, 17,* 497-500.

Harrison, C. (1987). *Student service: The new Carnegie unit.* Princeton, NJ: Carnegie Foundation for the Advancement of Teaching.-

Kilpatrick, W. (1918, September). The project method. *Teacher's College Record,* 319-335.

Melchior, A., & Bailis, L. N. (2002). Impact of service-learning on civic attitudes and behaviors of middle and high school youth: Findings from three national evaluations. In A. Furco & S. H. Billig (Eds.), *Advances in service learning: Vol.*

1. Service-learning: The essence of the pedagogy (pp. 201-222). Greenwich, CT: Information Age.

National Youth Leadership Council. (2004). *G2G: Growing to greatness.* St. Paul, MN: Author.

Newmann, F., & Rutter, R. (1985-1986). A profile of high school community service programs. *Educational Leadership, 43*(4), 65-71.

Westheimer, J., & Kahne, J. (2000, April). *Assessment and the democratic purpose of schooling.* Paper presented at the American Educational Research Association conference, New Orleans, LA.

Section V

INSTITUTIONALIZATION OF SERVICE-LEARNING IN HIGHER EDUCATION

CHAPTER 10

ANCILLARY TO INTEGRAL

Momentum to Institutionalize
Service-Learning and Civic Engagement

Karen McKnight Casey and Nicole C. Springer

ABSTRACT

Indications that the service-learning and civic engagement movements have prospered in recent years are found in the proliferation and array of publications ranging from the popular press to scholastic publications and online journals and Web resources. Evidence of growth is apparent, yet does it speak to trends toward institutionalization? The authors of this chapter examine the trend toward the institutionalization of service-learning and civic engagement, tracing its roots from a few outliers or "pioneers" to what it has become today. Presentation of national indicators and regional accreditation criteria create an evidence-based foundation for making service-learning and civic engagement an integral facet of higher education.

Advancing Knowledge in Service-Learning: Research to Transform the Field, 207–222
Copyright © 2006 by Information Age Publishing

(Mechanical Engineering) Design Day helps area student:
Specialized cycle gives man better mobility, freedom

—Martin, *The State News* (2003)
[A headline in a university newspaper]

Helping to plant a garden to grow food for the VOA (Volunteers of America) kitchen
was an extension of math, science, social studies, and language arts lessons the stu-
dents were learning in school. But it also was a lesson in life.

—Leach, *Lansing State Journal* (2006)
[From an article in a daily newspaper]

These quotes from newspaper articles provide a form of evidence relevant to service-learning and civic engagement far different than what is provided by refereed journals, juried presentations, and/or other scholarly publications to which the reader might be accustomed. While nonacademic in nature, these articles are valuable, serving to highlight service-learning in the higher education and K-12 arenas. They help lend credence to the assertion that the service-learning and civic engagement movements continue to build momentum.

Evidence of national and international interest in service-learning and civic engagement abounds in the numbers and types of scholastic publications, dedicated conferences, seminars and colloquia, as well as Web-based and other online resources such as clearinghouses and listservs. Campus Compact, the premier organization for service-learning and civic engagement in higher education, will celebrate its 20th anniversary in October 2006. This is a milestone anniversary that speaks to the appreciation of its work. Campus Compact has encouraged campuses across the United States to build cultures of civic engagement and has developed and promoted tools to help. In 2003, The Higher Learning Commission of the North Central Association of Colleges and Schools, a regional accreditation body, revamped its criteria for accrediting colleges and universities in its region, specifically addressing civic and community engagement and service in Criterion Five, while also acknowledging the role of service-learning pedagogy to promote effectiveness within other criteria. The sixth edition the Book of Professional Standards and Guidelines (Council for the Advancement of Standards in Higher Education, in press) features standards for service-learning. In February 2006, The Carnegie Foundation for the Advancement of Teaching, a hundred-year old, congressionally chartered, nationally recognized, independent policy and research institution, "whose charge is to do and perform all things necessary to encourage, uphold, and dignify the profession of the teacher and the cause of higher education" (Carnegie Foundation for the Advancement of Teaching, 2006), invited colleges and universities to apply to participate in the new Community Engagement Elective Classification. This proliferation of evidence, products, and resources, documents both interest and a trend toward institutionalization of service-learning pedagogy and practice. This chapter will examine that trend as it pertains to higher education.

HISTORY/BACKGROUND

In examining the trend toward the institutionalization of service-learning and civic engagement, it is important to acknowledge the persistent question of whether or not institutionalization is preferred or even desirable. Kendall and Associates (1990) explored questions of institutional support in sections dealing with institutional policy issues and the history and future of service-learning (parts IV and V) in the first volume of *Combining Service and Learning: A Resource Book for Community and Public Service.* Stanton, Giles, and Cruz (1999) raised the same question regarding the benefits of institutionalization in the preface of *Service-Learning: A Movement's Pioneers Reflect on Its Origins, Practice, and Future.* These authors noted that until the 1980s, service-learning advocates were a small, marginal group within higher education. Is such marginalization somehow advantageous?

In the chapter "Passing the Torch," Stanton and colleagues (1999) interviewed pioneers who offered differing views on the desirability of institutionalizing service-learning. Some expressed concern that bringing service-learning into the mainstream would somehow dilute it, or cause it to lose its edge or mission of social change (Stanton et al., 1999). Others, such as Harkavy and Duley (Stanton et al., 1999), proposed that integrating service-learning into the framework of higher education could change the delivery of higher education for the better. Parallel discussions, questions, and views were discussed by Kenny, Simon, Kiley-Brabeck, and Lerner (2001), where ultimately they stated the function of service-learning as "a critical cornerstone of outreach scholarship" (p. xi). Corresponding issues were raised by Kezar and Rhoads when they viewed service-learning in higher education through a philosophical lens (2001).

While respectful of opposing views, the authors of this chapter support the perspective of those pioneers, editors, and writers who are proponents of institutionalization. If one sees institutionalization as means to make service-learning a "part of a structured and usually well-established system," as defined in the *American Heritage Dictionary of the English Language* (2000), versus a means to "assimilate or homogenize" (*Roget's New Millennium Thesaurus,* 2006), then the benefits to the pedagogy and culture of engagement are clear. Noninstitutionalization can lead to fragmentation, inconsistency, perceived lack of value and rigor, and in the long-term, sustained marginalization. Incorporation of service-learning into the core and fabric of college/university practice is not predestined to lead to a focus away from social change if care is taken to build in parameters and structures to support this agenda. Integration into the mission and operation of the institution does not negate change, but can provide a platform and mechanism to effect it from within.

PRIMARY INDICATORS OF
NATIONAL MOMENTUM TOWARD INSTITUTIONALIZATION

Although additional indicators may provide evidence toward the incorporation of service-learning and civic engagement into the institutional culture of higher education; two national indicators and one regional set of accreditation standards provide unique, consistent validation. These are:

1. Campus Compact Indicators of Engagement Project;
2. Carnegie Foundation for the Advancement of Teaching: Community Engagement Elective Classification; and
3. The Higher Learning Commission: North Central Association Accreditation Standards.

Campus Compact Indicators of Engagement Project

This Indicators of Engagement Project is an outgrowth of the work of Hollander, Saltmarsh, and Zlotkowski (2002) and others who investigated indicators of engagement in higher education. The project was funded in 2002 by a 3-year grant from the Carnegie Corporation of New York for the purpose of documenting and disseminating evidence of the institutionalization of engagement at a range of college and university campuses. The result of these collaborations has already produced two monographs with a third publication forthcoming, all of which highlight best practices, and a toolkit titled, *Strategies for Creating an Engaged Campus: An Advanced Service-Learning Toolkit for Academic Leaders* [Strategies Toolkit] (Hollander, Burack, & Holland, 2001). The collective work provides parameters for all colleges and/or universities that wish to measure the level and value of their engagement.

The Indicators of Engagement Project utilizes 13 indicators of engagement:

1. Mission and Purpose
2. Academic and Administrative Leadership
3. Disciplines, Departments, and Interdisciplinary Work
4. Teaching and Learning
5. Faculty Development
6. Faculty Roles and Rewards
7. Support Structures and Resources
8. Internal Budget and Resource Allocations
9. Community Voice
10. External Resource Allocation
11. Coordination of Community-Based Activities
12. Forums for Fostering Public Dialogue
13. Student Voice (Campus Compact Website)[1]

While it is not expected that all colleges and/or universities will demonstrate evidence in each category, the greater the number of criteria addressed and the greater the depth of involvement in each, gauges the institutional commitment to engagement. These 13 indicators corresponding to those outlined in the *Strategies Toolkit*, are defined as follows:

1. **Mission and purpose** that explicitly articulates a commitment to the public purposes of higher education;

2. **Administrative and academic leadership** (president, trustees, provost) that is in the forefront of institutional transformation that supports civic engagement;

3. **External resource allocation** made available for community partners to create richer learning environments for students and for community-building efforts in local neighborhoods;

4. **Disciplines, departments, and interdisciplinary work** that incorporate community-based education, allowing it to penetrate all disciplines and reach the institutions academic core;

5. **Faculty roles and rewards** that embrace a scholarship of engagement that is incorporated into promotion and tenure guidelines and review;

6. **Internal resource allocation** that is adequate for establishing, enhancing, and deepening community-based work on campus—for faculty, students, and programs that involve community partners;

7. **Community voice** that deepens the role of community partners in contributing to community-based education and shaping outcomes that benefit the community;

8. **Enabling mechanisms** in the form of visible and easily accessible structures (i.e., centers, offices) on campus to assist faculty with community-based teaching and to broker community partnerships;

9. **Faculty development** opportunities that are available for faculty to retool their teaching and redesign their curricula to incorporate community-based activities and reflection on those activities within the context of the course;

10. **Integrated and complementary community service activities** that weave together student service, service-learning and other community engagement activities on campus;

11. **Forums for fostering public dialogue** that are created that include multiple stakeholders in public problem solving; and

12. **Pedagogy and epistemology** incorporate a community-based, public problem-solving approach to teaching and learning (Hollander et al., 2001).

These indicators are designed to serve both as a springboard and a means of assessment. They are applicable to the individual institution, but are not to be taken as prescriptive (Hollander et al., 2001).

Embedded in the *Strategies Toolkit* is the articulation of the need for colleges and universities to assess their work in service-learning and civic engagement. Featured as a resource in the toolkit is the article "Exploring the Challenge of Documenting and Measuring Civic Engagement Endeavors of Colleges and Universities: Purposes, Issues, Ideas" (Holland, 2001a). The article provides a compelling argument for the need to assess effectiveness of service-learning as a vehicle for civic engagement. Holland posits that this effort should come under the same scrutiny for academic rigor as other efforts, and should prove its quality and value to the institution and to the public that it serves.

While the participating in the Indicators of Engagement Project and adopting the *Strategies for Creating an Engaged Campus* certainly are not required of campuses, their grounding in evidence-based practice and rigor, and their targeting of university administrators rather than individual faculty and/or practitioners, speak to the momentum toward institutionalization.

Carnegie Foundation for the Advancement of Teaching: Community Engagement Elective Classification

On February 28, 2006, the Carnegie Foundation for the Advancement of Teaching invited colleges and universities across the United States to apply for selection to participate in the new Community Engagement

Elective Classification. The background of this initiative was described as follows:

> In 1970, the Carnegie Commission on Higher Education developed a classification of colleges and universities to support its program of research and policy analysis. Derived from empirical data on colleges and universities, the "Carnegie Classification" was published for use by other researchers in 1973, and subsequently updated in 1976, 1987, 1994, and 2000. (Carnegie Foundation for the Advancement of Teaching Web site, 2006)

Revisions occurred in 2005 that served to measure institutions not only by size and type, but "based on what is taught, to whom, and in what setting" (Jaschick, 2005). These revisions allowed for the vastly different sizes and missions of individual institutions to be seen as comparable in certain situations and settings. The introduction of the classification on engagement in 2006 dovetails with the 2005 revisions and exemplifies a significant enhancement of the benchmarking criteria: for the first time the classification measures engagement, most notably service-learning and civic engagement.

For those colleges and/or universities participating in the initiative, the documentation process for the new classification is to be conducted in two stages. The first requires the institution to describe a set of entry or foundational indicators, which examine institutional identity and culture and institutional commitment. The questions in these areas are not dissimilar from the Indicators of Engagement outlined by Campus Compact. Those institutions able to outline the foundational indicators adequately are asked to provide descriptions, data, and examples of focused engagement activities within the categories of curricular engagement and outreach and partnerships. According to the Carnegie Web site,

> *Curricular Engagement* describes teaching, learning, and scholarship which engage faculty, students, and community in mutually beneficial and respectful collaboration. Their interactions address community identified needs, deepen students' civic and academic learning, enhance the well-being of the community, and enrich the scholarship of the institution.

> *Outreach and Partnerships* describe two different but related approaches to community engagement. The first focuses on the application and provision of institutional resources for community use benefiting both campus and community. The latter focuses on collaborative interactions with community and related scholarship for the mutually beneficial exchange, exploration, discovery, and application of knowledge, information, and resources (research, economic development, capacity building, etc.). (Carnegie Foundation for the Advancement of Teaching, 2006)

Key to the process of institutionalization is the intent by Carnegie that it "ensures an institutionalized approach to community engagement" (Carnegie Foundation for the Advancement of Teaching, 2006). The questions in the pilot survey focused heavily on service-learning and civic engagement.

Participation in the documentation process for the elective classification will not be without challenges. Institutional characterizations of civic engagement and outreach, for example, may or may not precisely coincide with the definitions put forth by Carnegie.

Michigan State University (MSU) was one of 13 institutions to participate in the pilot study in July 2005. Key MSU administrators and practitioners were actively involved in discussions leading to establishing the criteria for the pilot study. Expanded discussions and networking helped to pinpoint the requested criteria and shed light on detail required in collecting data and examples to ensure alignment with the requirements for conducting an internal study for the report.

The challenges in participating in the pilot study were seen as minimal in comparison to the benefits. The level of scrutiny required to participate in the study compels the institution to take a realistic and critical look at itself in relation to engagement, thus illuminating the need to document and/or devise an institutional, embedded approach to engagement. In addition, given the perceived prestige of the Carnegie Classification System for Higher Education, participation in documenting such a classification study was viewed as value added for the college/university, and clearly helped to promote institutionalization of service-learning and civic engagement.

The Higher Learning Commission: North Central Association Accreditation Standards

The Higher Learning Commission (HLC) of the North Central Association of Colleges and Schools (NCA) is the accreditation body for the more than 1,200 institutions of higher education in the north central and midwest regions of the United States, including the majority of universities in the Big Ten Athletic Conference. In 2003, the HLC/NCA revamped its criteria for accrediting or reaccrediting institutions within its jurisdiction to become the following:

- Criterion One: Mission and Integrity
- Criterion Two: Preparing for the Future
- Criterion Three: Student Learning and Effective Teaching

- Criterion Four: Acquisition, Discovery, and Application of Knowledge
- Criterion Five: Engagement and Service (Higher Learning Commission, 2003, pp. 5-7)

Of particular note is the addition of the specific criterion addressing Criterion Five, Engagement and Service: *As called for by its mission, the organization identifies its constituencies and serves them in ways both value* (p. 7). This indicator speaks to the importance placed on multiple forms of engagement with the public, which include service-learning and civic engagement. Moreover, the revisions and additions to the criteria in general speak to service and engagement in other categories. In asking the institution to articulate vision and mission as part of Criterion One, HLC/NCA (2003) specifically asks the college/university to "recognize the ... greater society it serves" (p. 4). In Criterion Four, the organization is asked to articulate that "it realistically prepares for a future shaped by a multiple societal and economic trends" (HLC/NCA, p. 6). These criteria, coupled with a wide berth given colleges and universities in addressing Criterion Three, necessitate and afford opportunities to convey the institution's commitment to and implementation of service-learning and civic engagement in the crucial context of accreditation.

MSU was one of the first Big Ten universities to undergo the HCL/NCA accreditation process under the new criteria. MSU undertook its self-study in 2004-2005, with a visit from the NCA team occurring in February 2006. As the pioneer land-grant institution, which makes community service and inherent part of its mission, MSU references public service and engagement throughout the report. Service-learning and civic engagement specifically are articulated throughout the MSU report, appearing prominently in Criteria Three, Four, and Five (Michigan State University, 2006). The inclusion of service-learning in Criterion Three (Student Learning and Effective Teaching) and in Criterion Four (Acquisition, Discover, and Application of Knowledge) particularly speak to the integration and value of the pedagogy (MSU, 2006).

While the HCL/NCA does not accredit institutions in all parts of the United States, its groundbreaking work in establishing and implementing criteria that speaks to service-learning, service, and engagement paves the way for institutions under its purview to articulate and forge ahead in the documentation and implementation of service-learning and civic engagement. Successful accreditation is a driving force for any college or university, and as such, will serve to promote implementation. In addition, willingness of NCA to delve into these arenas may provide impetus for parallel accreditation bodies in other parts of the country.

Engagement Explicit in the Mission

As noted in each of the three primary indicators of momentum, the articulation of service and engagement in the mission and purpose of the institution is critical to institutionalization. In the fall of 2005, during her Sesquicentennial Convocation Address, MSU President Lou Anna K. Simon announced "Boldness by Design: Our Working Mission Statement and Strategic Imperatives," as a means of defining what it means to be land-grant in the 21st century. The working mission statement illuminates the growing importance of engagement at MSU (2005b).

Michigan State University is a national public research university that was created as a state land-grant university and is funded in part by the state of Michigan. The mission of the school is to advance knowledge and transform lives by:

- Providing outstanding graduate, undergraduate, and professional education to promising, qualified students in order to prepare them to contribute fully to society as citizen leaders;
- Conducting research of the highest caliber that seeks to answer questions and create solutions in order to expand human understanding and the well-being of all living things; and
- Undertaking outreach and engagement and economic development activities that are innovative, research-driven, and lead to a better quality of life for individuals and communities (Michigan State University, 2005a).

Michigan State University is a member of the prestigious American Association of Universities and is recognized as one of the top 100 research universities in the world. The university performs its work statewide, regionally, nationally, and internationally. The university is an inclusive, caring academic community, known for its strong traditional academic disciplines and professional programs and enthusiasm for collaborative, cross-disciplinary enterprises that connect the sciences, humanities, and professions in innovative ways to address society's rapidly changing needs. MSU's strategic imperatives provide details for implementation:

- Enhance the student experience—by continually improving the quality of academic programs and the value of an MSU degree for undergraduate and graduate students;
- Enrich community, economic, and family life—through research, outreach, engagement, entrepreneurship, innovation, and diversity;

- Expand international reach—through academic, research, and economic development initiatives and global, national, and local strategic alliances;

- Increase research opportunities—by significantly expanding research funding and involvement of graduate and undergraduate students in research and scholarship; and

- Strengthen stewardship—by appreciating and nurturing the university's financial assets, campus infrastructure, and people for optimal effectiveness today and tomorrow (Michigan State University, 2005a).

The mission statement and the first four of the *Strategic Imperatives* address service-learning and civic and community engagement. Boldness by Design provides a platform for institutionalization: it is more than rhetoric (Michigan State University, 2005b). Rather, it serves as a blueprint for which effort will be benchmarked. While the mission and imperatives will differ from one institution of higher education to another, the framework provided by such a set of statements helps to give form to the work and supports. Kent State University and Cleveland State University, for example, have issued presidential statements on community service and civic engagement, respectively, which incorporate mission statements and articulation of intent and evidence. These and similar presidential declarations also serve to exemplify progress towards institutionalization.

UTILIZATION OF STANDARDS

Further evidence of efforts to institutionalize service-learning can be found in the development of standards for implementation. Thorough examples of course-related standards can be found at the University of California, Berkeley (UC Berkeley), Service-Learning Research and Development Center and the University of Utah Service-Learning Hub at Lowell Bennion Community Service Center. While the approach to establishing and implementing the standards and designations vary, they are consistent in the use of faculty input on these items and the clear expectation that only courses meeting the determined criteria will be considered service-learning. UC Berkeley utilizes definitions and a matrix established by the Faculty Policy Committee on Service-Learning (University of California, Berkeley, n.d.). In the case of Utah, a "Service-Learning Course Submission Process" is in place, and faculty apply each semester to have individual courses recognized as service-learning (University of Utah Service-Learning Hub, n.d.)

Standards for courses, when adopted, can be viewed as an indicator of institutionalization, and as a toolkit of sorts for the design and implementation of service-learning. However, standards implementation can be challenging. In order to align with its mission and practice, each college/university will need to examine national recommendations, as well the practices of peer institutions, through its own unique lens. In institutions with long histories of service-learning, careful attention may need to be given to addressing instances in which a long-term practice approximates, but does not precisely meet, standards in order to afford both respect to the work of pioneer faculty and/or the needs of community constituents. In isolated cases, the grandfathering in of a particular course may be beneficial. The determination and issuance of standards need to be derived through a deliberative process that includes the voices of faculty, practitioners, administrators, applicable university governance, and community partners.

The Council for the Advancement of Standards in Higher Education (CAS)

In 2004, the CAS convened a committee to assist in the development of standards that would address a range of service-learning programs. Chaired by Dorothy I. Mitstifer, executive director of Kappa Omicron Nu, this committee outlined a set of standards that was later included in the 2005 edition of the *Book of Professional Standards for Higher Education*. The principles outlined by the CAS service-learning committee delineated standards by both mission and program. The CAS subcommittee defined *mission* as follows:

> The primary mission of Service-Learning Programs (S-LPs) is to engage Students in experiences that address human and community needs together with structured opportunities for reflection intentionally designed to promote student learning and development. The mission of S-LPs must address human and community needs defined by the community. (Mitstifer, p. 7, 2004)

S-LPs must:

- Incorporate student learning and development in their missions;
- Enhance overall educational experiences;
- Develop, record, disseminate, implement, and regularly view their mission and goals;

- Have mission statements that are consistent with the mission and goals of the institution and with the standards in this document; and

- Operate as integral parts of the institution's overall mission (Mitstifer, p. 7, 2004).

The audience for CAS is national, rather than that of a single institution so the standards developed were broad-based and recognized that colleges and universities may have differing definitions and means of implementation. This acknowledgment of differences and the high quality of the standards serve to make them appealing to colleges and/or universities seeking to adapt the standards according to individual needs.

Standards and recommendations for program, leadership, organization and management, human resources, financial resources, facilities, technology and equipment, legal responsibilities, equity and access, campus and external relations, diversity, ethics, and assessment and evaluation were all addressed in a manner that speaks to the range of institutions, but also the need for institutionalization (Mitstifer, 2004).

TRANSFORMING FROM ANCILLARY TO INTEGRAL: CHALLENGES AND REWARDS

Coverage in the popular press, the echo of the voices of the pioneers of service-learning, the development and promotion of national indicators and standards, the articulation of service and engagement in the mission and strategy statements of institutions, the call for measurement and assessment—all demonstrate the trend to institutionalize service-learning and civic engagement in higher education. The movement of service-learning and civic engagement in higher education from ancillary to integral is exciting and rewarding, but it is not without challenges. Care must be given to increase the growth of evidence-based practice so as to coincide with the academic rigor embedded in the disciplines. Attention must be given to reward the efforts of faculty engaged in the work. Documentation and reporting of faculty participation, as evidenced through the MSU Outreach Engagement Measurement Instrument and other instruments for recognizing the teaching and implementation of service-learning courses in the promotion and tenure process, are all essential to institutionalization.

Careful attention must also be given to maintaining the student and community voices, which are germane and crucial to practice. The need for student input in the service-learning and civic engagement process is recognized in the Indicators of Engagement Project, included in the Carnegie Classification Pilot Survey, and articulated in the CAS standards. However, without orchestrated and systematic attention to that voice, it could become overlooked in the faculty and administrator-driven cultures prominent at some institutions.

The importance of maintaining the value and the voice of the community is addressed most recently in *Engaging Campus and Community* (Peters, Jordan, Adamek, & Alter, 2005). This volume speaks to the practice of public scholarship beyond service-learning alone, addressing the need to value the knowledge of the community partners and incorporate that knowledge and expertise into the work. This need is expressed in all of the higher education indicators, methods of measurement, and standards.

The recently developed tools, such as Campus Compact's Indicators, the Carnegie Elective Classification, and CAS Standards, and internal catalysts, such as MSU's Boldness by Design mission statement and strategy framework, help to propel and maintain the integration of civic engagement and service-learning into institutions of higher education. This encouraging development will help institutionalize practice, clearly moving service-learning and civic engagement from ancillary to integral.

NOTE

1. Campus Contact Web site: http://www.compact.org/indicators/detail.php?id=1

REFERENCES

American Heritage Dictionary of the English Language. (4th ed.). (2000). Boston: Houghton Mifflin.

Carnegie Foundation for the Advancement of Teaching. (2006). *The Carnegie classification of institutions of higher education.* Retrieved May 2, 2006, from http://carnegiefoundation.org/classifications/index.asp?key=1213

Council for the Advancement of Standards in Higher Education. (in press). Retrieved May 3, 2006, from http://www.cas.edu

Higher Learning Commission: A Commission of the North Central Association of Colleges and Schools. (2003). *Institutional accreditation: An overview.* Retrieved May 3, 2006, from http://ncahigherlearningcommission.org/download/2003Overview.pdf

Holland, B. A. (2001a, March). *Exploring the challenge of documenting and measuring civic engagement endeavors of colleges and universities: Purposes, issues, ideas.* Campus Compact Advanced Institute on Classifications for Civic Engagement. Retrieved May 3, 2006, from http://www.compact.org/advancedtoolkit/pdf/holland_paper.pdf

Hollander, E., Burack, C., & Holland, B. (2001). *Strategies for creating an engaged campus: An advanced service-learning toolkit for academic leaders*. Retrieved May 3, 2006, from http://www.compact.org/advancedtoolkit/

Hollander, E. L., Saltmarsh, J., & Zlotkowski, E. (2002). Indicators of engagement. In M. E. Kenny, L. A. K. Simon, K. Kiley-Brabeck, & R. M. Lerner (Eds.), *Learning to serve: Promoting civil society through service-learning* (Vol. 7, chap. 3). Norwell, MA: Kluwer Academic.

Jaschik, S. (2005, November 18). The new Carnegie classifications. *Inside Higher Ed*. Retrieved May 3, 2006, from http://www.insidehighered.com/news/2005/11/18/carnegie

Kendall, J. C. & Associates. (1990). *Combining service and learning: A resource book for community and public service: Vol. 1*. Raleigh, NC: National Society for Internships and Experiential Education.

Kenny, M. E., Simon, L. K., Kiley-Brabeck, K., & Lerner, R. M. (Eds.). (2001). *Learning to serve: Promoting civil society through service learning*. New York: Kluwer.

Kezar, A., & Rhoads, R. A. (2001). The Dynamic tensions of service learning in higher education: A philosophical perspective. *The Journal of Higher Education, 72*, 148–171.

Leach, H. (2006, June 3). 3rd-graders plant seeds to start soup kitchen's garden project. *Lansing State Journal*. Retrieved June 13, 2006, from http://lsj.com

Martin, K. (2003, April 25). Design day helps area student: Specialized cycle gives man better mobility, freedom. *The State News*. Retrieved May 3, 2006, from http://www.statenews.com/article.phtml?pk=17498

Michigan State University Web site. (2005a). *Boldness by design: Strategic positioning of Michigan State University*. Retrieved June 26, 2006, from http://strategicpositioning.msu.edu/Design_Glance.asp

Michigan State University. (2005b). *Boldness by design* [Brochure]. East Lansing, MI: Author.

Michigan State University. (2006). *HCL/NCA (North Central Accreditation Association) re-accreditation self-studies at MSU: The self-study report*. Retrieved May 3, 2006, from http://accreditation2006.msu.edu/report/index.html

Mitstifer, D .I. (2004). Standards for service-learning programs. *Service-learning: Its opportunity and promise, 15*, 7–16.

Peters, S. J., Jordan, N. R., Adamek, M., & Alter, T. R. (Eds.). (2005). *Engaging campus and community: The practice of public scholarship in the state and land-grant system*. Dayton, OH: Kettering Foundation Press.

Roget's New Millennium Thesaurus (1st ed.). (2006). Boston: Houghton Mifflin.

Stanton, T. K., Giles, D. E., Jr., & Cruz, N. I. (1999). *Service-learning: A movement's pioneers reflect on its origins, practice, and future*. San Francisco: Jossey-Bass.

University of California at Berkeley. (n.d.). *UC Berkeley Service-Learning Research and Development Center*. Retrieved May 3, 2006, from http://gse.berkeley.edu/research/slc/

University of Utah Service-Learning Hub, Lowell Bennion Community Service Center. (n.d.). *Faculty*. Retrieved May 3, 2006, from http://bennion.slpro.net/index.cfm

ADDITIONAL READING

Billig, S. H., & Furco, A. (Eds.). (2002). *Service-learning through a multidisciplinary lens: Vol. 1*. Greenwich, CT: Information Age.

Clearinghouse and National Review Board. (2002). *Evaluation criteria*. Retrieved April 12, 2002, from http: www.scholarshipofengagement.org

Holland, B. A. (2001b, November). *Measuring the role of civic engagement in campus missions: Key concepts and challenges*. Speech presented at ASHE Symposium on "Broadening the Carnegie Classification's Attention to Mission: Incorporating Public Service," Richmond, VA.

Michigan State University. (1993). *University outreach at Michigan State University: Extending knowledge to serve society*. Report by the Provost's Committee on University Outreach. East Lansing, MI: University Printing.

Michigan State University. (2003). *Campus sustainability report*. Report by the Office of Campus Sustainability. East Lansing, MI: University Printing.

University Outreach. (1996). *Four dimensions of quality outreach* (UO-02). East Lansing: Michigan State University.

ABOUT THE CONTRIBUTORS

Martha Balshem is professor of sociology at Portland State University. She is the author of *Cancer in the Community*, an ethnography describing her community health education research in a working class community in Philadelphia. She has served as coordinator of PSU's Freshman Inquiry Program, associate director at the Western Association of Schools and Colleges, and director of PSU's Center for Academic Excellence.

Rick Battistoni is professor of political science and public service at Providence College. For the past 17 years, Rick has been a leader in the field of service-learning, especially as it relates to questions of civic education and engagement. From 1994-2000, he served as the founding director of the Feinstein Institute for Public Service at Providence College, the first U.S. degree-granting program combining community service with the curriculum. He has also developed and directed service-learning efforts at Rutgers and Baylor Universities. His major service-learning publications include *Civic Engagement Across the Curriculum: A Resource Book for Faculty in all Disciplines*.

Shelley H. Billig, PhD, is vice president of RMC Research Corporation. She directs the Carnegie Corporation of New York national study of the impact on service-learning on civic engagement as well as several other research studies involving service-learning, citizenship, and educational reform. She has coedited and/or authored 10 books and multiple articles on service-learning and other K-12 educational reform topics.

Karen McKnight Casey is the director of the Michigan State University (MSU) Center for Service-Learning and Civic Engagement. She is responsible for facilitating university initiatives that provide academic, curricular and cocurricular, service-based learning and engagement opportunities for MSU students. Casey also directs the MSU America Reads/America Counts federal work-study projects and serves as an adjunct faculty/specialist in the Department of Family and Child Ecology and as a field instructor for the School of Social Work. She is active on the board of Michigan Campus Compact and a number of university and community committees and boards. Casey has multiple years of professional experience in both higher education and within community agencies, allowing for unique perceptions and expertise in promoting and implementing service-learning and civic engagement.

Beverly Cleary is a graduate student in the counseling psychology program at Villanova University. She is a recent graduate from the Psychology Department in the Social Science Division at Widener University. Beverly was one of the first students to complete the educational psychology service-learning program. She has worked as a research assistant with Dr. Simons on this project for the past 3 years.

Peter Collier has been involved in the national service-learning movement for the last 14 years due, particularly, to an interest in how educational experiences impact high school and college students' identities as citizens. He has published service-learning related articles in *Teaching Sociology, Sociology of Education, and the Journal of General Education*. Dr. Collier has also been active in developing educational materials and assessment tools for service-learning classes. He was a coauthor of *Serving and Learning: A Student Workbook for Community-Based Experiences Across the Disciplines*, (2005 Stylus Press and American Association of Higher Education). He has participated in the PSU STRT program since 2001, and currently serves as the faculty-in-residence for scholarship at the Center for Academic Excellence at Portland State University.

Georgia Davidson, MA, is former special education teacher in Lansing, Michigan, and Harrisburg, Illinois. She has a 28-year career in student affairs administration including positions at the University of New Hampshire, Boston College, and at Michigan State University. Her experience has included work in residence life, admissions, student life, judicial affairs, and service-learning/civic engagement. She is currently the associate director of the Center for Service-Learning and Civic Engagement at Michigan State University, focusing on service opportunities for students within the Greater Lansing community.

Frida Díaz Barriga Arceo serves at the Faculty of Psychology of the National Autonomous University of Mexico. She has a degree in psychology, a master's degree in educational psychology, and a PhD in education. Her research and teaching areas are curriculum development and assessment, instructional psychology, teacher assessment and training, constructivism, and higher education teaching. She is the author or coauthor of *Curriculum Design Methodology for Higher Education, Introduction to Teaching, Teaching Strategies for a Meaningful Learning: A Constructivist Approach, and Teaching Assessment*. She has supervised degree and postgraduate dissertations at national or international higher education institutions. She has been a consultant and has participated in educational projects in several institutions such as the ILCE, the UNESCO, the La Salle University, the Universidad del Valle de México, and the University of Monterrey.

Pablo Elicegui is executive director of the National Service-Learning Program at the Ministry of Education, "Educación Solidaria." He is also senior researcher at Centro Latinoamericano de Aprendizaje y Servicio Solidario (CLAYSS), conducting research and publication projects, and supervising PhD and masters dissertations. He was formerly under-chief for research and teacher training area, with the School and Community National Program of the Ministry of Education, Argentina, in charge of research activities and supervision of seminars and workshops. Recent publications include: *El rol docente y el trabajo en equipo a partir de proyectos educativos vinculados a la comunidad* (Elicegui & González) and *Algunas consideraciones sobre calidad educativa en la experiencia argentina del aprendizaje-servicio* (Elicegui & González).

Devon Fliss was inspired to become a special education teacher after serving as an AmeriCorps volunteer as a literacy outreach coordinator. She recently graduated from the secondary education master's in teaching program at Western Washington University. Throughout her terms with AmeriCorps and her work pursuing her teaching certificate, she came to realize that the connection between community and school is vital in education. She looks forward to inspiring her students and community members through service-learning.

Erin Gaulding is a student in Western Washington University's Secondary Education Master's in Teaching program, where she is pursuing her middle school humanities endorsement. As a Project Connect learning facilitator, she worked with groups of middle school boys at a food bank and salmon restoration site and was unceasingly impressed by the level of seriousness with which they took their work. Her experience with service-learning taught her the importance of scaffolding and guidance and also that a sense of ownership greatly influences students' desire to do their best and contribute to the community in a positive way.

Alba González is the senior researcher for Centro Latinoamericano de Aprendizaje y Servicio Solidario (CLAYSS) conducting research and publications projects. From 2000 to 2001, she was chief of the research and teacher training area at the School and Community National Program, Ministry of Education. She was in charge of the research activities and the supervision of seminars and workshops that offered training on service-learning to more than 20,000 teachers of all the country. She is author of seven popular primary, middle and high school textbooks on social sciences. She has coauthored several articles on service-learning and supervised the edition of more than a dozen Ministry of Education publications on service-learning.

Angela M. Harwood, PhD, is professor of secondary education at Western Washington University where she teaches curriculum and instruction courses. She has a special passion for middle school education and has collaborated with local schools to help them implement service-learning approaches. She also facilitates a faculty fellows program for Western's Center for Service-Learning, where she assists faculty from across the university in their pursuit of mastering service-learning pedagogy.

Kevin Kecskes is director for community-university partnerships in the Center for Academic Excellence at Portland State University. He has been involved in community-based work and K-12 and higher education for 25 years. His recent publications focus on cultural theory and partnership development, faculty and institutional development for civic engagement, and ethics and community-based research. He recently edited *Engaging Departments: Moving Faculty Culture from Private to Public, Individual to Collective Focus for the Common Good*, to be published by Anker Publishing in 2006.

Amanda Moore McBride, PhD, is assistant professor at the George Warren Brown School of Social Work, director of the Richard A. Gephardt Institute for Public Service, and research director of the Center for Social Development (CSD) at Washington University in St. Louis. She is principal investigator for the Global Service Institute research initiative, implementing an international research agenda on civic service. Her scholarship focuses on civic engagement and civic service, with four primary areas of research: inclusive civic programs and policies, international service and global citizenship, youth service as youth development, and the relationship between civic service and asset building.

María Nieves Tapia is director of Argentina National Service-Learning Program, "Educación Solidaria," at the Federal Ministry of Education. She is also founder and academic director of Centro Latinoamericano de Aprendizaje y Servicio Solidario (CLAYSS), the Latin American Center for Service-Learning, which was founded after the 2001 political crisis in Argentina. In 1991, she was appointed chief of advisors at the National Institute for Youth and was responsible of the first Presidential Project on Conscientious Objection and Substitutive Social Youth Service. In 1994, she began to work in the social sciences curriculum area at the Ministry of Education. From 1997 to 2001, she designed and directed the first service-learning program in the country. Recent publications on youth and service-learning include "*La solidaridad como pedagogía*" (Buenos Aires), "*Aprendizaje y servicio solidario*" (Madrid), and "*Educazione e solidarietà*" (Roma).

Diana Pacheco Pinzón serves at the Marist University in Merida (Universidad Marista de Mérida), where she is the academic vice-rector and director of the service-learning program. Her academic career includes a psychology degree from the National Autonomous University of Mexico, a master's degree in education from Michigan State University, and a PhD in education from Yucatán Autonomous University. Her research and teaching areas are experiential learning, instructional psychology, curriculum development, and professors' development and evaluation in higher education. She is the coauthor of *Teaching and Continuing Education of Civil Engineering, Curriculum Design Methodology for Higher Education*, and *Service-Learning: A University Educational Approach for Community and Solidarity Values*.

Suzanne Pritzker is a doctoral student at the George Warren Brown School of Social Work and research associate at the Center for Social Development at Washington University in St. Louis. She is engaged in research on civic engagement and political attitudes among low-income youth and families and on service-learning as a means to increase civic outcomes among K-12 students.

Susan Root, PhD, is a senior research associate at RMC Research Corporation with extensive experience in teacher education and service-learning. She was professor of education at Alma College in Michigan and a teacher educator for 23 years. Dr. Root was a regional director of the American Association of Colleges for Teacher Education's National Service-Learning in Teacher Education Partnership (NSLTEP). She has conducted several studies of the effects of service-learning on undergraduates, prospective teachers, and K–12 students. She is currently project director for an international study of the effects of Project Citizen on student civic development and for a study of the impacts of Western State College's Teacher Quality Enhancement project.

Robert Shumer, PhD, former director of the National Service-Learning Clearinghouse at the University of Minnesota, is currently assessing higher education/K-12 partnerships in four states. Dr. Shumer teaches courses on experiential learning and service-learning, as well as on the qualitative research process, youth development, and school-to-work issues. He received his PhD in education from UCLA.

Lori Simons, PhD, is an associate professor of psychology in the Social Science Division at Widener University. She teaches courses in educational psychology, community and counseling psychology, and tests and measurements. For the past 4 years, Professor Simons has developed and evaluated an educational psychology service-learning program. She has presented at international, national, and local conferences including the International Civic Education Research Conference and the National Service-Learning Conference. Her recent research has focused on the effects of service-learning for community recipients and K-5 teachers, multicultural service-learning and student development, and interdisciplinary service-learning and civic engagement.

Nicole C. Springer, MA, is an alumnus of Michigan State University. Before graduate work at MSU, Nicole attended Concordia College where she worked closely with the Office of Student Leadership and Service, and later served as an AmeriCorps VISTA in Moorhead, Minnesota. Nicole is currently an academic outreach specialist in the Center for Service-Learning and Civic Engagement at Michigan State University where she is involved in outreach, research, curriculum development, and advising students related to service and engagement opportunities.

INDEX